Praise for *Giving 2.0*

"At last! This terrific book cuts through the jargon to demystify philanthropy, proving what's possible when givers put their hearts and minds to issues that really matter. Laura Arrillaga-Andreessen's profiles in great giving are beautifully rendered, her insights fresh and compelling, and her practical how-to's pitch perfect. *Giving 2.0* should become the indispensable guide for everyone who's ready to make the most of what they have to give!"

—Sally Osberg, president and CEO, Skoll Foundation

"Through vignettes of individual and family philanthropists, Laura Arrillaga-Andreessen, a great philanthropist and leader in her own right, captures both the passion and the tough analysis and decision making necessary to turn that passion into results. In a highly engaging style, she covers the value of having clear goals for one's own philanthropy; the importance of supporting an organization's real needs, even for quotidian back-office functions; and how to undertake appropriate due diligence and evaluation. *Giving 2.0* offers a bounty of valuable information for donors of all levels."

—Paul Brest, president, William and Flora Hewlett Foundation, and coauthor, *Money Well Spent*

"Laura Arrillaga-Andreessen has made a great contribution to the philanthropy of this country, combining personal experience and passion with professional insight to create a deeply valuable resource that will help families throughout their philanthropic journeys. *Giving 2.0* is a book that provides rich stories, inspiration, and information relevant to all as they continue to give generously of both time and money."

—Carol Larson, president and CEO, Packard Foundation

"*Giving 2.0* opens the door to a new era of philanthropy in which everyone, at every giving level, can combine new and innovative approaches with the power of the Internet to achieve positive social impact and personal joy, whether by helping their neighbors next door or across the world. It offers a rare perspective from one of philanthropy's most thoughtful leaders that makes it essential reading for anyone who wants to make giving a meaningful part of his or her life."

—Leslie Crutchfield and Mark Kramer, coauthors, *Do More Than Give*

"Research shows that happiness comes from spending time connecting with others, not just having or spending money. *Giving 2.0* shows how connected the world is, and how to determine the role you'd like to play in changing the world. Whether donating time, money, skill, or voice, *Giving 2.0* can show you how to gain greater happiness and fulfillment from your efforts."

—Jennifer Aaker, coauthor, *The Dragonfly Effect*, and professor, Stanford Graduate School of Business

LAURA ARRILLAGA-ANDREESSEN

.·.

GIVING 2.0

.·.

TRANSFORM YOUR GIVING AND OUR WORLD

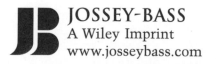

JOSSEY-BASS
A Wiley Imprint
www.josseybass.com

Published by Jossey-Bass

A Wiley Imprint

989 Market Street, San Francisco, CA 94103-1741—www.josseybass.com

Jossey-Bass books and products are available through most bookstores. To contact Jossey-Bass directly call our Customer Care Department within the U.S. at 800-956-7739, outside the U.S. at 317-572-3986, or fax 317-572-4002.

Wiley also publishes its books in a variety of electronic formats and by print-on-demand. Not all content that is available in standard print versions of this book may appear or be packaged in all book formats. If you have purchased a version of this book that did not include media that is referenced by or accompanies a standard print version, you may request this media by visiting http://booksupport.wiley.com. For more information about Wiley products, visit us at www.wiley.com.

Library of Congress Cataloging-in-Publication Data

Arrillaga-Andreessen, Laura.

    Giving 2.0 : transform your giving and our world / by Laura Arrillaga-Andreessen. —1st ed.

      p. cm.

    Includes bibliographical references and index.

  ISBN 978-1-118-11940-2 (cloth); ISBN 978-1-118-14856-3 (ebk); ISBN 978-1-118-14857-0 (ebk); ISBN 978-1-118-14858-7 (ebk)

    1. Charities.   2. Endowments.   3. Humanitarianism.   4. Social action.   I. Title.

II. Title: Giving two point zero.

  HV48.A77 2012

  361.7'4—dc23

2011029319

Printed in the United States of America

FIRST EDITION

HB Printing 10 9 8 7 6 5 4 3 2 1

To the Givers
I love most in this world:
Marc Andreessen and John Arrillaga Sr.
I am who I am because of you.

For Frances Arrillaga
1940–1995
In celebration of a beautiful giving life

CONTENTS

INTRODUCTION

*A philanthropist is anyone who gives anything—time, money, experience, skills,
and networks—in any amount to create a better world.*

For all of us who give, there are moments, people, events, and experiences that prompt us to take action; that inspire us to live outside ourselves. When we are so moved, we can no longer stand back passively and watch injustice, cruelty, and inequality; we have to *do something* to make the world better.

My own first inspiration came from my family, and in particular my mother. Frances Arrillaga was my best friend, my mentor, my soul mate. In her living, she inspired me, and in her dying, she showed me a new life path. I took the tragedy of losing her and transformed it into my life's greatest blessing—my giving.

Giving was more than a part of my mom's life. It *was* her life. She sat on multiple nonprofit boards (serving as chairman on several of them). She co-founded two nonprofits and ran the family foundation she and my father created. With a radiant smile for everyone, she found it easy to recruit volunteers for causes and organizations she supported—but she'd never ask anyone to do anything she wouldn't do herself. She had an astonishing sense of purpose, and she created an extraordinary community around her. Watching her on visits to local nonprofits was inspiring—everyone loved her. Seeing how she helped set up and build new organizations encouraged me to think that perhaps one day I could do the same. I saw how her light drew others to her side. I saw her purpose, her passion, and her peace. And I wanted to live the life she'd led—to share her purpose, her passion, and her peace.

The day my father, brother, and I learned of her illness, I quit my job, deferred my Stanford MBA, and stayed at home to take care of her. Watching my mom in unbearable pain, unable to do anything about it, was the hardest experience of my life. That's when I learned the reality of human suffering and what it felt like to be completely powerless. Yet I also realized that while forces we cannot control may be ranged against us, they should never stop us from fighting on. What mattered, I discovered, was not achieving the next goal for myself, but making life better for those around me—whether I knew those people or not.

As my mom grew sicker, I became petrified. I felt horribly isolated and yet scared to ask for help, for fear of appearing weak. Then something happened. People came from all over our community to share how my mother had touched their lives. They brought homemade dinners, flowers from their gardens, prayers, and kindness. I discovered that in asking for help, I could give others the opportunity of doing something to help me—just as I was helping my mother.

Devoting myself to her care taught me how to live outside myself. Even in the worst hours of her suffering, my mother showed me, and those around her, grace, gratitude, and unconditional love. Through the terrible experience of losing her, I gained the deep understanding of suffering, compassion, humility, and selflessness that is the force behind my giving.

Her illness also taught me that passion, while driven by our hearts, must be supported by research, goals, and sound strategies. My family and I knew we had to do everything we could to fight her disease. Even if ultimately unsuccessful, our efforts might one day help save someone else's life. Applying these lessons to my giving has been challenging— such moments of learning can be intensely painful as well as frustratingly difficult. But they're also beautiful opportunities for transformation, because they give us fresh perspectives and take us on new paths in how we live and how we give.

Just twenty months after receiving her diagnosis, my mother was gone. But as hundreds of people—many of whom I'd never met—came forward to offer their condolences, I learned of her immense contribution to our world, of the selflessness with which she'd given her time and energy. And in those last days, I experienced a profound realization of the reason I was born into my family and what my future should hold. I made a promise—to her, to God, and to myself—that I would keep her light shining brightly, turning her pain and my grief into something positive, helping her spirit live on through me.

In doing so, I was not alone. For I'm blessed to be the daughter of two extraordinary philanthropists, and my father, John Arrillaga Sr., is one of his generation's most generous. For more than two decades, he's devoted at least half of his time to giving. He uses the expertise acquired through a career in real estate development to bring to fruition dozens of essential building projects for local schools, universities, and nonprofits. And with the profits from his business, he funds a huge portion of their general operating costs.

Since losing my mom, he and I have become the best of friends and effective partners in our family's philanthropy. Every day, we get together or talk by phone about how he and I can do more to transform our world for good or about the giving plans I'm making with my husband, Marc. Sometimes we drive around to visit the sites of my father's nonprofit building projects (he is famous for walking campuses and hallways and picking up any trash he finds along the way).

Intensely private and humble, my father has spent much of his life giving, permitting no acknowledgment of his tremendous generosity. He's accepted only one of the countless philanthropic awards bestowed on him—Stanford University's highest volunteer honor, the Uncommon Man Award. Even then he insisted that the awards dinner (an event attended usually by several hundred) should include just eight people (Stanford's president and his wife, the provost and his wife, and our immediate family). His commitment to giving bonds us more closely, and his unconditional love has supported me in my philanthropic aspirations and actions.

My parents embody the philanthropic spirit at its finest, both individually and as one. Together, they created the Arrillaga Foundation, and together they contributed to countless causes. They were an incredible team, supporting each other's efforts at every turn. My mom was the public face of their giving. My father was the silent force behind her volunteerism, supporting all her efforts, providing her with an essential platform of stability, resources, and love—support he now gives to me as I strive to live up to their shining examples.

My parents are my philanthropic heroes. Perhaps you feel the same about yours. Perhaps you, too, want to emulate their beliefs and values. Or it could be that you're driven by other experiences; things that have touched you in a significant way—battling a disease, losing a loved one, caring for a sick child. You may have witnessed or experienced the horrors of domestic abuse, poverty, or discrimination. Or maybe your life was changed by something far from your own world—something you read in a newspaper article or saw in a disturbing television report.

What inspires you may also be positive—the peace and strength of a religious community or the natural beauty of a landscape. The generosity of a friend or colleague may have moved you, or a stranger may have funded your college scholarship. On any day of the week, you could have a conversation with someone or observe something that could change your giving path forever. Each of these moments represents an opportunity, a responsibility, and a privilege.

* * *

We give from the heart—our most powerful engine for action. And we give because it makes us feel good (in fact, medical tests have shown that giving stimulates a part of the brain that gives us the same gratification as when we eat food or have sex).[1] We live in a frenetic world, with incessant demands on our time, money, and energy. At home we care for spouses and children and support aging parents; at work, we face constant pressure. Even when times toughen and wallets shrink, we stretch our resources to help those with even less. (In 2009, at a time of deep recession and personal hardship, annual individual giving in the U.S. still averaged almost $2,000 per household).[2] But what never ceases to astound me is that through everything, one powerful, beautiful force persists: our giving. And why? Because giving *feels good*.

But feeling good in the moment doesn't necessarily accomplish our greater goal—making the world a better place. Too often the warm glow that drives us to give is not backed by knowledge, research, and strategy. We write checks, but we rarely find out exactly how our money is used. We unknowingly waste resources—reinventing the wheel when we could be learning from others—and ultimately at the expense of those we are trying to help. As you probably already know, giving away money is easy—doing so effectively is much harder.

Today, while big problems demand increasingly complex solutions, the world's philanthropic resources are ever more tightly stretched. We need to do more with less. We need to channel precious philanthropic resources into innovative ways of giving—learning constantly, partnering with others, pooling funds through collaborative giving, inventing new, entrepreneurial models of social investment, and applying more rigorous performance measurement to everything we do philanthropically. For between the signing of a check and the delivery of vaccinations to a family in Liberia or better education to low-income sixth graders in Detroit lies a complex set of decisions, strategies, and infrastructure, all of which contribute to the impact of the money itself.

It was the desire to help other philanthropists navigate these complexities that shaped my philanthropic path. For the past fifteen years I've been developing support systems and designing giving "products"—organizations, networks, and resources—that I hope will educate, empower, and inspire anyone who wants to give (myself included) to do so—and more effectively. This book is an important part of those efforts, and I plan to donate all of my royalties from its sales to charity.

My first big step on this philanthropic path came soon after my mom died. I knew I wanted to create an organization to support other philanthropists—but in the meantime, I needed support of my own. As I set out on this journey, I'd never felt so alone or unprepared. I had no idea where to start and, aside from some of the seasoned philanthropists I knew through my parents, I could find no community of givers with whom to share ideas, compare stories, and figure out how to proceed. There was no organization to join that could teach me (or the countless new potential philanthropists born of Silicon Valley's 1990s technology revolution) how to give more strategically, how to pool resources for greater impact, and how to learn through doing. No gathering place existed where individuals like me could share passions and exchange ideas about what had or hadn't worked. Like many individual donors, I felt frustrated and isolated.

So I decided to create a new organization—one through which philanthropists could get together and support each other while learning how to give more effectively and dive more deeply into certain social issues. I called it the Silicon Valley Social Venture Fund (SV2). In SV2, I wanted to help people make investments that were relatively small financially but big in terms of expanding their own skills. At SV2, donors (we call them *partners*) gain hands-on experience by working directly with nonprofit leaders and fellow philanthropists. We invest time in educating ourselves, bringing in field experts to talk about the issues we fund. We not only give and pool our money; we collaborate on grantmaking decisions and use our skills and knowledge to help the cutting-edge nonprofits we support become more effective and scale up their operations. The success of our partners in doing this sends a powerful message: you don't need to donate huge dollars to have a huge impact.

The experience of setting up and running SV2—along with my volunteer and board service for a number of nonprofit organizations—gave me part of the grounding I needed to help my father steward our family's philanthropic resources. However, this was just the beginning of my learning journey.

When Stanford Graduate School of Business (GSB) invited me to join its faculty in 2000, I embarked on a formal study of "strategic philanthropy." Researching and teaching at Stanford has taken me deep into the world of individual giving, philanthropic foundations, venture philanthropy, corporate philanthropy, global social investing, and social innovation. Over the past decade, I've taught some amazing students, a few of whom have even gone on to found or run some of the organizations that appear in this book.

As I became immersed in the world of academia at Stanford and the world of practitioners in the professional philanthropic field, I was struck by the gap between the incredible knowledge and insights of my academic colleagues and the extraordinary generosity and vision of my philanthropic sector colleagues. To create a hub where these two communities could share their wisdom, I founded a new university center—Stanford PACS (Center on Philanthropy and Civil Society)—which I now chair.

Working as both a hands-on philanthropist and an academic, I've become what I call a *pracademic*—part practitioner, part scholar. And over the years, immersed in philanthropic pursuits, I've gained confidence in my abilities. But I often think of those early days, when I assumed everyone knew much more than I did and wondered how on earth I could ever gain enough knowledge and experience to be an effective philanthropist. Even with my Stanford education, I felt overwhelmed by how much material I needed to absorb. At board meetings, when I was often the youngest person in the room, I was reluctant to ask questions for fear of sounding hopelessly uninformed.

What I've learned, of course, is that there are no questions unworthy of asking—in fact, it's a good thing to further your knowledge or challenge norms. And even though I'm sometimes still shy about asking for feedback and results from my gifts, I try to remember that it's all part of empowering the nonprofits I fund to do better. Yet, fifteen years into my giving, I still feel that all philanthropists out there (myself included) could benefit from greater support—more knowledge about what works and what doesn't; a resource from which they can learn about different issues and explore new models of giving; something to show us all not just how to make gifts that feel good but how to make a real difference with those gifts.

The result is this book, and the following chapters address the hundreds of questions that individual givers have asked me over the years about issues we've all faced. This book won't tell you *why* to give (if you've started reading it, you already have a giving heart). But it will tell you *how* to give, and it will provide you tools with which to give more effectively.

Writing this book has transformed my own philanthropy from "giving 1.0" to "giving 2.0." For me, it's been a chance to renew, evolve, and reenergize my giving—to go from being reactive to proactive, to create a strategy that capitalizes on past giving experiences but also embraces new philanthropic activities. I hoped to tap into the amazing reach of the Web and overcome my fear of engaging in the world of social media. I wanted to deepen my exploration of volunteerism, different giving vehicles, social entrepreneurship, advocacy funding, and family foundation best practices. I aspired to have the impact of my giving go beyond the emotional rewards of the moment to something that would be intellectually and spiritually satisfying over the long term.

Over the course of my career, I've made gifts that were spectacular successes and ones that were miserable failures. I've made gifts whose impact I can measure accurately—and ones for which I couldn't tell you what happened to the money if my life depended on it. But I've tried to learn from every experience. And when I look back on the timid, uncertain girl that I was when I started giving, I realize I'm much more optimistic, ambitious, and empowered today than I was back then.

Part of that empowerment has come to me through writing this book. Even as an experienced giver, the process of setting down the range of philanthropic options, formulating the right questions to ask, and coming up with tools for making gifts with greater impact has fueled my appetite to achieve more. It's given me the courage to formulate plans that are much bolder than those I would have made even a few years ago. I hope it will do the same for you.

* * *

Giving 2.0 is a book for anyone who gives anything at all—money in *any* amount, time, skills, networks, or expertise. While you'll find industry terms used throughout, it talks clearly and simply about different forms of giving. A "Jargon Buster" section at the end of the book demystifies the language that often makes the "strategic philanthropy" described in so many books seem intimidating. And because giving is so deeply personal, I present no formulas or mandates on how you should give. Instead, I offer up an ocean of possibilities for enhancing whatever path you choose to take, helping you design a giving life that's suited to the way you live and expresses who you are.

Here's how it works: each chapter takes you through a different form of giving, highlighting opportunities, considerations, and challenges. It explains how to define your aspirations, take stock, change direction, renew existing strategies, acquire critical skills, and create or participate in exciting new models of giving. It shows you how to maximize the impact of your gifts while strengthening your personal connection (the emotional force behind your generosity) to social transformation.

The "Making It Happen" section at every chapter's end provides an extensive set of questions you can ask yourself and others, as well as suggestions and things to think about when considering the form of giving covered in the main text of the chapter. These sections will help you construct your goals and how you can go about achieving them. They'll suggest ways of planning your giving, either alone or with your partner, spouse, friends, or children.

Since many volunteers and donors learn their values from their parents, each "Making It Happen" section also includes a component called "For the Family." "For the Family" shows you how to instill these values in your children and how, through a host of different activities, you can pass philanthropic values down to future generations.

In Chapter Three, I show you how to start a giving journal to track your donations of time and money (an essential thing to do if you want to increase your impact). But I also refer to this journal at various points throughout the book, and Appendix I provides an extensive list of questions and suggestions to help you build your own giving journal. As you go through each chapter, the "Making It Happen" sections give you a portfolio of questions, ideas, and innovations to consider and apply to help you develop your journal, as well.

This book is itself a journey—early chapters focus on volunteering and direct giving, discussing what you can do to make gifts of time or money more rewarding for those you support and for yourself. Other chapters show you how to engage in collaborative giving, or how you can participate in exciting newer models of philanthropy that support entrepreneurs using market-based models to bring about lasting social change. Later chapters tackle more complex forms of philanthropy, such as setting up an unstaffed family foundation or embarking on advocacy. They also provide advice on things such as how to establish a board of directors or what to think about when considering starting a nonprofit.

Yet, no matter how straightforward or complex the type of philanthropy being examined in it, each chapter shows you how—even with just a few hundred dollars or hours of your time—you can participate. You may not, for example, have the wherewithal to engage in advocacy right now. Yet I'll show how you can donate to organizations that are conducting advocacy, or go online and use social networking websites to create your own campaign for a cause you care about.

Some chapters feature forms of giving established decades ago— tried and tested models such as donor-advised funds, charitable trusts, and tithing. Yet while some systems for giving may have existed for more than a century, they may be new to you. Even if they're familiar, you can adapt them to your current goals or use them as a way to set yourself more ambitious ones.

For better or worse, we all become creatures of habit, and I'm no exception. I've found that my own giving needs a reboot every few years. Sometimes I find myself funding organizations year after year without really knowing what work they're doing, or giving reactively based on the requests of friends and family, rather than pursuing my own passions. At other times, the chaos of work and family life means I neglect my own philanthropic learning—something I always regret. Here's where your giving journal can be a critical support tool. By keeping it up to date, you can keep yourself on track.

Throughout the book, you can also follow the giving journeys of the committed and talented individual philanthropists profiled in each chapter—how they found their passions, how they made their giving decisions, their first volunteering experiences, and what they did to make their philanthropy more meaningful and have more impact. These individuals don't conform to the traditional image of a philanthropist—that of a wealthy older man making large gifts to prestigious institutions. Today, in fact, women play a leading role in philanthropy. In a 2009 national survey, almost half the women surveyed said they made the family's decisions on which nonprofits to give to and how much to give, while more than 80 percent of men say they defer to their spouses on giving decisions.[3]

I believe that *anyone* who gives *anything* is a philanthropist. After all, the word itself derives from the Greek *philanthropus*, which translates as "love of humankind"—and there's nothing in this definition to suggest we need to give away huge sums of money, if any money at all, to make a difference.

The women, men, and organizations featured in this book have been chosen not because they are necessarily more effective than others or because their causes are more important, but because together they illustrate this century's true philanthropic community in all its glorious diversity. Some donate a few hundred dollars a year using online tools, while others give only their time and expertise. Some have joined forces, pooling their funds to give thousands of dollars collectively. Others tap into the expertise developed by professional foundations to make significant personal investments. A few have even established impressive nonprofits or philanthropic funds. All have married their passion with their knowledge.

Following their journeys will, I hope, help you think about your own. For me, however, their stories were just a beginning. Trying out ideas inspired by the stories of others is how I continue to develop my philanthropy. I hope you'll do the same. In an age of "giving while living," it's a time to experiment, to renew existing forms of giving, and create new ones that are uniquely yours.

It's also important to think of giving as an evolutionary process. I find it's helpful to treat every gift not as an independent transaction but as a single note that contributes to a lifelong symphony of philanthropic action—a whole greater than the sum of its parts. And whether you're giving money, time, skills, or compassion, the opportunities you'll encounter at different times come with varying levels of complexity— each of which you may embrace at certain stages in your life. Things that worked at one time may not be appropriate at another. Your passions may turn you on to one cause early on in life, while another draws your attention later. You might start modestly, giving to a nonprofit whose work you admire, and intensify your impact by serving on its board. You might even decide to found your own philanthropic or nonprofit organization.

So when do you begin this journey? When do you start acquiring the knowledge needed to enhance your giving? When should you think about doing more with your time and skills? When should you stop simply worrying about the world's problems and start looking for innova-tive ways of helping solve them? When should you renew or even rein-vent your giving? The answer to all these questions is the same—NOW. If you can manage your personal financial investments more effectively, you can manage your philanthropic ones more effectively, too. If you're able to learn from what you read in books or online, you have the ability to learn more about how to have a bigger impact. We can all do more to support people who strive to solve the world's problems and even to help develop those solutions ourselves. We can all transform our giving for the better—let's start right now.

∴

One final note: Throughout the book, whenever you see a Web logo in the margin of this book (as in the margin here), please visit the Giving 2.0 website: www.giving2.com. There you will find direct links to (and in some cases additional information on) the organizations featured in this book, as well as ongoing updates on developments in the world of individual giving. This site will serve as a living, evolving hub, hosting giving blogs (mine and those of inspiring individuals and other philan-thropic leaders), interviews, and videos, as well as providing updated references. The Giving 2.0 website also will host a wide range of links to organizations, articles, books, publications, and other resources to use for inspiration, education, action, and community. A section dedicated entirely to this book will have a chapter-by-chapter breakdown for related ideas, resources, and links to help take your giving to the next level. This site will also serve as an online community for philanthropists at all levels to meet and share information—a virtual home for givers globally.

GIVING YOURSELF

A Donation More Valuable Than Money

Jump in and engage—add value by giving your time, experience, skills, and networks.

G iving is a universal opportunity. Regardless of your age, profession, religion, income bracket, and background, you have the capacity to create change. Everything you do, from spontaneous acts of kindness to an hour of your time, constitutes how you give. Indeed, making a gift of time, coupled with expertise and compassion, is a powerful way to make a positive impact on our world.

Hector Chau is one of millions transitioning out of the workforce and, as such, redefining his professional and personal relationships to his community. Now retired and living in Westchester, a neighborhood of western Los Angeles, Hector lives on a pension that doesn't leave him a large amount of money to give to charity. Hector is an active philanthropist, however, as he gives away something even more valuable—his time. Hector volunteers with a program called Tax-Aide, an initiative launched in 1968 by AARP, an organization that provides services to people over the age of fifty. Tax-Aide helps low- to middle-income taxpayers—many over the age of sixty—complete their yearly filings, with volunteers like Hector leading them through the process.

Born in Mexico, Hector has been living in the United States since 1977, when he moved from Mexico City to Santa Monica with his family. Hector, his wife Olga, and their three children (aged nine, eleven, and thirteen)—were all on holiday in California. Olga and the children were enjoying themselves so much that they told Hector they wanted to move to America. "We decided that since we were in a democracy, we should take a vote on it," says Hector. "And I lost, four to one."

Hector had left his home town of Tuxpan on the Mexican Gulf Coast once before to live in the United States. He attended a Texas high school funded by the Presbyterian Church, and later graduated from the University of Texas at Austin. After leaving college, Hector moved back to Mexico City, where he married his Texas-born university sweetheart and got a job with an accounting firm where he remained for the next sixteen years. He later worked as a salesman for an equipment manufacturer, a job he loved, as he enjoys meeting people and hearing about their lives.

In his new role as a volunteer, Hector is able to enjoy so much of what he loved in his profession. The Tax-Aide program has not only drawn Hector back to the accounting world; it has also given him a chance to make new friends. In between tax seasons, he exchanges jokes and letters, keeping in touch with his fellow volunteers via email. He also meets a wide range of people among the clients who use the Tax-Aide service. There was the hundred-and-two-year-old man who still managed to drive his car to the center, with his girlfriend (in her nineties) beside him. And the young aspiring actress who claimed her breast implants as tax-deductible items since she'd had them done to improve her chances of getting work.

"Sometimes we get our heartstrings pulled, and sometimes it's simply fun," says Hector. Cheerful and outgoing, Hector still loves meeting different people and finding out about their lives. Working in sales afforded him this opportunity during his career; volunteering has restored it in retirement. "It's very satisfying when you're helping someone and then, when you see them next time, they're doing well," he says.

Hector is one of millions of Baby Boomers who've decided to take up volunteering or increase it in retirement. For some, it's a chance to give back to society. For others, it means they can continue to learn and develop while meeting new people and expanding their horizons. These opportunities help countless high-energy retirees enhance their self-esteem and fill the void that can open when people give up paid work.

Thousands of new opportunities to do volunteer work emerge all the time, and not just for retirees, whether it's making the occasional call for a nonprofit or helping construct libraries in a developing country. And these opportunities are mushrooming thanks to the power of the Internet. With the connectivity of the Web and online search tools, you can tap into a new world of community service, finding activities that match your skills and organizations that meet your goals.

Volunteering does not have to be a lifelong commitment (although it can be). You might start by doing a couple of hours a week playing dominos with a senior citizen and end up on an intensive six-month school-building project in an impoverished African village. You can work directly with people, giving your compassion and care, or help a nonprofit by giving your legal, financial, or marketing expertise. But you'll make a bigger impact and get more out of it if you think carefully about the kind of work you want to do, how much time you have to devote, and how your skills and experience can best be used. As with any form of philanthropy, planning, tracking, and taking stock are critical first steps (find out how to do this in Appendix I, Creating Your Giving Journal), because if you establish the right volunteer relationships, your involvement will provide your greatest personal connection with giving.

A GIFT TO YOURSELF

In search of happiness, we read about everything from how we need to simplify our lives to avoid stress to how we should eat well, exercise, and surround ourselves with positive people. We are all obsessed with being happy, it seems. And after all, who doesn't want to be happy? Well, it turns out that one of the things that make us happy is giving. And volunteering is no exception. What's more, volunteering even appears to be good for human health.

That's right—volunteering could lead to fewer pills and fewer trips to the doctor. The 2010 "Do Good Live Well Study" found that people who volunteered through their job rated their physical and emotional health more positively than nonvolunteers.[1] Some 92 percent of the respondents said they were satisfied with their current physical health, compared to 76 percent among nonvolunteers. And 72 percent of volunteers claimed to have an optimistic outlook on life—tellingly this was true for only 60 percent of nonvolunteers. Moreover, 68 percent of volunteers reported that volunteering made them feel physically healthier.

Other evidence supports the observation that helping others brings benefits to those doing the helping. In a paper on the subject, Stephen Post, a renowned bioethicist, cites work conducted by researchers at Brown University Medical School.[2] The researchers studied members of Alcoholics Anonymous, the largest self-help group in the United States, to assess the difference between individuals who helped other alcoholics recover and those who didn't. The study found that those who were helping others were far less likely to relapse in the year following treatment. Post also points to studies that show teenage girls who volunteer are less likely to become pregnant or take drugs, and these young women are more likely to do better at school and to graduate. A similar review conducted by the Corporation for National and Community Service (CNCS) found that states with higher rates of volunteerism also had lower rates of heart disease.[3]

What's more, among the many studies that Post cites in his paper, research shows how people who volunteer tend to have fewer of the symptoms of depression. "We are perhaps substituting happiness pills for the happiness that flows from pro-social opportunities and more authentic community," he writes.

Even if you're already healthy of mind, body, and heart, the volunteer spirit brings with it countless rewards. For a start, the more you take on, the more you'll find you have time to do. Being happier as a result of giving will increase your productivity at work, enrich your relationships at home, and put your own problems into perspective by focusing on the greater problems of others.

And volunteering can bring thrills rarely found elsewhere—particularly when volunteers get to see the difference they are making. "Some people say there's a pop or a spark," says Michael Lombardo, describing the moment when his volunteers see the turning point in a student's progress. "They often talk about seeing a new light in the child's eyes."

Michael is CEO of Reading Partners, a nonprofit providing one-on-one tutoring for K–6 students from low-income communities (it was one of SV2's early grantees and a recipient of a Social Innovation Fund, or SIF, investment). Reading Partners volunteer tutors (retirees, full-time parents, high school students, and working professionals) spend twice-weekly sessions with individual children, forming a close bond with them, watching their journey through frustration and disengagement toward understanding, excitement, and pride.

"We can all remember times as children and adults when we finally *got* something we were trying to understand," says Michael. "And the real emotional nourishment for our volunteers is seeing the kids have that happen on a weekly basis—not only make a huge stride in their learning but also receive a huge boost to their confidence."

As well as giving you emotional nourishment, community service also helps you maintain your skills during a period of unemployment, while demonstrating your energy and initiative to potential employers. When you're looking for work, volunteering can expand your network of contacts. On an event committee for your city's art museum, for instance, you might meet another volunteer whose company has job openings. Meanwhile, feeling productive can help keep your spirits up at a time when it's easy to become discouraged.

It's worth noting some of these benefits. Has volunteering helped you make new friends or find a community of like-minded people, for instance? Have you been able to attend lectures or events that you might not otherwise have known about? Has volunteering helped you get a new job or led to other service work? It's this personal contact that makes volunteering so rewarding—in helping others, you help yourself.

For Hector, the Tax-Aide program has given him more than a chance to brush up his accounting skills. "I like meeting different people," he says. "And part of the procedure is that, once you've finished a return, someone has to audit it to make sure it's all correct and that you haven't missed anything important. While you're waiting for someone to do this, you have four or five minutes to chat with people—and those moments are fun."

Community service as a family is also a way of introducing your children to giving and the idea of caring for others, while also showing them how they can contribute to solving some of your community's problems. For your children, taking on new challenges—whether that's helping plant trees on a neglected street or going on a fifty-mile bike ride to raise money—helps them learn new skills, gain greater self-confidence, and become more responsible. However, before embarking on any social adventure with your child, it's a good idea to sit down together and decide as a family what projects or causes you want to spend time on. You could even select four or five possibilities and vote on it—thus, as Hector Chau did, giving your kids a lesson in democracy in the process.

Volunteering as a family takes many forms. You could involve the whole family or just a few members. You could take on a challenge for a day—or embark on something longer term. You could participate in an adoption-type program, through which your family might take on responsibility for helping an individual in the community on an ongoing basis—a recent immigrant, perhaps, or an elderly person without relatives (community organizations and churches can help facilitate these relationships).

Volunteering as a family is a great way to spend time together. Equally important, however, is the fact that when families work on community service projects, it provides a real opportunity for you to teach and transmit values to your children. This exposure has a more powerful and enduring impact on them than simply talking about the importance of giving. This was confirmed by a 2011 study called "Heart of the Donor."[4] It found that of people who grew up with parents who were frequent volunteers with nonprofits, almost half (49 percent) had volunteered with a nonprofit in the past year, and of those with parents who occasionally volunteered, 31 percent are volunteers. Among those who never saw their parents volunteer, only 20 percent do so now.

Whether you're going to volunteer alone or with your family, you should think about what you're embarking on as a true commitment—not being paid for your work makes it no less an obligation. So be realistic about what you promise to do. At too many nonprofits, volunteers come and go, many of them losing interest or leaving when another more exciting activity presents itself. Volunteering is a serious business—the business of transforming and saving lives. I've never been paid for my work at SV2 or Stanford PACS (Center on Philanthropy and Civil Society), for example, but because of the impact of what we do, I work just as hard as I did when I worked in the for-profit sector, if not harder. You may experience the same thing—how passion can amplify your commitment. But practically speaking, if you'd never walk out on a paid job, you should treat your gifts of time and expertise, regardless of their scope, with the same level of seriousness.

THE VALUE OF COLLECTIVE PASSION

When Alexis de Tocqueville, a French philosopher and political scientist, traveled across the United States in 1831, he was deeply impressed by American volunteerism. He witnessed Americans' ethic of coming together to solve problems collectively, working in unison to improve life for those in their communities. Nearly two hundred years later, ever-growing numbers of Americans give their time, energies, knowledge, and experience to organizations and causes that they believe can improve life for their fellow citizens, tackle injustices, and help protect the natural environment. More than 63 million Americans, or almost 21 percent of the population, volunteered in 2009, according to the CNCS—that's 1.6 million more people than volunteered in 2008. And the numbers are growing particularly fast among certain sections of the population. Since 1989, for example, the volunteer rate among sixteen- to nineteen-year-olds, in terms of hours given, has almost doubled, according to the CNCS.

If you're among the many millions who volunteer, you may not think of what you're doing as making a financial donation. But in a sense you are. For collectively, the value of those millions of hours given runs into the billions of dollars. According to the CNCS, the monetary value of volunteering services in 2009—which totaled more than 8.1 billion hours—was almost $169 billion. And, that assumes an hourly wage value of roughly $20—probably a huge underestimation of the actual value of volunteer time and expertise.

Behind every single one of these dollars is an individual such as Hector Chau, bringing individual gifts of time and talent. According to a survey conducted by the National Society of Accountants in 2009, the average fee for tax preparation is $229. During the tax season, Hector completes about seven to ten returns a day. This adds up. The AARP says that, every year, Tax-Aide volunteers such as Hector are able to help more than 2.6 million taxpayers to file their federal, state, and local tax returns. At an average of $229 per return, that's almost $600 million—an astonishing amount of money, and all given free of charge by AARP's army of more than 34,600 volunteers.

Volunteers are also essential in times of trouble. In the wake of the devastation of Gulf Coast hurricanes Katrina, Rita, and Wilma, for example, more than 110,000 national service volunteers, along with 648,000 community volunteers, contributed more than 9.6 million hours. These volunteers helped transform the relief, recovery, and rebuilding efforts—removing debris, creating shelters for the homeless, running call centers for those in need, coordinating benefits, and establishing schools and youth programs. The CNCS values these efforts at more than $200 million to the Gulf Coast states. We've also seen a rise in the number of volunteer efforts that support our troops overseas and veterans as they return home.

As these statistics and examples demonstrate, by giving your time, knowledge, and experience—whether your skills are as a lawyer, a construction worker, or a parent—you're providing an essential service that would otherwise not be delivered or would have to be purchased.

Of course, sometimes it's hard to calculate the value of service in monetary terms. Some even say it's wrong to do so, arguing that putting a cash price on volunteering cheapens its worth. Others suggest that to measure volunteering in this way implies that volunteers simply replace paid workers—when in fact their gifts can be far more valuable in human terms.

This can be true, too—for sometimes a service is simply too precious to measure. Take volunteer initiatives such as the No One Dies Alone program, through which volunteers provide a companion service in hospitals and hospices to terminally ill people who have no friends or family and face the prospect of death on their own. The volunteers provide a comforting presence, talking to the dying individuals, reading poems, singing quietly, or simply sitting in silence while warmly holding their hands. How can you put a monetary value on such a gift—a gift that embodies the very essence of human kindness?

A BEAUTIFUL LIFE

When I think of volunteering and community service, I remember my own first experience as a rather awkward thirteen-year-old girl in knee socks, a white middy blouse, and pale blue skirt, holding the hand of a silver-haired woman—my mother. "But Mom," I whispered to her as we waited in the lobby of Family & Children Services, a nonprofit organization located just off California Avenue in Palo Alto. "Why do we have to be here now? I need to go home and do my homework."

I was in the seventh grade. It was my first week of school, and I had at least four hours of math, English, and history studies ahead of me. My mother smiled with the patience only a parent can give to their child. "One day you'll understand why I brought you here," she said. I stayed by her side, and we remained at the center for a couple of hours. I learned about young people facing the trauma of leaving foster care, about children who'd been physically or mentally abused, and of teens who'd been separated from their drug-abusing parents. It was my first realization that not everyone grew up in families as happy and loving as my own. I saw for the first time the difficulties so many people face in society.

As an adult, I do understand the importance of giving time to your community and to broader society. But it was my mother who first showed me the way. My mom, a sixth-grade teacher when she met my father, continued to teach at a local public school until my older brother was born. When we were little, she stayed at home to look after us, but from the moment she stopped working she started volunteering. Blessed with the good fortune of not having to bring in a second paycheck for our family, she started to use her time to help others.

That journey started in a very hands-on way, as nursery and grammar school volunteer. Then, when I was in middle school, she worked with the school's parents association, and helped organize, and even chair, some of the school's fundraising events. By the time I reached seventh grade, she'd started serving on school boards and nonprofit boards, including that of Family & Children Services. Eventually, she developed her own expertise, and she went on to co-found two nonprofits.

With two master's degrees from Stanford, she also gave a gift of intellect along with her time. And she was dedicated, starting at 7 a.m. and often working until 11 p.m., spending more than eighty hours a week on her unpaid service work—while also caring for two children and my father. Few of the organizations she worked with were high-profile. She believed in the importance of providing basic services to help disadvantaged people succeed in society.

She gave her time in a very targeted way, concentrating on education—whether by serving in educational institutions (some of which my brother and I attended) or working with community institutions such as Vista Center (then the Peninsula Center for the Blind and Visually Impaired), which helps people living without full sight to enjoy rich and rewarding lives.

What was so impressive about my mom's volunteering was the way she developed her service work. She started out by simply giving her time in a very emotionally driven way and grew into a passionate nonprofit entrepreneur, an institution builder, and a community leader (while also running our unstaffed family foundation with my father). Everything she did was related; everything she did gave her experiences she could use when tackling the next nonprofit challenge.

She certainly inspired me to do the same. At school, I was always deeply proud when she was giving a speech. I wanted to be just like her. I used to say to myself, "One day, I will serve on a board," even though at the time I knew little about what that really entailed. Because of her, and the philanthropic leadership of my father, my notion of normalcy when I was growing up was grounded in the idea that everyone should live a life of service. Like all things—from exercise and reading to respect and generosity—what you learn when you're young stays with you throughout your life.

GETTING OUT THERE

So should you clean up trash in a park or prepare food in a soup kitchen, or should you offer legal or accounting services to the nonprofit that organizes environmental cleanups and manages hunger relief programs? Should you edit the text for a nonprofit community news website, help that same organization to procure free advertising, or raise money for it in a telethon? If you have certain skills, it might make sense to work on the administrative or production side of things. On the other hand, working in a housing shelter for a couple of days might give you a better understanding of the realities of poverty, informing your other giving activities.

None of these are easy questions to answer—and today's vast volunteering options can seem overwhelming. You could distribute fliers to promote a social justice campaign or check in patients at a free health clinic. You could help build a database or hand out water and supplies at an emergency aid station. But given the multitude of possibilities, before embarking on volunteering it's important to spend some time taking stock and assessing how to balance your personal passions with public needs. This could help you make a bigger impact and get more enjoyment from volunteering—which will encourage you to do more of it.

First, assess what you have to give—and do so broadly. Remember, everyone has *something* to give. And your ability to share your expertise is not limited by the discipline of your professional life. You might be a lawyer, but if you also love reading and writing poetry, you could volunteer in a classroom, introducing children to poetry. You might be a political consultant, but you love the outdoors, so could lead a summer wilderness trip for impoverished urban kids. It's about being in touch with your natural talents, hobbies, and interests—and finding a way to put them to use for good. Even if you feel you don't have many skills to offer, you can use your networks, bringing others together for an event or rallying friends, family, or colleagues to volunteer with you.

Next, think about the level of commitment you'll be comfortable with—how often you'll be able and willing to volunteer, as well as the length of your commitment, whether a month, or a year, or on an ongoing basis. Clearly these decisions depend on whether you're working or not, whether you're single or caring for a spouse and children, whether you're a student or you've just retired.

One way to get an idea of how much time you could devote to volunteering is to write out a list of all the activities that take place during your average week. Mark down the times when they have to be done and look for gaps that could be filled by volunteering. Do you have an afternoon on weekends when, instead of window-shopping or watching TV, you could visit a senior center or help renovate a school? If you're a student, are there times when, instead of hanging out at the campus café, you could spend a morning teaching children to read or helping clean up a local river? If you're an unemployed professional, could you set aside time from job hunting to help a nonprofit manage its budget or launch a marketing campaign?

Sometimes you might wonder how you can possibly fit volunteering into your schedule. Well, you might be surprised to find that it's perhaps at times when you're under greatest pressure at work or stress at home that doing something for others does most to relieve your stress. Even if it's hard to leave the house because you're caring for young children, or your health limits your physical abilities, stepping out of your own world and into the wider world—even if it's only for a few hours—will help put your own challenges into perspective.

You can also volunteer from home. Just as the Internet is transforming the working world, it is providing new "virtual volunteering" opportunities—from remote tutoring to producing material for marketing campaigns or helping a nonprofit write thank-you letters to donors.

If you're a professional journalist, for example, you could become a "mentor editor" at the Op-Ed Project, sharing your writing acumen with female and minority academics hoping to publish their first op-eds. These volunteers help increase the number of new voices in public discourse (more than 80 percent of opinion pieces published in major newspapers are by men—something the Op-Ed Project wants to change). Even without technology or professional skills, there are things you can do from home, such as joining the global movement to knit toy bears for orphans around the world.

Knowing exactly how much time you have to give and where you can give it will help you find opportunities that will fit in with your personal and professional schedule. After all, the last thing you want to do is make a commitment you're unable to meet, or to overstretch yourself so that other parts of your life start to suffer. As with anything, striking the right balance between your volunteering time and your other commitments is essential. However, it's always possible to make time for volunteer work—regardless of how busy you are or think you are. As any volunteer already knows, the more you do, the more you can do.

HANDS IN GLOVES

When it comes to volunteering, recognizing what you have to give is only part of the equation. The other part is finding out what's needed and how your particular skills, knowledge, and experience can help fill the gaps. So do some research to find out whether what you have to offer is something the nonprofits you'd like to work with actually need—you may have plenty of experience and skills, but they may not necessarily be useful to every organization you approach.

If you come from the business world, you may have expertise and knowledge in areas such as the law, finance, accounting, marketing, or strategic planning. But remember that you may also have an awful lot to learn.

For a start, nonprofit organizations have to operate in a resource-constrained environment where the kinds of support systems the business sector relies on, such as IT help desks and videoconferencing facilities, are often absent. They must also interact with a far broader range of stakeholders than businesses (including local governments, other non-profits, foundations, universities, community groups, and clients) when trying to get things done. Working within a consensus-building or col-laborative culture can be challenging in this environment, as can moti-vating people who are driven not by money but by purpose.

And compared to the for-profit sector, decisions regarding the alloca-tion of a nonprofit's funds are far more emotional, depending on a complex range of social and cultural factors rather than purely financial or economic considerations.

So if you come from the business world, it's important not to assume you know more than your nonprofit colleagues. But if you can tackle these issues successfully in a nonprofit environment, you can make an important contribution while also improving your management skills—something you can take back with you to your workplace. If you do, you're joining a powerful force. VolunteerMatch alone has 2.5 million registered members and has made 4.5 million volunteer referrals since 1998.

Then think about what you want to get out of volunteering. You may want to meet people or even a potential life partner, in which case joining a team working on the construction of a new youth center or getting involved in volunteering at your place of worship might be right for you. Or perhaps you prefer working alone, in which case you might want to work on building a Facebook presence for a nonprofit or provid-ing an organization with IT support.

Volunteering is also one of the best ways to add to your knowledge and experience. You might be looking to build up your résumé so you can make a career transition, in which case you should consider oppor-tunities that give you the chance to polish specific skills or gain exposure to a certain industry, such as health care or education. Or perhaps you want to combine volunteering with the chance to travel.

Finally, think about what form you want your volunteering to take. Do you want to work directly with the people being helped by nonprofits or who work at nonprofits? Do you want to give your compassion in the form of caring for others (for example, teaching people with Down's syndrome to swim)? Do you want to take on physical work (repainting a community playground or cleaning oil from birds after an oil spill)? Or do you want to put your mind to work (for example, by giving legal training to those working on immigrant assimilation)?

Be prepared for rejection, too. Many nonprofits—especially if they are well-known institutions—already have sufficient numbers of volunteers. And you may not have the specific expertise that a nonprofit needs. It's great to approach volunteering as a way of building your own skills— but to be useful, you must be able to fill an organization's requirements. Good intentions don't necessarily make for good results.

These days, nonprofits are becoming much more professional in how they take on volunteers. Some may even screen you, as a company might when assessing a job applicant, particularly when they're looking for help in areas such as technology or legal matters. Even if you're applying for a position that doesn't require specific skills, remember that managing new volunteers takes a nonprofit's time and energy. It may simply not have the capacity to handle your presence.

However, don't let this deter you. You may just need to spend a little more time finding the right place for your skills and energies. Or you might have to do a bit of advance preparation to show you understand a nonprofit's objectives and the needs of the people it serves. There will always be plenty of organizations out there that can benefit from your time. And working for a nonprofit that really needs your help and to which you can make a real contribution will be far more satisfying for you and everyone involved.

SEEK AND YOU WILL FIND

The good news: it's easier than ever to find the right volunteering opportunity. For a start, you can look around in your local community. Find out whether the nonprofits operating near you match the issues you're concerned about, and whether or not they need extra help. Your local community foundation, Junior League, or Rotary Club may be able to suggest organizations to approach and even make an introduction.

If you're nearing retirement and want to start or increase your volunteering, your company may be able to help. Many larger companies have programs that help employees move from the for-profit world into the nonprofit sector. Senior Corps (part of the Corporation for National and Community Service) matches people over the age of fifty-five with organizations in need of help and trains new volunteers so that they can be more effective.

The foundation world has also stepped in to encourage postcareer volunteering. Created by Civic Ventures and funded by the John Templeton Foundation and the Atlantic Philanthropies, the Purpose Prize awards $100,000 each to ten individuals over the age of sixty who are finding innovative ways of addressing difficult social problems. A program called Encore Careers helps people in the second half of life find new work with a sense of purpose—paid positions that combine job satisfaction with a chance to help others. For younger people, Global Citizen Year provides a formalized program that helps high school graduates spend a "bridge year" living in developing nations working on social problems before they attend college.

Of course, sometimes it's a conversation that gets the ball rolling. "The moment I retired, I went and told my neighbors," says Hector Chau. "One of them was already active in the [Tax-Aide] program, so he immediately suggested that I join." The neighbor told him about training sessions that took place every year; on retiring that September, Hector took the test for prospective volunteers and passed with flying colors.

Meanwhile, the Web has provided a new and efficient way of connecting volunteers of all ages with community opportunities. Just as Web-based job boards have revolutionized employment searches, online tools now bring together volunteers and organizations that are looking for help. Take Catchafire, a New York City–based for-profit social mission business and a certified B-corporation (a new type of organization that uses for-profit models to generate social benefit). On Catchafire's website, you can browse organizations and match your skills with their needs. The website even tells you how much money a certain number of pro bono hours will save the organization.

The CNCS also has a tool on its website that allows you to enter your charitable interests and zip codes and search for volunteer opportunities. VolunteerMatch has a similar search engine (in fact it's the number one search result for the word *volunteer* on Google and Yahoo, with more than 100 million pages served in 2008) while UniversalGiving has hundreds of screened and validated international volunteer opportunities available on its website. For young people, DoSomething.org presents all kinds of options and matches people with grants and the chance to volunteer.

But the Internet does more than matchmaking. Social networking allows volunteers to use their activities to raise money, too. One organization pioneering this approach is Crowdrise, launched in 2010 by actor and philanthropist Edward Norton, producer Shauna Robertson, and Robert and Jeffrey Wolfe, who founded the offbeat online retailer Moosejaw (Crowdrise's cheeky slogan is "If you don't give back, no one will like you"). As well as empowering fundraisers, Crowdrise boosts volunteers' fundraising potential. Inspired by the charity walkathon or marathon concept—in which participants raise money through networks of friends—Crowdrise's founders believe individuals or teams of volunteers should be able to attract funds in the same way, whether they're working in an American homeless shelter or helping build a school in rural Africa. Crowdrise calls it "Sponsored Volunteerism."

On the site, you create a project page for yourself or your team through which to showcase your volunteer activities by uploading text, photos, and videos. Using your email accounts, Facebook friends, or Twitter accounts, you let friends and family know what you're doing and ask them to sponsor your activities, with amounts as small as $25. You can also search for projects and join existing teams, either by volunteering or donating. Once your page is up, anyone can join your team or donate to your cause. So while you're giving your time, you're also using your volunteering to raise financial resources from others. It's a turbocharged form of volunteering, powered by online social networking.

Alicia Chastain, a San Francisco–based designer and one of the individuals with a Crowdrise page, is on the board of BayKids, where she began as a volunteer editing videos for the nonprofit. BayKids works with local hospitals to teach digital filmmaking skills to hospitalized children, helping them find new ways of expressing themselves. "More than once I went home in tears," Alicia writes on her page. "Not because it was sad, but because of the sheer will and courage these kids have. It is humbling." Alicia uses her Crowdrise page—which includes a video—to encourage people to give to BayKids.

The sponsored volunteering concept is catching on fast. But whether you're using the Web to find volunteer opportunities or to combine your volunteer activities with fundraising, the Internet has made it easier than ever to give your time. A whole world of community service exists—and, with a click of your mouse, you can now become part of it.

GETTING ON BOARD

Another important form of volunteering is serving on nonprofit or foundation boards. However, as with any form of philanthropy, giving some thought to your decisions matters. Your choice of nonprofit board, as well as how you engage with it, can make your presence more or less effective for both you and the organization.

If you approach it thoughtfully, you can absorb the best practices of one board and take that experience to another board. What I learned while on the board of Menlo School and Castilleja School (the high schools my brother and I respectively attended), I was able to bring to another local private school, Eastside College Preparatory School. I first encountered Eastside on an SV2 site visit, after which the school became one of our first SV2 grantees. Unlike Castilleja and Menlo, at Eastside every student was on full scholarship and the first in their family to be headed for college. My experience with Eastside, other educational institutions, and the other nonprofit boards on which I sat informed the way I led the boards of SV2 and the Stanford PACS (Center on Philanthropy and Civil Society).

Serving on a nonprofit board is a tremendous responsibility, and attending meetings and going to events is just the beginning of your stewardship. As a board member, you need to become fully engaged with an organization and contribute to its evolution directly with your time and expertise. You need to work closely with the nonprofit's executive team to help it achieve its goals and tackle its challenges. Then, as well as making a contribution, your service can become a critical part of your philanthropic journey, helping you acquire knowledge and skills you can use not only in your giving but also in your working life.

If you're an active philanthropist or community participant, chances are that at some point you'll be asked to join the board of a nonprofit or foundation, and an invitation to serve should be considered an honor. However, before accepting, ask yourself some questions. Is the organization one whose values you share? Are you passionate about its mission? Are the individuals on the board people with whom you'd like to collaborate? Does it have a strong leader at the helm, and what are its plans for the future? Is it in need of special skills and expertise that you can provide? As with volunteering, think about what you can bring to the table in terms of skills, experience, knowledge, and networks—are those a good fit with the organization's needs?

In addition, find out what kind of board it is, what commitment is expected of you, and what the board's activities involve. Does it exist purely for fundraising? Is it simply bringing together high-profile individuals to give the organization public credibility? Or is it a working board, with members who participate in the organization's evolution?

Another important consideration is how you'll support the organization financially. If you serve on a nonprofit board, you should be prepared to make a stretch gift to support its work (whatever *stretch* means to your personal finances), as board leadership in fundraising is important in setting an example for other donors. Often a measure of success for a nonprofit is what percentage of its board members are annual donors, as well as giving to its events, capital campaigns, or endowments—the sector "gold standard" being 100 percent. Many nonprofits raise a large portion of their annual operating funds from board members, and while they may not state this, the expectation may be implicit. So when joining a board, expect to be asked to support all of the above. You should also be willing to ask others in your networks to do the same.

Many boards do, however, have representatives either from among the people they serve or the broader community, as well as philanthropists and field experts. If your service falls into this category, you may not be required to give the same amount financially as other board members, but you may be required to raise the same amount. So it's a good idea to join a board only if you feel sufficiently committed to the organization's mission to do this.

Regardless of your role on any nonprofit board, pay attention so you recognize when your interest shifts, your ability to give time diminishes, or you are simply burnt out. Others can always bring fresh energy, resources, and expertise to an organization. Instead of drawing out your service because you feel obligated to fulfill a specific term, treat this as an opportunity for the nonprofit to acquire a new board member who may be able to bring different skills and connections to the table. Boards need regular renewal, as well.

Some boards are what I call "reporting boards," and their meetings can be unrewarding events. To me, it seems a waste of time, talent, and philanthropic capital to call together meetings of an extraordinary group of people (often key leaders in the community and industry) and proceed to talk at them (rather than with them) for several hours, with staff members reporting on items that could easily be distributed as preparatory materials. So find out how the organization structures its meetings and whether it gives members concise, informative reports in advance as background for the key issues to be discussed. Investigate what role the board plays in strategic planning and core decision making, as well as in coming up with new ideas and different ways of thinking about an issue.

When I chair a board, I structure meetings so as to make the most of the intellectual capital of those in the room, keeping introductory remarks and presentations to a minimum and maximizing time for group discussions and brainstorming. Leaders who fail to do this are missing a huge opportunity to tap into the expertise of board members and to engage them fully in the organization's mission and goals. So make sure that the chair of any board you sit on uses the time and talent of board members productively. This will make the experience far more valuable to both you *and* the organization.

WORKING FOR GOOD

Ben Amaba, a senior sales executive at IBM, is a particularly active volunteer. He not only serves on boards at universities and research organizations, but also speaks at Engineers Week and at career days for many Florida schools. Among the activities he loves most is getting schoolchildren and students fired up about studying math, science, and engineering. Among the many letters of thanks Ben has received from the young students he speaks to is one from an eight-year-old boy named Bryan. In his handwritten note, Bryan told Ben: "Just like an earthquake you rocked the classroom." These words are music to Ben's ears. "That's when you know you made a difference to somebody's life," he says. "I can't even put into words how I feel when I get those kinds of letters."

Ben is the son of a Filipino immigrant who joined the U.S. military early in his career and later worked in logistics and finance for the U.S. Navy. His father's story, says Ben, is one of the reasons he feels passionate about volunteering. "The U.S. had a program where they would let Filipino citizens join the navy to help them improve their quality of life," he explains. "And what motivates me is to bring the same opportunities to others that the U.S. presented to my father and to the world."

For Ben's family, many of those opportunities came in the form of the education and training provided by military officers (themselves volunteers) to minority families. "My dad couldn't speak English," says Ben. "He didn't even know what a checking account was. But senior officers came to the house to provide special programs to minorities in the navy. They were helping the ones coming in and, growing up, we saw that this was just normal behavior. That's why I'm drawn towards service rather than just writing a check."

Ben uses the knowledge and experience he's gained from his professional career to encourage students—from kindergarten through to postgraduate level—to consider careers in scientific and technical fields. Working through the Science, Technology, Engineering, and Mathematics (STEM) Education Coalition, Ben regularly finds himself in classrooms using his enthusiasm to inspire the students sitting in front of him. Sometimes this involves taking children from kindergarten to meet postdoctoral students. "I have five-year-olds that go to universities and build things and see prosthetics and ergonomics," says Ben. "And these kids are amazing—they're listening and understanding more than we think they are."

But while Ben has been giving his knowledge and experience to others, he's also been acquiring it. When he first started going into classrooms, he had to spend many hours preparing for the sessions, but he is now a skilled presenter. For Ben, his ability to help change young people's future never ceases to amaze him. Six months after he received the letter of thanks from Bryan, Ben saw him in the street and stopped to say hello. The eight-year-old explained again how much he'd enjoyed Ben's talk, but confessed that he didn't want to go into technology, math, or science. He wanted to be an attorney. However, after Ben's talk, he said, he'd got a new idea. "He told me he'd worked out how to make himself happy while also making me happy," explains Ben. "He said: 'I'm going to be a patent attorney.'" Ben was astonished—not only that, as a result of his class session, Bryan had spent several months thinking seriously about his career, but also that an eight-year-old had learned what a patent attorney was. "It's phenomenal," he says. "I think I dropped my groceries."

Becoming adept at teaching and presenting is just one of the skills you can acquire by volunteering in a field related to your work. You can also gain professional experience that might otherwise not be open to you. If you work in a law firm at a junior level, for example, it's unlikely that you'll work directly with clients until you have advanced within the firm. Doing pro bono work for a nonprofit could be a way of getting direct client experience, giving you the kind of interpersonal, leadership, and project management skills that would be difficult to acquire on the job at an early stage in your career.

What's more, volunteering can help you advance in your career, demonstrating your abilities to the people you report to and proving you're ready to take on greater responsibility. Corporate community projects—whether rebuilding homes for flood victims or teaching under-privileged children to read—bring people from various parts of the business together to work on charitable projects and thus are great ways to build your teamwork skills. These activities also provide networking opportunities. Who knows, as a second-year analyst in a bank, you could find yourself hammering nails into a wall with your chief strategy officer.

The corporate sector certainly has more to contribute than money. This was reflected in the Palindrome Pledge—an initiative of Palindrome Advisors—in which, in March 2011, one hundred global corporate leaders committed to change the way they give to the nonprofit sector by taking more prominent roles in the board management or operations of nonprofit organizations and by helping them with their business and management needs.

Large companies—who often see volunteering programs not only as part of corporate philanthropy but also as a way of building workforce skills—have developed sophisticated mechanisms to make it easier to organize their employee volunteer resources. IBM, whose employees worldwide have donated more than 11 million hours since 2003, harnesses the power of the Web to maximize these efforts. Ben Amaba and his coworkers can tap into IBM's On Demand Community, an online hub that helps employees and retirees assess their skills and then decide what kind of volunteer work they'd be best suited to do. Once they've figured this out, they can search the site for opportunities based on their interests and the amount of time they have to give. They can take online training courses to prepare themselves and track their volunteer work on the site by logging their hours.

Through links to documents, videos, and online presentations, employees learn new skills, make the most of their volunteer time, and share knowledge between volunteers, helping spread the experience of those who've gone before. "We use it to store our presentations," says Ben. "And not only is it information that is reusable by other people across the world, but I'm able to contribute to it as well."

Of course, not all companies have the resources to develop a system such as IBM's. But even if you work at a small company, you may be able to encourage your IT department to set up an intranet—an internal website—where volunteers in the company can share information. If there's an existing corporate intranet, you might persuade IT to add a volunteering micro-site to it. And if neither is possible, you could set up a volunteering page for your company on a social networking site such as Ning or Facebook and encourage colleagues to add their stories and experiences, as well as links to useful information.

Make sure you know what your employer is offering, too. Many companies will help connect employees to volunteer opportunities and give them a certain number of paid working hours a year to devote to this. Some even match your volunteer hours with dollars in the form of a donation to the nonprofit you've been assisting. Others offer more extensive volunteer opportunities. Some consulting firms send executives on overseas volunteer missions, for example, to work in developing countries on projects with nongovernmental organizations or nonprofits.

And if you cannot find a program in your own workplace, look into other ways of discovering how to put your professional skills to work for good. The Taproot Foundation, for example, helps business professionals donate skills in areas such as strategic planning, management, human resources, marketing, design, or IT to nonprofits in need of those skills.

If you own a business, remember that offering volunteer work to your staff brings many benefits. In addition to developing their skills and teamwork, it can help you recruit and retain the best employees at a time when—particularly for younger people—there's an increasing desire to work for companies who invest in their communities as well as in their economic success. A volunteering program can also help you establish your brand in the local, or even global, community. And all corporate volunteer programs help make the company a larger part of its employees' lives, which fosters loyalty.

To maximize your impact—particularly on the communities you're trying to help—you need to manage such a program carefully. A study by Deloitte, a consulting firm, found that only 38 percent of companies work with nonprofits to measure the impact that their employees' time is having.[5] Yet such measurement is critical, as it quantifies the benefits of community service to your employees and ensures that their individual skills are being used in the most appropriate way.

Organizations such as the Taproot Foundation and Senior Corps can help. They work with companies to design volunteer programs for employees and retirees. Organizations such as United Way can provide your company with information on local volunteering opportunities and will match your company with appropriate nonprofits in your area. They facilitate these connections by building a volunteer opportunity search box on your intranet, and providing toolkits to help educate managers and employees. Using existing resources, you can create new ways of giving in your company.

VolunteerMatch offers Web-based tools that can be used by an organization of any size to help manage, track, measure, and increase the impact of corporate volunteering programs. The American Red Cross's "Ready When the Time Comes" program helps partner companies train and prepare their employees for large-scale disasters, so they can act as reserves that can be called in to help when necessary. The Entrepreneurs Foundation works with companies nationally to set up both volunteering and giving programs, as well.

These programs and others help companies and employees not only increase the impact they can have on the communities in which they operate but also develop a stronger, more motivated workforce with better skills, improved teamwork, and leadership abilities. Through volunteering, companies can build their relationship with the local community while also enhancing their own human resources. It's what the business world would call a win-win.

MAKING IT HAPPEN

What to Ask Yourself When Considering Volunteering:
- How much time do you want to give?
- How often do you want to volunteer—for example, a month every year, an evening a week, or a couple of hours every weekend?

- Do you want to volunteer with someone as a bonding experience—perhaps your spouse, your children, or a friend?
- Are you looking to use volunteering as a means by which to meet new people for social or professional reasons?
- Do you want to give kindness and care—such as by reading stories to kids suffering from terminal illnesses—or do you want to put your mind to work—for example, by helping a nonprofit develop a marketing plan?
- Do you want to work directly with the people being helped by nonprofits or do you want to work with staff members at nonprofits?
- If you want to work with nonprofit staff, what are the most appropriate skills and knowledge you can offer them that they currently lack?
- What does the nonprofit you'd like to volunteer with need, and is this need something you can offer and something you want to do?
- Will your volunteering create value for both you and the nonprofit?
- How will you measure the success of your volunteering—these measures may include a certain amount of money raised at an event, a child's test scores improving over a semester, or a more beautiful community space?

What to Ask Organizations You'd Like to Volunteer For:
- What does the organization need in the way of skills?
- How does the organization manage its volunteers?
- Could you talk to one or a few other volunteers to learn about their experience of working with the organization?
- What are examples of volunteering they can give you?
- Does the organization do any training or introductory programs for volunteers?
- What learning opportunities are there at the organization?
- Does the organization need volunteers to work in the field helping to deliver its services, or does it need writers, publicists, IT specialists, or other types of volunteers to help run the organization itself?
- Who will supervise your work or be your point of contact?
- Does the nonprofit have the capacity to manage your presence as a volunteer?

What to Ask When Considering Board Membership:
- What type of board is this—a fundraising board, a titular board (a group of high-profile individuals who give the organization credibility but are not

necessarily active participants), a working board (high-engagement individuals who participate in building the organization), or a strategy board (with members involved in strategic decisions but rarely in implementing the strategy)?

- Who makes decisions—the executive committee, the board chair, the chief executive, and/or the nonprofit executives? Does the entire board have a say?
- How many meetings take place each year?
- Can you see past agendas to assess how much of the board's time is spent participating in strategic decision making rather than listening to staff presentations?
- Can you talk to a few current board members or attend a meeting, or both?
- Is the board created primarily for fundraising? If so, meetings may entail mainly listening to reports, with decisions driven solely by staff (if you're passionate about the mission and committed to your fundraising responsibilities, this should not discourage you from becoming involved).
- Does the board have a "give or get" policy, requiring board members to either give a minimum amount of money themselves or to raise an equivalent sum from others? (Don't let such a policy put you off, but make sure you can meet fundraising levels expected of board members.)
- What are the fiduciary responsibilities of the board, and what is the oversight process for managing and allocating organizational resources transparently and effectively?
- What is the board's annual process for assessing the performance of the CEO or executive director?
- What is the board's annual self-assessment process?
- How often does the organization create a strategic plan, and what is the board's role in creating the plan?
- Does the organization have directors and officers (D&O) insurance to protect board members in the event of a legal dispute?
- Will you have time outside of the board meeting schedule to support, advise, and work with the organization's staff?
- Are board members expected to give names and addresses of friends to the organization? (This is often a requirement of serving on an event committee or chairing an event.)
- Are you willing to introduce ten of your friends to the organization? (It's a good idea to join boards only if you feel comfortable doing this.)

- How does the community view this board and its organization (this can influence your effectiveness in supporting it)? Ask five to ten people from different parts of the community before agreeing to join.
- Are board members expected to serve on one or more board committees as well? If so, how often do board committees meet and what are committee members' responsibilities?
- Are board members expected to do work outside the board committee meetings?

Innovation Lab—Ideas to Test:
- Talk to local nonprofit leaders about which volunteers at their organizations have been most effective and why.
- Ask friends or colleagues what their most rewarding volunteer experiences have been and why.
- Go online and choose one volunteer opportunity through a matching service.
- Take stock of your skills (whether business, creative, technical, or in communications) and offer them to one of the nonprofits you are already funding.
 • Attend a meeting of your local Rotary Club, Junior League, Elk's Lodge, Lions Club, AARP chapter, or any other volunteer or religious organization and see if a giving community can enhance your own gifts of time.
- Select one of your most rewarding volunteering experiences and talk about it with people you know through a social network such as Facebook or Twitter. Ask people to comment on your story, and you may receive valuable insights into the volunteering experiences of others.
- Help a nonprofit expand its existing volunteer program, or help a nonprofit create one.
- If your company has no volunteering program, find out how you could start one.

For the Family:
- Take your children on a site visit to one of the nonprofits with which you are currently or considering getting involved.
- Consider taking a "volunteer vacation" with the family to a location that is interesting to you all.
- Take your family to a beach or public park cleanup. Then take them all out for a pizza as a reward for hard work.

- With your children, make a list of things each of them is good at and likes to do. Then think of ways that your children can put their own talents to work to help others.
- Find out if there are any nonprofits in your area that allow teens or college students to sit on the board, as board fellows or volunteer members, or are willing to pilot such an opportunity. Nonprofits who serve youth may be especially interested.
- Spend a weekend afternoon with your children helping a local food bank with a physical capacity issue—such as crating a ton of oranges or packing a hundred food packages for families in need. You can easily do this activity with one or two other families, which will increase both the impact and fun.
- Create a "volunteering circle"—like a giving circle for time instead of money. Partner with two or three other families who have children of similar ages and with whom you already enjoy spending time. Choose an issue area that's important to all of you, and plan monthly volunteer projects focused on that issue area. End each volunteering session with a potluck dinner at a circle member's home.
- Make volunteering around an important family event or holiday a tradition.
- Ask the religious institution you attend if it has any community activities that you and your kids can become involved with.

And Remember:

- Your offer of time and skills may not necessarily be accepted by a nonprofit—the organization may already have enough volunteers or may not have the capacity to manage your presence (free help—including student interns—can be costly to nonprofits in terms of staff time and energy).
- Not all organizations can legally allow people under the age of eighteen to volunteer (this is not true for every organization, and some nonprofits do accept younger volunteers).
- There's no shortage of nonprofits to volunteer at, so if your talents don't fit the first place you offer them, don't stop looking.
- For a nonprofit, volunteers can present a significant management burden, so if you're considering volunteering, make sure the organization is able to accommodate your presence and that you have something of value to offer (this is true to an even greater extent for teenage volunteers and college student interns).

- An organization to which you're also donating money may feel obligated to accept your offer of voluntary help, whether from you or from a family member. It's your responsibility to make sure you're meeting an unmet need and that you'll be helping rather than hindering its work.

- Often nonprofits turn first to board members for professional expertise, but some have board committees with nonboard volunteers (particularly in areas such as investment, audit, marketing, social media, and fundraising).

- Serving on a board is just one of countless ways you can serve an organization—fundraising requirements need not be a limiting factor in your engagement.

- If you're leaving a board, be honest about why (critical feedback can be among the most valuable gifts you can give an organization).

- Activities in which your children participate can provide excellent opportunities for volunteering, such as coaching Little League or other sports teams, helping create costumes for a dance recital, or being a troop leader for Boy Scouts or Girl Scouts.

- For many nonprofits, offers of time, skills, and talent are even more valuable than offers of money.

- Volunteer work can include the most unglamorous tasks. You may find yourself cleaning out a storage room, addressing envelopes, or making photocopies. No matter how inspiring the cause, the work can be emotionally challenging, physically challenging, or unstimulating—but changing people's lives for the better makes it more than worthwhile—it's exhilarating.

2

CONNECTING THE DROPS

New Ways to Make a World of Difference

*Turbocharge your giving through connectivity—use the virtual world
to bring about change in the real one.*

Seema Bhende inherited her family's deep commitment to personal
giving. Born in Michigan and raised in New York state, she now
lives in Seattle. But her philanthropic roots lie far away—in the Indian
state of Punjab. There her family played an active role in the shaping of
modern India, participating in protests against British rule, founding two
newspapers, and contributing to post-independence peacemaking. Seema
often remembers the struggles of her family—which lost several members
in the post-independence violence—when thinking about how she wants
to help create a better world.

In 2009, when she moved to Seattle from Manhattan with her
husband for a new job, she'd had to leave the StepUp Women's Network,
a philanthropic group she'd volunteered with back in New York. So,
soon after arriving on the West Coast, Seema—who'd always been
involved in community service—began a search for a new nonprofit. As
a starting point, a friend had recommended an event at the Seattle Public
Library hosted by the Young Professional International Network, an
organization that unites executives in their twenties and thirties who have
a passion for the world around them.

At the event, she heard Adnan Mahmud—a thirty-two-year-old
Microsoft program manager who had moved to the United States from

Bangladesh—talk about the nonprofit he'd recently founded with his wife, Nadia Khawaja. Jolkona Foundation, Adnan told the audience, was pioneering a new form of philanthropy—one in which donors could make gifts in small amounts and yet see the impact of every single donation, whether giving $40 to educate a girl in Afghanistan for ten months or $200 to pay for a prosthetic limb for a worker in Bangladesh. In an innovative addition to its portfolio, Jolkona even allows donors to help support its operating costs with gifts that cover items such as one month's utility bills or the cost of holding a Jolkona strategy meeting. Whatever they choose to give to, donors can track what's happening to their donation and receive proof of its impact.

To do this, Jolkona harnesses the power of technology. First, donors do everything online, learning about issues and choosing causes or individuals to support. Using an interactive map, donors take an online tour of the world in search of projects, and they make their gifts over a secure payment system. Every time the partner nonprofit spends funds on a project, the donor is notified via email and can log on to see a video, photograph, or story about the person or community the money has helped.

Gifts range from $5, which buys medicine to prevent a child in India from dying of diarrhea, to $50, which buys a solar cooker for a family in Tibet, or $300 to upgrade a pond in Malawi, providing a livelihood for women fish farmers. Small amounts add up, too, Adnan told the audience. *Jolkona*, he explained, is a Bengali word meaning "a drop of water"—and in this new form of philanthropy, drop by drop, donors create a ripple that spreads outward, generating a significant movement of social change.

At the end of Adnan's talk, "I was blown away," Seema says. "He was saying you don't need to be rich to be a philanthropist." While Seema had always given her time generously, she had never thought of herself as a donor, let alone a philanthropist. Now here was an organization helping to create a new generation of philanthropists with smaller financial resources than their predecessors but more technologically savvy—people giving sooner rather than later and wanting to connect more directly to their gifts.

Seema liked the way Jolkona provided donors with tangible evidence of what happened to every dollar they gave. "In the past, I've often cut small checks to friends running marathons but I had no idea how the money was used," she admits. "It's like buying a box of cereal—you want to know what's in it before you eat it. So if you're an active consumer, shouldn't that apply to everything you consume?"

Seema realized she'd found what she'd been looking for—an entrepreneurial nonprofit that was rethinking the whole concept of philanthropy. She also realized she could contribute her professional experience in corporate social responsibility and marketing to the nonprofit's growth at an early stage in its life. "I wanted to be part of a movement that was changing the way people view philanthropy," she says. "And not being an older person with thousands of dollars to give away, this felt very tangible." So as the session ended, she approached the stage, introduced herself to Adnan, and asked him how she could get involved.

THE POWER OF THE WEB

In the 1990s, a new force started connecting people across the globe in ways that had previously been impossible. That force was the Internet. People could buy things from and sell to individuals they'd never met—without using a middleman. Those looking for romantic partners could post their wish lists, descriptions, and photographs, and view potential dates. With so much data newly available on a mass scale, people could share knowledge, creating virtual encyclopedias in a way that was unprecedented only a few years earlier. Big corporations could solicit ideas from inventors, academics, and even customers via open source websites.

Fundraising changed too. Strangely enough, the philanthropic world was slow to wake up to the potential of this new instrument of change. To be sure, charities and foundations established websites, describing their activities and providing ways for potential donors and grantees to contact them. However, it wasn't until the rise of social networking technology—and a new generation driven to make a difference—that the Internet became a significant tool for the philanthropic community.

Gradually, philanthropic leaders have embraced this tool to engage donors. The Rockefeller Foundation has forcefully shown the Internet to be more than a store window for charities; it brings everyone into the business of social change. To solicit new problem-solving ideas, it formed a partnership with GlobalGiving, an online donor marketplace, and InnoCentive, an online research organization established by Eli Lilly, the pharmaceuticals group, which offers financial rewards to any scientist or developer with a breakthrough idea. In the philanthropic version pioneered by the Rockefeller Foundation, the problems are social and economic, such as lack of access to health care, water, food, and economic opportunity.

The model challenges everyone from nonprofits and funders to researchers and entrepreneurs to use open innovation or crowdsourcing to approach social, environmental, and economic problems, whether that's finding a cheap method of purifying water or devising an affordable rainwater harvesting storage tank for people in developing countries. "If you want an answer, ask everyone," says the Rockefeller Foundation on its website.

Here again, the Web is bringing individuals into the process of change-making. A few years ago, if you had an idea for water purification or rainwater harvesting and storage, where would you have gone to have this idea evaluated or adopted? Tracking down the right nonprofit or foundation to approach would have been impossible for most of us. Now you can just go online.

Others have also embraced this new, open, tech-enabled approach to social change. In 2007, to tap into what it called "citizen-centered" problem solving, the Case Foundation—established by Steve and Jean Case—launched the "Make It Your Own Awards," a competition in which applicants submitted ideas for making a difference in their communities. In its research, Case had found that many people felt disconnected from the public sector and nonprofit institutions whose mission is to solve community problems. So it decided to use the Web to seek ideas from within the community itself—whether from individuals or small groups—and to award funding to the best of those ideas.

Competitions that solicit ideas are not new to the world of philanthropy. But the Case Foundation's version gave the concept a new twist—with the help of the Internet. "In a first, a major foundation is offering the public a direct role in deciding who should receive some of its money, a process typically shrouded in mystery," wrote the *New York Times*'s Stephanie Strom at the time.[1] In the competition, individuals from all over the country submitted their ideas through the foundation's website and, for the top four finalists (who each received $35,000 in total), members of the public conducted the judging via an online voting system. Giving ordinary citizens a role in helping a foundation choose how to spend its money represented a significant move away from the old world, in which large institutions decided what was good for society.

The Make It Your Own Awards have since closed, but they were soon followed by other examples of philanthropic crowdsourcing, such as JPMorgan Chase's annual Chase Community Giving program. Through Facebook, the bank allowed users to vote on which of the more than 500,000 participating nonprofits should receive a share of the bank's philanthropic funding. A Gift Vote feature lets users give additional votes to a friend. Meanwhile, the charities can create and edit their profiles online to tell their stories through videos and photos. In its first two years, Chase's Community Giving program gave $10 million to three hundred small nonprofits and community groups, and in March 2011 the bank committed $25 million and two years to the Facebook-based program.

The Rockefeller Foundation's open innovation initiative, the Case Foundation's citizen-driven competition, and the Chase Community Giving program are all part of a new wave of online philanthropy that engages you as an individual donor in a far more powerful way than if you were simply writing checks. Through the Web, you can become much more than a donor—you can become a high-impact philanthropist.

You can even take part in virtual fundraising events. Since 2005, the American Cancer Society, known for its walkathons, has staged walks

on Second Life, the virtual reality site. There you create an avatar (a
digital representation of yourself) to socialize, connect, learn—and now
give. During the society's annual Relay for Life of Second Life, you can
have your avatar "walk for charity" through cyberspace.

The amount of money that can be raised in this virtual world is rising
fast. In 2005, the Relay for Life of Second Life collected $5,000 with
just a few hundred walkers. In 2008, it generated $215,000—more than
the amounts raised in the three preceding years combined. Between 2005
and 2010, the American Cancer Society raised more than $800,000 in
Second Life. This is a large sum—but it's not the bequest of millionaires;
it's the aggregation of small amounts of time and money. By going online
to give, you can be part of this collective action.

It's very different from the days when to give in such small amounts
you had to put your dollars into the collection boxes rattled by charity
fundraisers on the street—and you'd have only the vaguest idea about
what would happen to your money. In the new Web-enabled era, donations are traceable, giving you the kind of accountability—with even the
smallest gifts—that was once available only to very large donors.

The virtual world also helps preserve the real world. If you're a
Second Life resident, your avatar can purchase and plant a tree from an
endangered species on a virtual island on the site—an innovative idea
devised by Plant-It 2020, the nonprofit late singer John Denver founded
to rebuild forests and assist the people who rely on them. For every tree
you plant in Second Life, the nonprofit plants a real one of the same
species in an appropriate location.

The Plant-It 2020 approach has something in common with organizations such as Jolkona—donor choice. Assisted by the Web, we, as
donors, get to choose the tree species we would like to have planted. And
as with Jolkona, the click of a mouse also gives us access to information—
in this case, about world forests, tree species at risk, and the problems
associated with deforestation.

One Web-based nonprofit, DonorsChoose, uses online giving to
encourage you to support projects in America's public schools. On the
site, teachers post descriptions of the projects they'd like to see funded—
whether that's updating a classroom map or providing students with a

digital camera—and you can pick the one to which you'd like to contribute.

As well as channeling and monitoring funds, a growing number of websites offer you a chance to become more deeply involved. Razoo.com, a social networking site, connects donors to nonprofits, helping them create fundraising campaigns and allowing them to share their stories with others online. Givezooks links you to nonprofits that promote their fundraising efforts online through social media networks. Meanwhile, Crowdrise allows you to create a page to promote your cause and then solicit funds—via email, Facebook, or Twitter—from friends, family, and other contacts.

Well known for its trailblazing role in online microlending, Kiva.org helps you make small loans to low-income entrepreneurs in the developing world. In its first five years, from 2005 to mid-2011, it facilitated more than $230 million in microloans from over 600,000 lenders (with a 98.79 percent repayment rate).

While Kiva (which was co-founded by Jessica Jackley, one of my former Stanford GSB students, and Matt Flannery) is in the business of making loans rather than engaging in philanthropy (you receive repayment of your loan), the idea is that you can quickly and easily make a difference to the life of an impoverished person in another country. And you can see—through stories and photos on the website—profiles of the people you've assisted and what your money has helped achieve (you can also donate to Kiva itself, which is a nonprofit organization).

As it's highly interactive and visually stimulating, online giving is a great way to engage your children or teenagers. With a budget of even $25 a month, philanthropy can become a family activity through a "Giving Night" on which everyone takes turns making the case for where that week's gift should go. This promotes giving as a family value and allows everyone to learn about new issues and causes.

Meanwhile, with more online philanthropic outlets emerging, philanthropy is following the model of online retailers. Brick-and-mortar stores make money by selling a handful of products at high prices in a street location, while online retailers such as Amazon, without the limitations of shelf space, can make hundreds of thousands of small sales in a cost-efficient way (including donations to nonprofits through their Wish List program). Similarly, online nonprofits can connect with hundreds of thousands of donors, regardless of their geographic location. Network for Good, for example, makes it easy for you to donate or volunteer to any of 1.2 million charities that can be found all in one place: online.

Because the Web lowers transaction costs so dramatically, it can combine thousands of small donations to produce extremely large sums. In 2010, online giving increased by 40 percent, according to Convio, which provides strategic consulting and software for nonprofits.[2] Online giving played a huge role in the assistance that flooded into Haiti after the 2010 earthquake, for example.

It was during the Haiti crisis that text message giving gained prominence as a means of donating money. And alliances have emerged between phone companies and charities, as in the United Kingdom, where (through a partnership launched in 2011 between Vodafone and JustGiving called "JustTextGiving") charities can receive donations by text, free of charge.

In recent years, mobile phone providers have partnered with major nonprofits such as the Red Cross to allow users to donate a few dollars to disaster relief through a simple text message. Television shows such as *American Idol* encouraged tens of millions of voting viewers to do this after the 2011 Japan tsunami, and at many charity events, the MC announces a "text now" moment during the proceedings to urge attendees to donate live (peer pressure helps, too, with some events posting the names of donors live on a screen for all to see).

As social networking technology evolves, more fundraising is taking place online, with individuals and nonprofits tapping into the fast mass communication networks available to them through microblogging sites such as Twitter. Through tweets, you can become a fundraiser, building a giving network and launching a campaign that reaches thousands of people instantaneously.

If you're using smartphone apps, you don't even need to be sitting at a computer. Take Foursquare, a mobile application through which friends connect with each other, check in to update their real-time locations, and receive points as they do so. The connectivity of this app has potential when applied to giving—and fundraisers, large and small, are tapping into this, launching campaigns whereby sponsors make a small donation every time a point is awarded for a Foursquare check-in. When Foursquare teamed up with Microsoft and PayPal to raise money for the Save the Children Haiti Relief Fund, more than 135,000 check-ins were logged, raising $15,000.[3]

Of course, social networking, Web-based, text message, and smartphone donations remain a small percentage of overall giving—but talking to my husband, Marc, who's on the board of Facebook and is an investor in Twitter, Groupon (which started life as an offshoot of online giving platform The Point), and Foursquare, I can see the vast role these types of companies are likely to play in the future of giving.

 For a start, giving online or through PayPal has been growing. And online companies are capitalizing on their subscriber bases to generate philanthropic funds—in 2010, Groupon used its online network of subscribers to help the Carnegie Museums of Pittsburgh attract new members by offering them year-long access to four of the city's museums along with guest passes and drinks vouchers, all for $40. Carnegie Museums advertised the deal on its Twitter and Facebook pages and sent text message links to its members. According to the *Chronicle of Philanthropy*, the initiative generated about 1,300 membership sales during the three-day buying period, more than doubling the membership of all four museums.[4]

As online gaming—a multibillion-dollar industry—has grown, so has its potential to give through games, particularly games such as Zynga's FarmVille—in which players grow virtual fruits and vegetables on their own farms. Zynga has used its popularity to attract charitable dollars, matching or outpacing bigger technology companies in raising money, according to the *Wall Street Journal*.[5] But instead of simply creating donation links, the company offers players the ability to buy virtual items to support relief efforts. For the Japan earthquake, for example, players could buy and raise crops such as daikon radishes, and the money they paid for the crops would be donated to Japan earthquake victims.

However, the Internet does more than facilitate philanthropic payments and donations. As philanthropists embrace the Web, they are ushering in a new era of openness and transparency. Take the decision announced by DonorsChoose in April 2011 to open up its database (which contains details of more than 300,000 classroom projects and more than a million anonymous donations) to Web developers and data analysts, invite them to use its information to build useful tools, and offer a prize for the best offerings.[6]

Most important, online companies such as Facebook and Twitter are redefining notions of privacy. With more people prepared to share information about themselves and their activities online, more opportunities are emerging to engage individuals in giving. Online, people increasingly define their social profiles not only by their favorite books, bands, and activities, but also by their social passions. And increasingly, these donors use sites such as Facebook and Twitter to talk about giving experiences and passions and to share related photos and videos with their friends and followers. As a report from the Monitor Institute and the Knight Foundation puts it, the Web plays a critical role in "harnessing the best network-centric practices, the ones that might unleash individual interactivity to achieve social impact at a scale and speed never before possible."[7]

The opportunities to harness these trends for good are enormous. As more people use social networking to connect philanthropically as well as socially, the percentage of funding generated online will grow. "It used to be the pennies we raised through UNICEF boxes," says Lucy Bernholz, a leading philanthropy blogger and founder of Blueprint Research & Design.[8] "Now you're talking about 15- and 17-year-old children who are savvy enough and committed enough to raise tens of thousands of dollars and sending it halfway around the world." In the fast-moving world of technology, constant upgrades, new functions, and improved applications will only make this easier. Then, small drops of giving will add up to something really big.

GIVING WITH DEEP ROOTS

Stories of her family's philanthropic history loom large in Seema's consciousness, forming a backdrop to her own giving. Her paternal grandfather was killed during an anti-British riot, while her maternal grandfather, Jagat Narain—committed to the pursuit of Indian independence—joined Gandhi's noncooperation movement in 1920. The movement resisted British occupation of India through nonviolent civil disobedience; it has since inspired civil rights movements across the world. It was no easy path, however. Many suffered at the hands of the colonial rulers, including Seema's grandfather, who spent several years in jail (missing the birth of his daughter, Seema's mother).

In 1981, tragedy descended on the family when Sikh terrorists assassinated Jagat Narain. Two years later, Seema's uncle, Ramesh Chandra, became the second family victim of the violence. Yet Seema's relatives maintained their focus on philanthropy. In fact, giving was how they responded to trauma and loss—relatives immediately embarked on charitable work, helping women who'd lost husbands during the conflict, while the newspaper initiated a fund to support victims of terrorist action.

Seema is proud of the courage and fortitude of her family. Moreover, she has a strong sense of the opportunities she's been given. Her parents were the first in their families to leave India and come to the United States. "I have a deep sense of appreciation of the life I was born into and how different it could have been if I'd been a girl in a rural village in India," she says. "That's carried with me and reinforced my commitment to giving." It also gives a special significance to Seema's favorite quote: "to whom much is given, much is expected."

For Seema, civic service started at a young age with the Girl Scouts and Interact, a young person's version of a Rotary Club. As a young professional, she spent more than a year in India with the Futures Group, helping implement USAID health programs promoting children's wellness, fighting HIV-AIDS, and improving maternal health through family planning. "India is where my most personal passion is," she explains. "And when women have child after child, their health deteriorates, and it creates financial challenges for families."

While in India, Seema also worked as an English teacher with the Kutumb Foundation, a nonprofit dedicated to slum children forced to work as day laborers. Their only opportunity for schooling is at night, so the Kutumb Foundation runs evening classes and activities for them. The experience prompted Seema to start an urban health program called KAFILA (which means "caravan of people" in Hindi) in partnership with the Lions Club. "While I was tutoring, I saw how malnourished the children were," she says. "They had difficulty focusing and many of them had jaundice or vision problems from vitamin deficiency."

It was a formative time for Seema—one in which she acquired skills and knowledge that have since proved extremely valuable. Working in India gave her new insights into some of the problems faced by poor populations in the developing world. It also gave her a chance to learn about her family's homeland.

After she returned from India, Seema wanted to use her passion for giving in a corporate setting, so she joined L'Oreal Paris as its director of strategic philanthropy and led the brand's corporate social responsibility efforts. Now in Seattle, she works in the Social Innovation Practice of Waggener Edstrom Worldwide, a global communications agency, working for corporate and nongovernmental organization (NGO) clients. "Philanthropy work doesn't need to be just about volunteering or donating money," she says. "There are companies, nonprofits, and international organizations that need young, talented people with business and NGO skills to help their organizations grow."

When Seema thinks back to her time in India, however, she recognizes the loneliness of many of those early giving activities. While working in the slums, images of the barefoot children she taught and the squalor in which they lived kept her awake at night. "If I'd do anything differently now, it might be to get more of my friends to work with me," she says. "Because I often did things alone, and that can be very intimidating."

So when she first met Adnan and learned about Jolkona, Seema realized she'd found a new way of giving, one in which everything could be shared, from experiences and knowledge to friendship and commitment. "The Internet changes everything," she says. "It turns philanthropy into a collective process."

Appropriately enough, Seema's first Jolkona donation was to support computer literacy, a program through which a $30 donation provides six months of computer training for a child in rural Guatemala. "My husband and I selected this program because we are both passionate believers in innovation and technology driving development," says Seema, who went on to volunteer as director of strategy for Jolkona. "We spend more than 75 percent of our days on computers, and the Internet enables us to work, grow, and explore. We wanted to provide that access to children." Seema and her husband also supported three Guatemalans, including a girl named Celestina. The couple received information about the girl's age, and about her family and her dream of becoming a teacher. "The feedback made me feel involved and impactful. And hopefully I was a small part in helping Celestina achieve her dream," says Seema.

For Seema, entering into the world of online giving was a further step in what has already been a rich philanthropic journey. It's never too early to start giving, and a $5 gift could set you off on a voyage that will become a lifelong venture. An hour spent volunteering would be another way to begin that journey. Your time, energy, and skills are powerful gifts.

SHRINKING THE WORLD

In December 2009, with Christmas approaching, Taylor Corbett, then a sophomore at Occidental College in Los Angeles, had an idea. Instead of exchanging holiday gifts with his family, he'd ask them to donate to projects through the Jolkona Foundation. "I could either get a sweater I'm never going to wear, or I could give a girl in Afghanistan an education—and when you do the math, it's clear that it's so much better giving a girl in Afghanistan an education." His family loved the idea. Taylor's mother gave the equivalent of a year's education for an Afghan girl to all her friends. Collectively, the family raised several hundred dollars.

Taylor is one of a new generation of philanthropists—young people who are exploring online ways of giving made possible through social media. A student, budding photojournalist, and fan of travel and summer road trips, Taylor is passionate about fighting poverty and promoting education. And as with many of his generation, philanthropic passions are as much a part of his online profile as his studies and hobbies.

Philanthropic interests help define who he is and how he connects with friends and family.

While at college, Taylor found what he learned of the world's problems—from global poverty to global warming—overwhelming. He felt unable to do anything to help. "In class, they said that when you have influence in business or are a leader in government, you can take your knowledge and apply it," he explains. "For me, that's not good enough. I don't want to wait thirty years—I want the opportunity to have an impact now."

Online philanthropy has given Taylor that opportunity. After his Christmas fundraising campaign, he became a Jolkona blogger, writing about causes that inspire him and connecting with other young donors. He also feels that the Internet has brought him closer to issues in developing countries that interest him. "It's made the world much smaller," he says.

Like a growing number of philanthropists, Taylor also places great importance on tracking the impact of donations. "Simply to give isn't enough," he says. "There's a level of responsibility that goes along with giving. We want to know our dollars are having the most impact—we want the most bang for our buck."

Taylor also likes the fact that his small donations can help transform the prospects of people in far-off places. "Ultimately, all these problems are at the level of individuals," he argues. "If you start thinking you have to solve global poverty single-handed, you get bogged down and nothing gets done. But if you can make just one girl's life better, it's a big step forward."

Empowered by this form of giving, Taylor has taken his involvement to new levels—in the real world. In 2010, he spent the summer in Bangladesh interning with BRAC, a microfinance institution that's one of Jolkona's nonprofit partners. There, he worked on a program giving ultra-poor people financial literacy classes and business training, as well as the assets—poultry, a cow, or fabric for sewing—they need to create a small business and graduate into the microfinance program.

"One thing that's really neat about Jolkona is that they're trying to rebrand what it means to be a philanthropist," he says. "You don't need to have millions of dollars or come from old money—anyone can be a philanthropist, and anyone can see the impact that their money is making."

AN EVOLVING MODEL

While online giving sites attract tens of thousands of enthusiastic philanthropists, the idea of connecting directly with individual beneficiaries is still evolving. One thing to remember is that while the Web has opened the doors to individual giving wide, online giving is not as direct and free as it might at first seem. For a start, social networking sites that direct money to charities may charge fees to cover the processing of credit cards and other administrative costs—and many take a certain percentage of each gift made through their portal. So be sure to investigate what that "cost of giving" is, prior to making your gift (that information should be on the organization's website).

When it comes to microlending websites, the relationship between online donors and the individuals they are helping is not entirely one-to-one. Take Kiva, for example. As some commentators have pointed out, the money lent to entrepreneurs in developing countries through Kiva's website is directed to borrowers through intermediaries—the microfinance organizations that are ultimately responsible for managing the loans.[9]

Jolkona also partners with nonprofits working on the ground in developing countries. These partners are carefully vetted by requiring submissions of financial information, lists of directors, and references. If a nonprofit's track record looks good, Jolkona creates a memorandum of understanding and conducts due diligence on the organization. Once accepted, nonprofit partners manage the online donations Jolkona receives.

Perhaps it's a good thing that intermediaries are still playing a role in directing our money to good causes. After all, leaving donors to choose how philanthropic funds are used can present problems. What if, for example, Plant-It 2020 donors pick too many of one type of tree and none of the most endangered species? What if online donors collectively generate only half the amount of money needed to complete a project? On the other hand, what if a cause pulls at people's heartstrings, prompting a wave of funding for an issue that does not in fact need vast financial resources?

And tackling poverty is a complicated business. It's great to give someone money or a loan to buy a plow to help increase their earning potential. However, if follow-up funds or money for things such as training and fertilizers fail to materialize, the farmer might not be able to make full use of that equipment. We need intermediaries on the ground to verify the validity of the organizations we want to give to and help us assess the impact our money is having.

Donor choices can have unintended consequences. Unsuitable or unwanted donations—such as expired medicine or canned food, inappropriate clothing or household supplies, or obsolete computer equipment—can create headaches for relief workers who've often had to use incinerators to dispose of items that could be dangerous or create bottlenecks in the relief supply system. As donors, our hearts might be in the right place, but we don't always know what's best for the individuals who are suffering or in need.

Some organizations have addressed the issue of donor choice with new options. The World Food Programme, for example, allows you to pick a designation for your money such as school meals for children or help for the survivors of specific disasters, such as the earthquake victims of Haiti. However, it also gives you the option of donating your money to "where it is needed most," leaving decisions on how the money is spent in the WFP's hands.

Intermediaries remain important, at least for now. And this is just as true in online giving as it is in other forms of donation. After all, a small farmer in Tanzania or a textile weaver in Pakistan may not have Internet access, be able to write you an email in English, or possess a bank account, let alone be able to receive a donation or loan online.

Yet if the one-to-one donor-donee relationship remains more romance than reality, e-philanthropy brings givers and receivers closer together than was ever possible before, expanding understanding between communities living in very different parts of the world. And we tend to be much more generous when we can grasp what others are experiencing.

The loans you make online might still go through intermediaries of various kinds. But the recipients of the money are real, as are the problems they face. Using the connectivity of the Web, they can tell you exactly what they need and, through photographs, videos, and email, you can track their progress and see how your money is improving their lives in a way that was once only possible by boarding a plane. As an engaged e-giver, you can become an educated and informed philanthropist.

INFORMED AND CONNECTED

As an academic and professional philanthropist, I find the Web one of my most important tools. When I joined the faculty at Stanford Graduate School of Business in 2000, no field-based courses on strategic philanthropy existed (apart from those on history or volunteerism). I had to start pretty much from scratch designing a program to prepare business school and college students for a philanthropic career. Even back then, when what was online was more limited, the Web helped me figure out which foundations would be exciting to publish cases on. I could push my research work further than would have been possible even a few years earlier, and I created courses on philanthropy that were far richer.

In today's world, the Web should be a critical tool for anyone who takes giving seriously. Through background material, images, and videos, you can find out what's really needed—whether it's nutritious food for drought victims in Africa or funds to hire extra counselors for a local teen rescue center. You can create your own information channels by signing up for newsletters. Through Google Alerts, you can select certain key terms such as "animal rights," "leukemia research," or "watershed protection" and receive daily or weekly notifications of the appearance of these words in blogs or news stories.

The amount of information available online is astonishing. On their websites, nonprofits post details about what they do and the social issues they address, often accompanied by photographs and video clips. What's so powerful about the Internet is that, as an individual donor, you can tap into the expertise of people who've spent years immersed in the kinds of issues to which you may want to contribute. Their knowledge constitutes a rich treasure.

Online, you can often find out which foundations are working in areas you're interested in and what nonprofits they fund. You can download their research and annual reports or check out the grantee sections of their websites to read about how they approach particular issues and which activities are proving most effective. Armed with this information, you can either donate to nonprofits that fit your goals (or, if they can receive public donations, the foundations that fund them), or use the knowledge you've acquired to inform your giving choices.

The Internet has given us something else that's new—transparency. Online, you can often find out how an organization allocates its annual budget, what it pays its executives, and how dependent it is on any single funder or set of funders. This has led to greater accountability, for the old command-and-control approach to information management is no longer possible when anyone can go online and find out how large organizations are funded and how they spend their money.

While it conveys positive information on developments in the philanthropic sector, the Web also exposes weaknesses. The world woke up to this reality after the terrorist attacks of September 11, when it emerged that not all of the hundreds of millions of dollars raised by the American Red Cross were going to the survivors and the families of those killed.

In fact, the Red Cross has always taken a portion of what it raises for any disaster and put it aside so that it has a pool of funds ready for use when the next crisis hits. However, it had not proactively communicated this to the American public. The misunderstanding led to a huge public outcry. Across the Web, debate raged about a bait-and-switch operation.

As a result, the Red Cross made an exception to its normal practice and announced that, in that instance, all contributions would fund the short- and long-term needs of those affected by the attacks. It has since introduced changes to its communications to make sure donors can see exactly how their contributions are spent and that they are notified when sufficient funding has been raised for any disaster response.

However, the incident transformed the philanthropic arena, dramatically raising the level of public transparency required of the entire sector. For the first time in history, the media—much of it online— became the mechanism for accountability for the philanthropic world. Empowered by the Internet, the day of the informed donor had arrived.

Online, you can even become a generator of information, too. In the past few years, rapid changes in technology have eliminated the need for technical know-how when producing and posting content online, whether text, audio, or video. Simple publishing tools mean almost anyone can now design a website, create a blog, or launch a fundraising campaign online.

But perhaps as important, the world of e-philanthropy has created another phenomenon—the emergence of new communities of givers. Donors to sites such as Jolkona can now share their giving experiences in the blogosphere. Users have become activists in important campaigns. In 2007, Witness (the human rights nonprofit founded by singer Peter Gabriel) launched a website called The Hub that helped anyone with a digital or phone camera capturing footage of human rights abuses to upload those as easily as on YouTube, giving them the ability to publish their images to a global audience. (The Hub has now moved the human rights–related media uploaded since its launch in December 2007 to an archive where all content is accessible, but the uploading and commenting functionality have been turned off.)

At the same time, people are using social networking sites such as Facebook and Ning (of which my husband is co-founder and chairman) to connect with others who share their passions. On Causes Exchange, for example, you can form an advocacy group, share your passions and ideas with others through email or Facebook, and create a virtual community of givers who can engage with your cause from anywhere in the world. You might use Causes as a platform to spread the word about an issue, inspiring and informing others virally. Or you could also select a beneficiary organization for donations from your group.

Another site, Jumo—founded by one of Facebook's founders, Chris Hughes—connects volunteers and donors with their causes. Anyone with a social mission or a nonprofit organization can create their own page, and users can post feedback on the site about different charities and issues, helping people evaluate different organizations and projects and donate online. However, depending on the individual policies of the website organizations, a percentage of your online donations may go to them for operations, profit, or credit card processing fees. While some are nonprofits, others are for-profit companies with a social mission.

For Seema, Jolkona's online giving model expanded her philanthropic community. "It's been fantastic to meet other philanthropists and read about their stories of giving through our blog, Facebook, and Twitter feeds," she says. "I now feel less isolated as a philanthropist because I'm able to engage friends and families in online campaigns for Jolkona."

Today's philanthropists might be widely dispersed across the globe. They might never meet each other in the real world. But online, they're part of a new movement of giving that, through small donations, access to information, and shared passions, is helping solve big problems. And this is just the beginning. In just a few years, terms like *online giving* and *e-philanthropy* will have disappeared. Just as in the world of business no one talks about *e-commerce* anymore, the Internet will be as vital to the activities of philanthropists as the telephone or electricity.

As the chapters of this book demonstrate, the Web permeates every form of giving, from microgiving opportunities and research resources to volunteer matching and collaborative forms of philanthropy. Riding the wave of the Web, philanthropy is undergoing an unprecedented transformation. And who knows where that will take it? What's certain, however, is that the world in which being a philanthropist meant commanding vast wealth and seniority is fast disappearing. The Web is bringing a new generation into the giving movement and creating a direct link between donors, other donors, and their causes. By connecting drops of giving, technology is connecting givers to create an ocean of change.

MAKING IT HAPPEN

What to Ask Yourself:

- How do you want to use the Internet—for giving, learning, community building, fundraising, or another philanthropic purpose?
- How much money can you allocate to your online philanthropy portfolio? (Even $100 could get you off to a great start and let you see your drops of impact begin their ripple effect!)
- Is the website you want to give through reliable and efficient?
- How can you use the Web to introduce your kids to giving?
- What blogs can inform your education about social issues around the world?

What to Ask the Online Nonprofits You'd Like to Fund:

- How much of your money will go to the specific individuals featured on its website?
- What intermediaries does the nonprofit use to distribute funds to the individuals featured on its website?
- What infrastructure is required to implement its model and what is required to sustain it?
- How does it finance its operational costs?

Innovation Lab—Ideas to Test:

- Take $250 and create your own online giving portfolio.
- Try investing 10 percent of your giving resources into specific giving products (such as funding books for a classroom in New Orleans) whose results you could measure.
- Commit an hour this weekend to learning about a social issue only through online research.
- Commit to reading and commenting on a social issue blog every day for a week or once a week for a month.
- Try using your social network (for example, your Facebook status update or Twitter account) to educate and fundraise for your favorite cause.

- If you live on your iPhone or Blackberry, find a way to incorporate your giving life (donations, research, tracking, and so on) into your mobile life.

For the Family:
- Online giving organizations provide a great way to teach your children about philanthropy. You could supplement their allowance on condition that their money is spent making online gifts, or set up an account for them on an organization such as DonorsChoose, UniversalGiving, or Jolkona Foundation (Jolkona has a special kids program) and give them small amounts of money for donations.
- If your children are old enough to use a computer, set aside one evening a week or a month where everyone in the family investigates a cause of their choosing and educates the family about it.
- Set up a family blog about the issues you care about and get your kids to post entries regularly.

And Remember:
- Personal information you put on the Internet remains there forever, so proceed with caution.
- The Internet is a constant source of innovation and new ways to give, so keep looking for what's out there. However, don't give to organizations without doing some research first and make sure you give through screened and validated sources.
- The dollar buys more in many developing countries than it does in the United States—your smallest donation can help change, or even save, someone's life.
- Small gifts online can be a great way to continue your giving throughout the year.
- You'll have no idea how enriching joining a social network or participating in an online campaign can be until you do it.
- You can be overwhelmed by the information out in the virtual world, so start with trusted sources such as well-established websites and those of large foundations and nonprofits, think tanks, and academic centers (though remember that research can sometimes be biased toward the social goals or political culture of the organization).
- The more you learn, the more you'll realize you don't know.

- As you search for knowledge online, you'll encounter approaches, strategies, events, and organizations you might otherwise never have known existed. As a result, your philanthropy may become more sophisticated—and you may also decide to take a new direction, refine your focus, or launch a new initiative.
- Online research is fun and limitless—like giving itself, it can become addictive!

CHARTING A COURSE

Smart Choices with Your Checkbook

Marry your heart and your mind—translate your passion into strategy.

On any Sunday, just before 7:30 a.m., Makeba and Damond Boatwright, a smartly dressed young professional couple, head toward the Catholic church of St. Michael the Archangel, Damond's place of worship. Built in 2007 in an Italianate style, it has a terracotta roof, a salmon pink façade, white stucco columns, and a gloriously decorated interior, with ceilings in deep blue, a marble pulpit, and rows of polished wooden pews.

An hour and a half later, after stopping for coffee and a glance at the Sunday newspapers, the Boatwrights can be found sitting in Makeba's church, the United Methodist Church of the Resurrection. Architecturally, this is a very different space from St. Michael's. A vast contemporary structure accommodating tens of thousands of worshippers, it looks more like an auditorium than a church (Makeba's first glimpse of it was at a jazz concert with the Kansas City Symphony). Services at Resurrection, which blend traditional and contemporary worship, accompanied by music—with choir and orchestra—also contrast with the solemn, formalized early morning mass of St. Michael's.

The two churches are less than a mile apart and only a few minutes' drive from the Boatwright's house. This is convenient for Damond and Makeba. If they need to, they can even dash home between sermons. "We value spending time together on Sunday," says Makeba. "So it works very well because by the time we're back home from both services, it's still only 10:30 a.m."

The ease with which Damond, a Catholic, and Makeba, a Baptist, have accommodated each other's religious denominations speaks of the couple's sense of unity. "We try to be learners," says Makeba. "This is just another opportunity for us to learn and grow." And their approach to spirituality extends to their joint giving. "It's given us more confidence in our marriage that we're able to agree on a set of principles and values to guide us," says Damond.

Damond and Makeba met in 2001, when Makeba was in medical school, at the suggestion of a mutual friend. On Thanksgiving Sunday at 1 p.m. (he remembers the date and time), Damond—now chief executive of Lee's Summit Medical Center—picked up the phone and the couple had their first conversation.

Three years later, they married and, says Damond, the conversation has not stopped since (something he puts down to the "spiritual law of attraction"). Bound by love, friendship, and values, the couple also share a deep sense of the importance of faith. And while proud of their African American heritage, they see philanthropy as part of something bigger. "Giving transcends who we are," says Makeba. At the same time, giving has brought good things to them both. "It's made our partnership so much stronger," says Damond. "And it's a defining anchor in our overall spirituality."

Giving is also a defining anchor of their marriage: Damond and Makeba put 10 percent of their joint monthly income toward charitable causes, through their churches and through the Greater Kansas City Community Foundation. Like so many of the best philanthropists, they started doing this after first defining their philanthropic goals, looking at the various giving options out there, and choosing donor vehicles that suited their incomes, their outlook on life, their giving philosophy, and their faith.

THE POWER OF TEN

Claude Rosenberg, a San Francisco philanthropist who died in 2008, was good at a lot of things. A top investment executive, he amassed his fortune by handling the money of others, founding Rosenberg Capital Management (which later became RCM Capital Management), a research-focused asset management firm. But Rosenberg was also a savvy and innovative philanthropist. When a German bank bought his firm, he not only set about giving away most of his money, he also made efforts to get other affluent individuals to do the same, researching his field using the same diligence he'd put behind his asset management business. In the process, he made a surprising discovery—the wealthy give away far less of their incomes than less affluent households.

In a Stanford University paper, he revealed that if a million affluent tax filers between the ages of thirty-six and fifty had given the same proportion of their assets as their less affluent peers did in 2003, they would have given away $12 billion more than they actually did.[1] If all of America's affluent donors had done this, a whopping $25 billion would have been added to that year's philanthropic pool of dollars.

As well as encouraging the wealthy to become more generous, Rosenberg turned an ancient idea—the practice of tithing by giving away a fixed percentage of income and assets—into something new. In 1998, he founded the NewTithing Group to encourage givers to see tithing as a new way to boost their giving. An online calculator, which took into account tax breaks, helped people to work out how much they could comfortably afford to give, according to their income, expenditure, assets, and future plans. Rosenberg's point was that, without doing the math, people tend to give money away in random amounts and so give less than they could afford to if they budgeted properly. "When donors eyeball, they probably lowball," he wrote.

Claude Rosenberg was not the only supporter of the concept of tithing. Tithing has deep roots. The word comes from the Old English word *teogoba*, or tenth, and the practice dates back to the early days of a wide range of religions including Judaism, Christianity, Islam, Sikhism, and Hinduism.

In fact, charity lies at the core of most religions (some 91 percent of all religious people give philanthropically)[2] and the responsibility to give appears in many religious texts. The Bible says: "There will always be poor people, therefore you need to be generous to them." The Torah reads: "Deeds of giving are the very foundations of the world." Meanwhile the Koran tells us: "Those who are generous by day and by night, both in secret and openly, will be rewarded by God. They have nothing to fear or regret."

For Hindus, hospitality and charitable giving are core tenets of the faith, with Hindu scripture requiring a person to walk outdoors before every meal and declare: "Is anyone hungry? Please come to take your meal!" Only then can the family eat. Buddhists espouse a similar philosophy. The Buddha once said: "If you knew what I know about *dana* (generosity), you would not let one meal go by without sharing it."

In its traditional form, tithing refers to the practice of giving away a proportion of an individual or family income—usually 10 percent—to a religious institution, with tithing seen by some as an act of worship. However, I agree with Rosenberg that tithing is a great way to give any percentage of your income away in standard amounts on a monthly basis. You may choose to tithe for nonreligious reasons, such as gratitude for your blessings or appreciation for organizations that have helped you and your family. And you can decide how often to tithe and the percentage right for you and your family—recognizing that your tithing practice may change alongside your financial situation. Rosenberg is not the only philanthropist to have revitalized this age-old practice. A new wave of tithing-type giving is the emerging response to the Giving Pledge, launched in 2010 by Bill and Melinda Gates and Warren Buffett, which invites wealthy individuals and families to give the majority of their assets to charity. Meanwhile, Bolder Giving, founded by Boston-based Anne and Christopher Ellinger, has launched a similar giving pledge for those who are not billionaires.

Since marrying, Damond and Makeba practice tithing as a couple. For Makeba, however, it started in her childhood. "I remember spending a summer with one of my aunts when I was in fifth grade and my allowance was about $4. She required me to put at least 40 cents in church that summer. So it's in my blood." Until he met Makeba, Damond's giving had mostly taken the form of volunteering. With time and skills as his main gifts, about 1 percent of his income went to his church and other spiritual and civic organizations, such as Habitat for Humanity and Big Brothers Big Sisters. "I made fewer financial contributions because I didn't have much means," he says.

Meeting Makeba changed all that. The day after they became engaged, they found themselves in a bookstore together. Rather than purchasing a guide to wedding planning, Makeba insisted they buy *The Hard Questions: 100 Essential Questions to Ask Before You Say "I Do."* "We sat down and went through the book, including a section on giving, religious belief, and how you work through all those things," says Makeba.

As they planned their life together, Damond and Makeba had tough conversations about the direction their giving should take. Makeba did not want to relinquish her commitment to tithing. Yet for Damond, it was an unfamiliar concept, representing a big change in his giving. "Tithing was a stretch in my thinking at the time, because I was contributing much less than that," he says. "So that was part of the substantive conversation we had together. But we prayed on it and decided it was the right thing for us."

After settling on the 10 percent figure for their donations, the couple started to work out how to distribute that money. Here, Makeba had to make a concession. She'd been raised in the belief that all the money she tithed should go to the church. Damond felt some of it should be given to other organizations. "After a lot of discussion, we got on the same page," says Makeba. "And the beauty of it was that we were able to work through all this together. I'm so happy that we've got that rhythm in our marriage and relationship."

Of course, not everyone who gives tithes in the traditional sense, that is, by donating 10 percent of their monthly income to charity. In fact, less than 7 percent of Americans do this, according to the Barna Group, which tracks trends in faith and culture. Nevertheless, 35 percent of all individual giving goes to religious causes and organizations, according to the GivingUSA Foundation in 2010.

Faith-based or not, there's something powerful in the practice of tithing, allowing you to be very measured about your giving. Even if you don't follow a faith, you can "tithe to humanity," "tithe to parentless children," or "tithe to the environment" and employ the same principles. You can change causes or organizations for your tithing from year to year. It's a way of taking stock and being more consistent—at least by amount—in the way you give. It's about systematically figuring out how much you can give from your income or assets. For the Boatwrights, tithing also brings peace. "We sleep well at night," says Makeba, "knowing that, no matter how much we bring in, 10 percent of that goes to different causes, whether religious or otherwise; to things we believe will make a difference to someone else's life."

TAKING STOCK

Whether tithing or not, everyone has experiences that inspire them to start giving. Like many, giving may simply be in your blood. Maybe your gifts to a school, hospital, place of worship, or other nonprofit express gratitude for an institution that's helped you or your family. If you've traveled—at home or abroad—perhaps you've been shocked by poverty and deprivation. Something you've read in a magazine or seen on television might have inspired you to take action. Or perhaps you met someone whose story prompted you to give.

Where do you start? Well, before moving forward you need to look back. It's something we rarely do—years can pass without taking note of what we're giving and what difference it makes. It's something I started doing a few years ago. I'd realized that for some time I'd not been feeling that great about my giving—at least, the financial side of it. Sure, when I raised the paddle at a friend's fundraising auction I experienced an immediate exhilaration, or when I received the thank-you letter for a donation, I felt that warm glow. But I had no idea where the money was going. Many of my donations were repeat gifts to causes my family supported. Others responded to requests from friends. Few adhered to any cohesive strategy.

This changed as soon as I started to take stock. When I looked back, I discovered that many of the gifts of which I was most proud were those that inspired, informed, and empowered other donors. I realized these gifts were part of a single mission—educating individual givers and helping further the philanthropic field. By analyzing my giving, I learned where my real passion lay and how I could do most to change the world. I also realized that helping others to become more effective givers would, through a ripple effect, dramatically extend the impact of my own philanthropic efforts.

My husband and I did the same for our joint giving, and we found a shared belief in supporting underfunded social needs or those neglected by others. These include emergency services and disaster preparedness research—services we believe benefit everyone. Marc and I also fund critical services for war veterans, safety equipment for police officers, and organizations that support families of the police and CIA officers who've lost their lives in the line of duty. We feel it's important to help protect those who protect us all every day.

Giving to these causes is something we've thought long and hard about. It's about balancing our support for immediate needs with funding long-term systemic change. But it wasn't until we took stock of our giving that we felt confident this was the right thing to do.

I haven't stopped doing this kind of analysis—I keep a journal on my computer desktop in which I jot down thoughts and experiences as they come to me. It's not difficult to do. Create a document on your computer, or buy a paper notebook to carry with you (I do both). Sit down for an hour and list all your giving activities over the past few years, whether donations in money, in kind, or in time (even if you've not kept records of gifts, if you've been claiming tax benefits for them, you'll find details in your tax filings).

Then see if any gifts stand out and ask what prompted them. Were they responding to requests from friends or colleagues, or to solicitation letters? Or to organizations asking you to renew gifts? Just because you've given to a nonprofit in previous years, that doesn't mean you owe it continued giving. If you're giving through a sense of obligation rather than choice, rethink your strategy, because if you get less satisfaction from giving, you may give less. But feeling good about your gifts—not only in the moment, but also in the long term—will help you get more from your giving. Your enthusiasm may inspire you to give more over time, as well as inspire friends, relatives, and colleagues to give, too.

Next, break down your giving portfolio into dollar amounts and look for patterns. Do you write lots of small checks, or do you make gifts online or via text message? Do you give regularly throughout the year, or all at once during the holiday season? Are you, for example, making ten gifts of $10 to $1,000 a year, or one of $25,000 and several of around $2,000? Are you making a multiyear pledge to an institution such as a hospital, your alma mater, or your child's school?

You might want to move from the scattergun approach to focusing on one initiative, organization, or program about which you're really passionate. This makes it easier to become involved in your cause, and helps you track how your money is being put to work.

In fact, keeping track is the next critical consideration. For any of the gifts you've made, can you say with any accuracy how those dollars have been used? If the answer is yes, and you're pleased with the results, then those are gifts worth continuing. But how about those you can't account for—donations that were part of your annual giving plan, tickets to charity events, gifts you make in honor of a late loved one, one-time disaster relief support gifts, or pledges to friends participating in for-a-cause walkathons. Where precisely did that money go?

Tracking what happens to your gifts is essential to being a successful, fulfilled philanthropist. After all, the money may end up being used for things you might not have expected—so either designate its purpose up front or be comfortable with it being used for any organization purpose (from utilities, furniture, and salaries to event marketing, donor relations, and conference fees). For example, if you're giving to an annual fund or an endowment campaign, your dollars could become part of a large interest-bearing principal used to fund operating costs. They might pay the fees of professional or celebrity fundraisers.

That's okay in some cases—perhaps that helps the organization run more efficiently or generate new funding. But you should ask whether celebrities have donated their time to the cause or are being paid—many donate their time, but check this as part of your due diligence process. And it's fair to ask how much of your gift will be spent on outsourced, professional fundraising—sometimes nonprofits pay companies to raise money or give them a percentage of whatever they raise as a fee, which in some cases can be high.

When faced with these kinds of choices, there's no right or wrong answer. Every situation is unique. Figure out what feels right for you and stick by it—but base your choice on knowledge. We put a lot of effort getting the best return on our personal financial investments—we should apply the same approach to our philanthropic investments.

Of course, in some instances this may mean saying no. This isn't easy. And the more you give, the more you'll probably be asked to give. Having a set of personal guidelines gives you a way to say no that's justifiable and easily understood by those who approach you for a gift. Being able to say no with respect and kindness is an important part of being a philanthropist.

One way to do this is to thank an organization for its efforts and say: "While I can't support you financially, I'll tell my friends and contacts about the important work you're doing." Then make sure you do so— what might not be a passion of yours could fit perfectly into someone else's giving plan.

Alternatively, explain that you have your own areas of focus, and describe your giving strategy (if you have a clear strategy, it shouldn't be hard to explain). You might also set up a "Friends Fund" for less strategic or one-off gifts—and at a certain point you may have used this up. In this case, explain this but also say that perhaps next year, you'll have another opportunity to give to the organization.

As well as taking stock of your monetary gifts, you should do the same with gifts of time, skills, and expertise. All three can be used wisely or wasted, so look at how your volunteering hours are spent. You could volunteer in your children's classroom or at your church, synagogue, temple, or mosque; you could sit on boards and event committees, tutor eighth graders online, or give strategic advice to nonprofits. But if you can't track your activities for any given year, the chances are you could be giving your human and intellectual capital more productively.

You also need to recognize what you're getting from giving, whether it's honoring family traditions or waking each morning feeling proud of your role in social change. Ask yourself what impact each of your gifts had on *you* and how your life has improved as a result. Did meeting the people served by a nonprofit you support change your perspective on their plight? Has giving to an organization allowed you to attend conferences or lectures about your cause? Have you been able to spend more time with family? Has your circle of friends expanded? Have these connections led to volunteer, career, or travel opportunities? Giving enhances our lives in many ways, but we rarely acknowledge them formally. I encourage you to do so (you'll find more suggestions in Appendix I, Create Your Giving Journal).

Giving also requires assessing what's working and what isn't. It means taking lessons from one gift and applying them to other areas of your philanthropy—drops of knowledge from individual experiences can irrigate every corner of your philanthropic garden.

This is important. As many have observed, philanthropy is society's risk capital. As a philanthropist you're an innovator (or partner to innovators). You're constantly searching for new ways of addressing the world's problems. And if something's not working, you should exit with grace—after all, you have more freedom than most to experiment. Unlike a business, you have no shareholders, customers, and investors to whom you're accountable. Unlike a politician, your position doesn't depend on voter choices. And very little, if any, government regulation governs how you express values, beliefs, and priorities through giving.

I'm not saying that as a philanthropist you are unaccountable—far from it; your tax benefits mean you have a responsibility to be accountable. But that accountability is self-imposed, not mandated externally. You're in charge of your success, and this is tough. But by constantly reviewing and renewing your activities, you'll come closer to achieving your philanthropic goals. Giving can be the start of a rich and fascinating journey—and the trip will work out infinitely better if you plan your route first.

MATCHING SOUL WITH STRUCTURE

Tithing, of course, is just one way to organize your giving. You might prefer to give on an annual basis, through either one-off checks or one of the many types of funds and trusts you can set up for your giving. So after you've decided why you want to give and what causes you want to support, you need to determine *how* to give. This means exploring specific giving vehicles. However, first, ask yourself a few general questions (you can add these to your giving journal)—the answers will help you choose the right structure for your philanthropy.

Start by thinking about what you have to give. Financial gifts come in many forms and are certainly not limited to cash. Assets you can give away include private company stock, publicly traded stock, real estate, privately held family businesses, art, mutual and hedge fund holdings. All may be donated, helping reduce your income tax, estate tax, and capital gains tax. (Check with the Internal Revenue Service website or your accountant or investment adviser for the most recent tax laws on giving.)

This is true of physical assets, too (to get the tax deduction on the fair market value of physical assets, the nonprofit's mission must relate to those assets). When you take your gently used clothing or furniture to a thrift store, you're giving away money you spent earlier. Nonprofits such as the National Furniture Bank Association and the Red Cross donate furniture to the needy living in empty homes, places not meant for human habitation, or houses whose contents have been destroyed by natural disasters or fires. Other organizations help companies renovating their premises move old office furniture to central warehouses, where it's sold to nonprofits at affordable prices. In some ways, of course, this is simply another form of recycling—and it's a great way to do it.

Next, consider the impact of tax deductions. Of course, few of us give solely to reduce our taxable income, but it's a wonderful benefit, if not impetus. If you know what tax deduction you're receiving on a gift, you might find you can afford to increase the donation amount.

Because the tax-deductible amount varies according to the type of organization you're giving to, it's important to know the difference between private and public foundations. These are both 501(c)(3) organizations, but a private foundation receives most of its funding from a single source, such as an individual, a family, or a corporation and makes grants to charitable organizations.

By contrast, public charities, or nonprofits, get at least a third of their funding from the public, government, and private foundations. Rather than making grants to other organizations, they tend to be service providers, engaged in activities such as educational programs, hunger relief, or health services. For this, they receive higher tax benefits.

It's also important to decide what level of control you want over your giving. Giving directly to a nonprofit gives you the most control (even if you do it through your family foundation). On the other hand, you might want to give your money more impact by pooling it with the funds of other donors through a venture philanthropy partnership (this is what SV2, the venture philanthropy organization I founded, does), another type of a giving circle (a collaborative group of donors), or a funding intermediary (an organization that regrants your dollars to organizations it has screened and validated).

Giving vehicles such as charitable remainder trusts and private foundations allow you to personally manage or leave investment oversight to a professional money manager while retaining control over the ultimate giving decisions. If you set up a trust, you'll need to decide who will govern it and how much you and your family want to be involved in running it. You might want to keep control of your philanthropic activities, for example, and bring your knowledge and expertise to bear on whatever you do. Or you might welcome the input of others with more or different experience than your own.

With a donor-advised fund, or DAF (these are managed by an organization such as a community foundation or the nonprofit arm of a financial institution), you can make a contribution of money, stock, or other select assets at any time and advise the foundation on which nonprofits to give that money to. Because you can donate the money without having to allocate it immediately, a DAF is a great way to get the immediate tax benefit for your gift without rushing into a decision or giving it all away at once.

DAFs have expanded rapidly. With tens of thousands of DAFs and billions of dollars flowing into and out of them—especially since 1999, when it became legally possible for financial institutions to have DAFs—they have become a powerful force in philanthropy. The 2010 "Donor-Advised Fund Report" found that in that year, DAFs awarded more than $6 billion in grants, the second-highest total in the six-year history of the study, while taking in \$5.9 billion.[3] DAFs had at least \$16.9 billion in assets in 2009, according to the *Chronicle of Philanthropy*.[4]

DAFs are a critical tool for philanthropy because fairly small amounts—\$5,000 to \$10,000—are required to start one (while the cost of establishing a foundation can run to tens of thousands of dollars because of legal, accounting, and reporting requirements). Most community foundations accept such funds in the range of \$5,000 to \$25,000, making it possible for millions of Americans to become more professional in their giving.

If your financial institution manages your donor-advised fund and you have private banking services, your money manager might be able to handle your philanthropic funds alongside your other assets. Look ahead, and before creating a donor-advised fund, find out if you can transfer your assets to another institution if you're not satisfied with either the first choice's financial performance or its support service. Also investigate what happens to your money after your death and ask the institution managing it whether the fund can be passed on to another donor (such as a family member or trusted friend), donated directly to specified nonprofits, or transferred to a different institution—sometimes the default grantee will be the institution's own unrestricted endowment.

When first thinking about the new resources we want to allocate each year, my husband and I decided that a donor-advised fund would give us the flexibility we were looking for. We set one up at the Silicon Valley Community Foundation (SVCF). First, since it's a public charity, we get the maximum tax deduction for our gifts. And while we're using the fund to make multiyear grants, our initial gift, which created the fund, qualified for the full tax benefit for that year. But more important, we can make a decision to give on a moment's notice. We can also make recommendations to the foundation as to what nonprofits we want to support in the long term. Another advantage of having an SVCF fund is that we can tap into the expertise of the foundation's grantmaking staff, who have deep knowledge of our community's needs and can advise us on which are the best-run nonprofits. In addition, we are part of a community that shares our giving values.

My husband and I have since created another donor-advised fund at Stanford University, which we use to support some of our Stanford projects. This vehicle provides us the same tax and community benefits as our SVCF Fund, but with the added benefit of Stanford's expert investment management. We have the option of allocating our Stanford fund resources either to specific university activities or to other nonprofits—though Stanford does not have the same nonprofit sector expertise that SVCF offers. We learned about Stanford's donor-advised funds from my father, who uses his own fund there to give to the university through supporting the construction and facilities projects he undertakes.

Of course, we can still make smaller gifts on our credit cards, via text messaging, or online. But the donor-advised fund provides us with an efficient way to keep track of our giving. At SVCF, we can log in to the website and track giving for both our fund and my family's donor-advised fund (which is also managed by SVCF) for current and past years.

Remember, too, that by working creatively, you can leverage your gift, using it to raise additional resources of all kinds for your cause. For example, if you set up a scholarship trust, you could volunteer your time and knowledge by helping with reunion fundraising or joining the school's alumni board. You could also direct skills toward your causes. For example, suppose you work for a company that produces software to manage data. Your company might help fund the software needed to set up a database for nonprofits. Company volunteers might even work with you to provide the necessary training.

Think about the duration of your philanthropy, too. Do you want it to last beyond your own lifetime? Or would you rather the funds were given away during a set period, and all according to your own wishes? And at what point do you want to give—now, at a future time, or at the same time every year? Do you want to give a lot right now, or a small amount every year? Or do you want to make a large bequest? You could set aside a lump sum for philanthropic purposes and weigh the pros and cons of a one-time gift or a cumulative giving strategy.

You also need to determine how public to be about your giving. Do you want to shelter your children from knowing how much money you have and give away? Or do you want to serve as an example, raising your children in a culture of giving and responsibility? Some forms of giving allow for total anonymity, but private foundations must list directors and officers on annual tax returns, which are public record. If you give to a nonprofit, funding intermediary, or venture philanthropy partnership, you can also donate anonymously, but you may give up some control over funding decisions.

While my parents gave anonymously, in most cases, while we were growing up, they became more public with their giving once my brother and I graduated from college. When Marc and I got engaged, we celebrated by making a public gift. We have decided to be public about all of our giving to demonstrate that giving while living is an important way to contribute to our world. And since we live in Silicon Valley—where people at early stages in their lives are creating so much wealth—we want to inspire others to give while they're young rather than waiting until retirement.

As you can see, there are plenty of questions to ask yourself when deciding which funding vehicle(s) will fit your requirements and how transparent you want to be with your philanthropy. These days, the options seem endless, with an explosion of new philanthropic structures and organizations (even experienced philanthropists may not be aware of them all). These opportunities can not only simplify your life—they can also help you learn about philanthropy, increase the impact of your giving, and take you beyond mere check writing.

BEFORE YOU WRITE THE CHECK

Direct giving gives you the most control as an individual donor—you choose a recipient and write a check. And if you give directly to a nonprofit, you can become involved with the organization, volunteering in addition to donating financially. However, if you want to be really strategic with your money, it's critical to do some research both before you write the check and when you want to continue to fund an organization. Just because philanthropy is a gift, that doesn't mean you shouldn't give a nonprofit the same scrutiny you'd give a for-profit company you planned to invest in.

This means educating yourself. Teach yourself about the issues you're interested in. If you want to support combating malaria, which countries are most affected by the disease? Are antimalarial drugs effective investments or is it better to equip poor families with insecticide-treated nets? Perhaps a combination of the two is most effective. Which nonprofits lead the field and where do they focus strategically and geographically? Are they tapping into other sources of funding, such as corporate philanthropy? Are they partnering with civil society groups, corporations, local governments, or religious institutions to establish reliable distribution channels? Have they secured enough institutional funding to ensure they'll be running in a year's time?

The good news is that finding this out has become much easier. As noted in Chapter Two, the Internet allows you to delve into an astonishing amount of information about causes, needs, nonprofits, and foundations, and also helps you navigate the thousands of organizations out there.

For a start, the Internal Revenue Service has an online version of Publication 78, which lists all the organizations it recognizes as eligible to receive tax-deductible contributions. Resources such as GuideStar and Charity Navigator provide online databases of tens of thousands of nonprofits, allowing you to search for information about a specific charity or look for organizations working in your area of interest. Other resources include Philanthropedia (which merged with GuideStar in early 2011), which ranks nonprofits based on experts' recommendations, and GreatNonprofits, which develops tools to find, review, and share information about nonprofits.

Personally, while I use GuideStar to view nonprofits' 990 tax forms, I don't use other charity rating services. (The Form 990 is the financial reporting that federally tax-exempt organizations file with the Internal Revenue Service. It provides information about a nonprofit's mission, finances, and programs.) And, as I write, some of the many rating systems out there were receiving mixed reviews. Find out what philanthropy sector leaders are saying about the effectiveness of these organizations before using them to shape your decisions. Regardless, I recommend doing your own research on organizations you're considering funding—what you'll learn in the process will enhance all your giving activities.

Next, delve a little deeper. This may mean calling up nonprofits and asking them questions—questions about their activities, their goals, what they've learned from their mistakes, what they consider their successes, and what they plan to achieve in the coming years (any nonprofit with a website should have the answers to these first two questions on its home page). You should assess a number of general areas, the most important of which include the nonprofit's operations, its financing and funding sources, its service provision programs, and its impact.

Of course, what you ask and how deeply you explore any of these areas depends upon a range of factors, such as the size of gift, your level of giving experience, and your knowledge about the organization. With small gifts, you don't need to do as much research as you might for a gift that will be a large portion of an organization's annual budget.

Other considerations can include your level of volunteering commitment with the organization, how long you plan on funding it, and how many years you've already funded it. For a nonprofit you've funded consistently over the years at a low amount, an intensive due diligence process is not always necessary. Nevertheless, monitor how it's refining its practices and improving its impact—is it building talent internally or has there been a recent leadership change, for example? Is there full board participation in funding the organization? Does it use advocacy to extend its impact to policy change?

Other things to look at include the nonprofit's breakdown between new and existing donors, and between small and large donors. Find out how often it loses donors. You can get a sense of this by asking the organization how many donors have given consecutively for more than one year and more than five years. Ask what the average number of years is that individual donors and foundation donors each give to the organization's annual or general operating fund, and what percentage of donors each year are new donors. Certain types of organizations, such as research institutions, universities, and nationally renowned nonprofits, tend to lose fewer donors than others—because of the breadth and sophistication of their professional and volunteer fundraising teams. Religious institutions typically have the highest return-donor rate, simply due to the ongoing, direct engagement of their members.

Remember, however, that nonprofit staff can be extremely busy. So if your gift represents only a small percentage of a nonprofit's operating budget, they may not have time for a discussion (you can still do a lot of research about the organization online). But if it's your first gift, or you're making a significant one (significant to you or the organization), make your search a detailed one. Talk to the development officer or chief financial officer or request a conversation with a board or clergy member. And don't feel intimidated—regardless of the stature or size of an organization, as a donor you deserve to have questions answered.

Of course, after creating a strategy for your giving, you may no longer want to give to some of the organizations you've supported in the past, but instead direct future giving to organizations you've encountered while researching your strategy. Don't worry—this is all part of how your philanthropy evolves and becomes more effective.

GLOBAL GIVING OPTIONS

As you put together your giving strategy, you may include global causes in your portfolio. While overseas giving remains a small percentage of overall philanthropy (just 5 percent, according to GivingUSA in 2010), in recent years, Americans—givers big and small—have gradually put more philanthropic dollars behind the world's problems. GivingUSA reported that in 2009 international giving had risen more than 6 percent (and estimates that it also increased 13.5 percent in 2010).[5] Part of the reason for the growing interest in funding overseas projects is a wave of global disasters, such as the Asian tsunami of 2004, the 2005 Pakistan earthquake, the Haiti earthquake of 2010, the devastating 2010 floods in Pakistan, and the catastrophic Japanese earthquake of 2011. And, thanks to online news and social media, awareness of these disasters is increasing.

As global citizens, we've watched these tragedies unfold with horror, and many of us have opened our wallets to make generous donations. As more of us travel internationally—whether for business, pleasure, or a family visit—all we have to do is pick up a local newspaper to learn about the country's problems. It's difficult to erase such images from memory, so it's hardly surprising that those of us who travel are coming back from trips and asking, "What on earth can I do to help?"

If you want to give more than a few dollars, plenty of organizations facilitate international grantmaking. Some community foundations facilitate overseas giving, and many U.S.-based intermediary organizations can regrant your money to international nonprofits or NGOs. Intermediaries help you get the tax deduction for your gift, which is not available when giving directly to overseas organizations. They also help identify appropriate recipients for your donation, conduct due diligence on them, and monitor performance after you've made your gifts.

Intermediaries include organizations such as Give2Asia, the Global Fund for Children, UniversalGiving, the American India Foundation, the Global Fund for Women, the Brazil Foundation, The Caledonia Foundation (which supports disadvantaged youth in Australia), the Resource Foundation (which focuses its grantmaking on projects in Latin America and the Caribbean), and CAFAmerica (which is part of Charities Aid Foundation dedicated to expanding global giving). Some intermediaries, including the Virtual Foundation and Global Greengrants Fund, provide grassroots funding to local activists around the world. Focusing on European causes are funds and organizations such as the King Baudouin Foundation United States, the American Ireland Fund (part of The Ireland Funds), and the Caledonian Foundation (which distributes funds to Scottish charities).

If you pursue this path, recognize that some may question why you're sending valuable resources overseas when most of us could find plenty of problems to fund near our own homes. Bill Gates faced this question when CNN's Fareed Zakaria quizzed the Microsoft founder on his giving strategy. "You're going to give away almost all your money," Zakaria began. "You're going to give away almost all of

Warren Buffett's money. Collectively that's tens of billions of dollars. You've chosen something very unusual. While most philanthropists gave their money away at home," Zakaria continued, "you chose not to do that. Why?"[6]

Gates argued that all human life should be valued equally. And he made a further point—reducing childhood deaths through improved public health slows population growth because parents no longer need large families to ensure some children survive into adulthood to take care of them later in life. "Amazingly, across the entire world, as health improves, then the population growth actually is reduced," he said.

As a nation's public health improves, so does governance. And with reduced corruption and increased adherence to the rule of law come other benefits such as lower crime rates and fewer incidents of terrorism. Slower population growth also eases pressure on natural resources and global water supplies and cuts our voracious demand for energy sources that produce greenhouse gasses—helping with climate change and global water stress that will affect us all.

What's more, bang for buck, global giving provides better value in developing countries because the dollar goes far further overseas. Take education. In the United States, a year's education could run to tens of thousands of dollars. In Afghanistan, according to Jolkona, a year's education for a girl costs just $40. Taking the top recommended organizations, GiveWell, an independent nonprofit charity evaluator (which Marc and I support with general operating funds), shows that in the developing world, it takes just $200 to $1,000 in health care costs to save a person's life. It compares this with the best U.S. programs costing more than $10,000 per child served and delivering encouraging but not overwhelming results.

Of course, this is not to suggest we should abandon home-based philanthropy. Neither should we assume that overseas nonprofits are more efficient and accountable than U.S. ones (and few developing countries have nonprofit sectors or traditions of philanthropy). Whether at home or away, all philanthropic organizations should be scrutinized before giving them money. However, new channels for global giving—particularly for young people and those with limited financial resources—

provide an eminently affordable way to have a substantial impact on people's lives.

At SV2, we ask nonprofits what type of funding structure would be most helpful to them. Most tell us that the hardest funds to raise are those needed for building up institutional infrastructure. So that's exactly what we decided to fund when we designed our grantmaking model.

Over time, I have learned to listen to and trust in the nonprofit leaders I support. The organizations we fund almost always know better than we do what they need. I learned that we should pay attention to what they say and act on that information.

The trouble is, we don't always do this. Driving us all, to some extent, is ego and emotion. And in philanthropy it's easy to feel that because we have the money, we should control how our dollars are spent. If you ever find yourself thinking this way, keep in mind philanthropy's ultimate prize—improving other people's lives and bringing about change, something that's possible only by learning from those we hope to help. Even if you come from a business background with skills that may be valuable to the nonprofit sector, remember that not all of your hard-won experience can be applied to philanthropy. As someone who's led a nonprofit organization, I can tell you that there's no sweeter music to your ears than hearing a donor ask: "What do you need funds for that you can't raise at the moment?"

Moreover, make sure the nonprofits you fund are asking the populations they're serving what *they* need. In the nonprofit world, well-intentioned organizations don't always provide services that really address underlying social problems. That could be because they're not listening. So ask any nonprofit you intend to fund how involved the people it's serving are in shaping its programs. For example, does an individual from that community sit on its board? What processes does it use to find out how that community can best be helped?

After all, if the nonprofits you are funding aren't serving the community successfully, then you can't be successful as a donor. Making a gift may make you generous and altruistic—but it doesn't necessarily make you effective. If you want to innovate and find new ways of making an impact, you must first become a good listener.

AN EASIER WAY TO GIVE

Soon after she moved to Kansas City, Makeba Boatwright's friends invited her to an event hosted by the Greater Kansas City Community Foundation. At the event, a lunch honoring the governor, Makeba found herself sitting next to Roxie Jerde, the foundation's head of donor and nonprofit relations. Though she didn't know it at the time, this lunch was the start of a new giving relationship for the Boatwrights, one that's helped them find the right type of giving vehicle for their tithing, opened up a world of philanthropic knowledge, and introduced them to a new giving community.

As the name suggests, community foundations focus on a specific geographic community or population. Rarely serving an area larger than a state, they tend to be focused on cities, or on counties, regions, or target populations—with the capacity to direct donor gifts anywhere in the country, and increasingly the world. A type of public foundation, a community foundation receives funds from many separate donors (including private foundations, corporations, and even local nonprofits).

The advantage of donating through a community foundation is that it can provide a range of services, reducing your administrative and legal costs. Because community foundations are also public charities, you'll receive a higher tax benefit than the one you'd receive giving to a private foundation. Since they're focused on specific communities or areas, they understand local needs and often have relationships with the most effective local nonprofits, and, therefore, can advise you on which organizations to fund. Many community foundations also incubate venture philanthropy partnerships, use technology to engage donors, pursue public-private partnerships, house giving circles, and even engage in advocacy. These institutions can provide a great entry point for firsthand experience of the potential of philanthropic innovations.

They also bring together a diverse community of groups and individuals, creating collaborative giving opportunities. And you can tap into the nonprofit expertise of the staff (the kind of expertise offered by a few private banks and advisories, but primarily to high-net-worth clients and often for a fee). Staffed by professionals who understand the process of making grants, evaluation, and administration, community foundations offer a variety of grantmaking structures and donor products.

The foundation continued to invite the Boatwrights to events, and after they learned what the Greater Kansas City Community Foundation offered donors, the couple arranged to meet with its executives to talk about establishing a donor-advised fund. "After I'd collected all the information from our accountant—which is a huge job—we realized we were giving money to all these different organizations and that this could make our lives easier," says Makeba.

Her hunch proved right. Using Damond's wages to live on, Makeba now puts her income into an investment account from which money is regularly transferred into the donor-advised fund. "I have a bank draft that occurs monthly, and we can very easily distribute money to different organizations," she says. "Then we go online and find a cause we want to give to. So it's made things much easier."

When it comes to investing their money, the foundation allows donors either to have their own financial adviser manage their fund or to select a mixture of funds, using one or more of the foundation's investment pools (such as an alternative investment fund, an equity fund, a fixed income fund, or a money market fund). "Our fund also accrues money, and we can be as conservative or aggressive as we want," explains Makeba. Watching the financial crisis emerge and endowments lose money, the Boatwrights didn't want to risk diminishing the source of their gifts. "We're being conservative for now," says Makeba. "And as things start improving, we'll get a bit more aggressive."

However, as well as providing an easy-to-manage, tax-deductible giving vehicle, the Boatwrights' investment with the Greater Kansas City Community Foundation has also connected the Boatwrights with other donors. Lunches, cocktail hours, and educational events featuring guest speakers provide an opportunity to discuss giving with other philanthropists and share ideas in a way they wouldn't necessarily want to at a dinner party or when out with friends. "We hate talking about money, but we really appreciate being around people who are giving, and feeling we're in a safe place to talk about philanthropy," says Makeba.

Most important, giving through the community foundation has enabled the Boatwrights' philanthropy to evolve. It provides research resources when they're considering giving to a new organization. Staff members have helped them come up with a mission to guide their giving. "We've narrowed it down to the things we're most passionate about," says Damond. "That's led to a more pragmatic and engaged approach to our philanthropy." And they get feedback on progress at their non-profits, as well as access to individuals in those organizations, which helps them build stronger relationships.

"It's opened up a new world for us," says Damond. "Early on in our marriage, we'd give money and didn't know what had happened to it. We were disconnected. Now we're very connected and engaged."

Like Damond and Makeba, you'll find that the most effective and rewarding philanthropy emerges through learning, knowledge, and continual renewal. Philanthropy is not just about generosity. It's not just about funding fiscally responsible nonprofits and maximizing tax benefits. We should also be thinking carefully about how and where to invest, and we should be choosing the right nonprofits and funding vehicles. Giving is successful only if the organizations we fund succeed, and part of our role as givers is to foster that success. So we should talk to our grantees, engage with our communities, and embark on learning to play a bigger part in the process of change. Just as we want our grantees to evolve as organizations, we need to keep transforming our own giving. Only then can our philanthropy be a truly powerful force in the world.

MAKING IT HAPPEN

First Steps: What to Ask Yourself:
- Where do you want to give?
  - What issue or issue areas are you most passionate about? Does your passion stem from a concern, an intellectual interest, an emotional response, or a personal connection?
  - Who are the people you want to help (age, circumstance, economic status, religion, education, background)?
  - What is the geographic area to which you want to direct funding?

- What types of services do you want to fund?
- What do you want to focus on—immediate needs, policy change, service provision, capacity building, or training and leadership development?
- What size of operating budget would you like a nonprofit you fund to have (a smaller or early-stage one, so your gift can have a significant impact, or a larger, better-endowed one, so longer-term sustainability is less risky)?
- What types of funding do you want to provide (endowment, capital, general operating, program, scholarship, infrastructure)?

- What do you have to give?
  - What financial assets do you have to give (cash, private company stock, publicly traded stock, life insurance plans, hedge fund gains, or real estate)?
  - What nonfinancial assets (art, furniture, computers, cell phones, or clothing) do you have to give?
  - Do you want to give time, intellectual capital, or other nonmonetary gifts, and how will that fit into your overall giving strategy (for example, do you want to give your time only where you also give your money)?

- When do you want to give it?
  - Do you want to give monthly, quarterly, every year at holidays, on your birthday, or at the same time every year? Or do you prefer to give as opportunities arise?
  - What's your philanthropic timeline? Do you want to make a large gift now, many small gifts over a long period of time, or a large bequest after your death?
  - Do you want your philanthropy to last beyond your lifetime, or do you want your funds given away while you're living?
  - If you want to make a bequest, do you want the funds given away within a set time period and all according to your own wishes?
  - If you make a bequest to a philanthropic foundation or fund, are you comfortable letting others make allocation decisions in your absence?

- How do you want to give?
  - How much control do you want over where your money goes?
  - Do you want to be public about your gifts? Or do you want to give anonymously, or through a family organization? (Bear in mind that access to information online makes anonymity difficult today, and the

names of private foundation board members are public knowledge,
as are the gifts foundations make.)

- Do you want to join forces with other donors and pool your funds?
- Does writing checks (which is transactional) work for you, or do you
  want to become more engaged with the organizations you fund
  (which is transformational—potentially for both you and the organizations you're funding)?
- How much personal engagement with your grantees are you hoping
  to have?
- Will you be disappointed if peers do not publicly recognize your gift?
  If you're giving overseas through a funding intermediary, it's unlikely
  you'll receive the recognition that comes with local or national gifts.

Innovation Lab—Ideas to Test:

- Arrange to meet with a leader at your place of worship and discuss new
  opportunities to merge your faith and desire for social impact.
- Bring together five members of your religious community and commit to
  helping your church, mosque, or temple improve one of its existing
  programs.
- If you are already involved with your local Rotary Club, Junior League,
  AARP chapter, or other service clubs, learn more about the nonprofits
  they fund and why they fund them. (And if you are not, consider joining
  one and getting involved with its grants committee or volunteer efforts.)
- Attend an event at or visit your local community foundation to find out
  what resources it has that could help you give more effectively.
- Schedule a date with your partner to discuss what you are most passionate about and why. Even if only one of you drives your giving decisions, having a structured conversation could take your giving in a
  different direction—including becoming involved in a new cause or organization together.
- Do some research on the history of your community, what its current
  needs are, and how other communities have successfully addressed
  those needs. Then introduce yourself to a local nonprofit that is working
  to meet those needs and learn more about how that organization
  approaches the problem. Together, you might be able to come up with
  a new approach to solving the problem.
- Over the course of a week, make notes on what community resources
  you use or take for granted. Then consider supporting the organizations
  that provide them to help others gain access to those services.

- If making overseas gifts, could you visit the part of the world where the NGO you are funding works? (This can be difficult to arrange individually, but you might be able to join a partner organization's trip or a delegation.) Such a trip can give you an entirely different perspective on your issue and make you a more informed grantmaker.

Choosing Your Vehicle for Giving:

- *Direct giving*: Donating directly to a nonprofit, you incur no external set-up costs or annual fees. Most nonprofits allow for anonymity by simply listing your gifts in their annual reports as "anonymous." And you retain control of your gifts. However, it can be harder to plan a strategy than it would be with the help of a community or a private foundation. And unless you are strategic, you may find most of your gifts are responding to solicitations rather than to organizations you've selected.
- *Giving to a private foundation*: A private foundation is a 501(c)(3) that receives most of its funding from a single source, such as an individual, a family, or a corporation. Private foundations make grants to charitable organizations and are required to give away at least 5 percent of their financial assets every year.
- *Giving to a public charity or nonprofit*: Unlike private foundations, these 501(c)(3) organizations get at least a third of their funding from the general public, including governments and private foundations. Rather than making grants to other organizations, they tend to be service providers. You cannot make a gift to a nonprofit exceeding one-third of its total annual operating budget (unless you channel the money through another public charity, such as a community foundation).
- *Giving via a federated program*: Some organizations pool your funds with those of others and distribute them to a variety of nonprofits. In their early years, funds such as United Way, Jewish Federations (formerly the United Jewish Appeal), Catholic Charities, or UNCF (formerly the United Negro College Fund) were often associated with ethnic and religious groups. These days, they're also community focused, basing their fundraising on workplaces and neighborhoods. You don't necessarily have to pool your money with that of other donors— some let you set up an individual fund from which to direct your grantmaking.
- *Giving to a funding intermediary*: This is a nonprofit organization which regrants donor funds to the ultimate beneficiary organization (a screened and validated nonprofit or NGO). However, intermediaries do much more than simply transfer funds between donors and recipients. First, they

pool your dollars with those of others. Second, they apply their expertise, connections, and on-the-ground knowledge to give you access to a portfolio of resources that are often inaccessible to individual philanthropists. Finally, they ensure your funds are directed to reliable, accountable organizations. Even if you're an experienced philanthropist, you might not have the expertise to invest wisely in places such as India or China or track the performance of your investments there. Intermediaries do this, working closely with nonprofits and assessing their performance so your money has the greatest impact.

- *Giving to a donor-advised fund (DAF), sometimes known as a donor-directed fund*: You can make your contributions to a philanthropic fund managed by an organization such as a community foundation or a financial institution. You can make a tax-deductible contribution to the community foundation at any time and advise on which nonprofits to give that money to. The organization that houses your DAF legally retains ultimate control of the fund, but in practice funds are almost always applied according to your wishes (choice of grantee must be in line with the foundation's investment policy). You can also set up a DAF through other third-party organizations such as funding intermediaries, banks, and fund managers. Before your funds have been distributed, community foundations can also invest them, bringing you a return and therefore more money to give away. DAFs afford you a degree of privacy—they're not public record (although their staff might recommend funding opportunities, and their board members may have access to a list of your grants). If your fund is at a local community foundation, it can give you insights into community needs and the most effective local nonprofits. If your fund is at your alma mater, its development staff can share new projects and funding opportunities across the university. A DAF allows for a certain amount of continuity since you can typically name one generation of successor advisers to the fund.
- *Giving to a donor-designated fund*: A community foundation may have personalized arrangements to create funds for which the donor has specified that income or assets be given to one or more specific public charities. Charities supported by a donor-designated fund do not change, unless the community foundation's governing body can prove that the fund is no longer meeting the needs of the community.
- *Giving to a supporting organization*: A separate charitable organization can be legally housed within another foundation or "sponsoring organization" (usually a community foundation or other public foundation). These organizations make grants supporting the work of the sponsoring orga-

nization, as well as to other nonprofits. The sponsoring organization appoints the majority of the supporting organization's board, manages the supporting organization's investments, and covers start-up costs and reporting—all of which are performed for a specific fee (typically more than that for a donor-advised fund, but rates may be negotiable depending on fund size). Aside from having staff, a formal infrastructure (including grantmaking programs), and separate legal status, supporting organizations operate like donor-advised funds, with the donor making recommendations for the grants.

- *Setting up a charitable trust*: A charitable trust helps you tackle both long- and short-term tax issues while you also ultimately still support the nonprofits of your choice. The basic form—the charitable remainder trust (CRT)—is an irrevocable trust (one that can't be changed without the consent of the beneficiary) that provides you with an annual income stream for a set period of time (a certain number of years or a lifetime). If you want to maximize your current income stream and income tax deductions, CRTs could be right for you. They also help avoid paying capital gains tax on stocks that are worth a lot more than you paid for them. Trusts come in many different forms—some more appropriate for newer philanthropists, others for the more experienced (see Appendix IV, Jargon Buster).

Note: All these different funding vehicles have important tax implications and multiple other considerations for donors. Always seek the advice of your accountant or the IRS website for the most current tax regulations before making any decisions. See Appendix II, Vehicles for Giving, and Appendix IV, Jargon Buster, for more information.

What to Ask the Nonprofits You Want to Fund:
- What does the organization do?
  - What programs and services does it offer?
  - Who are the people it aims to help and where are they located?
  - What are the greatest needs of those people and how does it assess those needs?
  - What other nonprofits are providing similar services and how do they differ?
  - What are the obstacles preventing the organization from achieving its goals and how does it aim to overcome them?

- How is the organization run?
  - What date was the organization founded?
  - What is its mission?
  - Who leads the organization, and how is the management team structured?
  - What skills of team members are most relevant to its mission?
  - Do any of the individuals in the communities it serves have a seat on the board or serve as advisers in any other capacity?
  - Who will oversee the program or project you want to fund?
  - What systems and infrastructure are in place to run the program or project you want to fund?
  - Would additional funding to increase the services it provides put a burden on the nonprofit's organizational capacity?
  - What is its greatest organizational challenge right now, and how does it plan to address it?
  - Has it experienced turnover of staff or board members in recent years?
  - Has the organization done any restructuring or other organizational changes in the past few years to become more efficient? And if so, what have the results been?
  - Are there any major changes planned in the near or intermediate term? If so, why and how will it know if they are successful?
  - Is the organization a start-up, experiencing rapid growth, or in a period of relative stability?
- How is the organization financed?
  - How do its revenue sources break down (such as fees for service, government grants, foundation grants, corporate support, and individual gifts)?
  - Who are its main funders?
  - What percentage of the organization's donors are supporting it for the first time? What percentage have been giving to the organization more than five consecutive years? (A high percentage may be an indicator of organizational stability.)
  - What nonfinancial support does it receive (such as free office space or pro bono legal, accounting, or consulting services)?
  - How does it rate its financial health—weak and in need of funds or healthy?

- What does it need funding for most urgently—capital (for building infrastructure and systems), income (for operating costs), or specific programs?
- If it doubled its funding in the next year, what would its growth priorities be?
- What does the organization need funds for that it can't raise at the moment? (These are frequently for the least sexy items, such as electricity bills, janitorial services, or accounting systems.)
- What are its biggest debts?
- How much does the executive director make and what percentage of the annual budget does that represent? (This is a calculation worth doing for all top executive positions.)
- How will it use your money—for running the organization itself or directly for the programs and services it provides, and what proportion of your funding goes to each of these?
- Will it pass your address (email, home, or office) on to other organizations? (Many nonprofits do this—so make sure you check privacy policies, including whether or not you have to check an opt-out box or make a formal request to be excluded from such lists.)
- If it uses direct mail, TV commercials, or other marketing tools to raise money, what percentage of the dollars raised end up as profits for those marketing companies?
- How does it plan to raise funds for the future?
- How does the organization assess its impact?
  - What has it achieved so far?
  - What have been the key indicators for that success?
  - What goals have not been accomplished according to plan? What plans are in place to still achieve those goals?
  - What systems does it have in place to measure the efficiency with which it's run and the effectiveness with which it delivers its programs?
  - What are the organization's annual and three-year future goals, and how does it measure whether or not it has achieved them?
  - How will achieving those goals help the community it serves?
  - What has been the organization's greatest setback and resulting "learning opportunity" to date?
  - What else could go wrong with its plan, and does it have a strategy to deal with such changes?

- In what form will you receive feedback on the project you want to fund?
- How does the organization maximize its impact?
  - What is its strategic plan?
  - How does it make the communities it serves aware of what it does?
  - Does it formally evaluate its own programs and operations? If so, what are the results, and if not, does it plan to in the future?
  - Does it have partnerships with any other organizations—nonprofits or organizations from other sectors, such as business or government?

Warning Signs to Note When Considering Funding a Nonprofit:

Think twice about funding an organization if you find that:

- Its executives cannot tell you what success looks like for the organization, and they've done no internal evaluation of their programs.
- The organization does not have full board participation in its giving, and not all board members practice fiduciary oversight.
- The nonprofit pays one or two inappropriately high executive salaries, or employs family members of the founder or executive director.
- The organization has had frequent changes of leadership in recent years.
- The organization has no individual on its team or board with expertise in accounting principles.
- The nonprofit is spending a high percentage of every dollar it raises on fundraising.
- The nonprofit's administrative costs are inappropriately high when measured against program costs.
- The majority of donors are one-time-only givers (as opposed to individuals or foundations who have been funding the organization for many years).

For the Family:

- Take $1,000 every year and create a family donor-advised fund at your local community foundation or bank. If the minimum fund amount is too high—they can be up to $10,000 at some community foundations—create a separate bank account you call the "[YourName] Family Philanthropic Fund." You can run it like a mini-family foundation: decide together which issues you want to focus on, have family members do some research, and share that with the rest of the family. Let each family member make one grant-making decision per quarter and make the case for why they think the family should donate to their chosen organization.

- Suggest your children try tithing—putting 10 percent of their allowance into a charity every month.
- Increase your child's allowance on the condition they give it away. Buy them a separate piggy bank so they can watch their philanthropic resource grow, and you can match their contributions with contributions of your own.
- Invite your religious leader to a family meal to talk to your kids about how your house of worship gives back to the community and how giving relates to your family's religious values.

And Remember:

- When you assess your giving, you may be frustrated to find how much of it is driven by others and how little is going to the causes about which you care most. Taking stock, therefore, will help you to focus on your own passions in the present and future.
- When giving directly, you may feel pressure to give hastily at the end of the fiscal year to secure tax deductions. To avoid making poor decisions due to time constraints, you could establish a general-purpose donor-advised fund to which you can donate immediately to get your tax deduction and allocate the funds more thoughtfully in the months that follow.
- Creating a strategy for your giving will make it easier to measure progress, or lack thereof, toward meeting a need, pursuing a passion, or tackling the problem. This will make giving more rewarding and exciting—enthusiasm you can share with others.
- It's okay to be disappointed about gifts you've made in the past—regretting making a poor giving decision in the heat of an emotionally-charged moment or giving to an organization or program that later fails doesn't make you a less generous person or a less effective giver.
- Holding an annual or quarterly meeting to develop a giving policy with your spouse—working out how much to give jointly and separately helps you pursue both your own and your shared interests.
- The more refined and focused your giving strategy is, the easier it is to say yes and no.
- Expect failure as well as success if you're trying new things in your giving.

- Read papers and reports on the issues you care about—an endless supply can be found online that can help you make more effective giving decisions.
- Look at foundations in the field and what organizations they're funding—they might be able to help you with your due diligence.
- Before funding an organization, do plenty of research—from online reading to having a conversation with nonprofit executives or board members.
- When you're funding for the first time, start with small amounts and set benchmarks for what that money should achieve. See how you enjoy working with the organization before making a bigger or longer-term commitment.
- When you make a significant gift (significant to both you *and* the non-profit), work with the nonprofit to set goals for what it will achieve with it. This will establish an expectation of accountability and transparency for your investment.
- Remember that if your primary gift is a bequest, you miss out on all of the benefits of giving while living!
- If you want a nonprofit to do a formal evaluation of your gift's impact, make this clear before donating and fund the evaluation as part of your gift—nonprofit resources are scarce and evaluations have financial and human capital costs, so make them worthwhile for you both.
- Continue due diligence on an organization even after funding it for many years—this will help you decide whether to withdraw your funding or increase your commitment.

4

DETERMINING A DESTINATION

Assess Your Aspirations and Impact

Envision your impact—defining goals and measuring outcomes will fortify your giving.

Minnesota-born Charlie Rounds believes that, as a privileged white male raised in a middle-class family, it would be "a sin to not use those advantages." And as a gay man, Charlie—with his partner Mark Hiemenz—is determined to use those advantages to help make the lesbian, gay, bisexual, and transgender (LGBT) community a prominent part of American philanthropy. "If we're going to take our place at the table and have equal rights, then the responsibilities that come with that are huge," he says. "And part of that is that the broader community needs to see we're out there and just as active in giving." For Charlie and Mark, impact is not only about affecting individual lives—it's about furthering a philanthropic movement by encouraging more LGBT individuals to become givers—and to do so publicly.

Charlie's community service started when, as a young man, he spent more than three years in central-western Africa volunteering with the Peace Corps, teaching English to French-speaking Cameroonian school students. He played another important role while in Cameroon. "I was the camp chef," he says. "I cooked for more than a hundred people over an open fire." It was no easy task, but it introduced Charlie to a diversity of races and faiths. Cameroon is a country with many religions, and Charlie had to accommodate Muslims who, during Ramadan, could only eat before sunrise and after sunset. "We also had a number of American Jewish volunteers, and it was the 1970s, so we had plenty of vegetarians," he says. "There was never a dull moment."

In 2002, Charlie married Mark, his longtime partner. While Minnesota did not allow same-sex marriages (and still does not, as of mid-2011), he and Mark held a public celebration of their deep love and commitment to each other.

Then, in December 2004, life changed again. At age forty-nine, Charlie sold the business he'd been running, a successful gay and lesbian cruise travel firm, leaving him and his three business partners a substantial profit. After the sale, he sat down with Mark, then forty-six and head of his company's corporate giving and volunteer programs, to discuss what to do with the money. "I said to Mark, 'We can keep it all and retire, we can give part of it away and retire five years from now, or we can give it all away and retire fifteen years from now," recalls Charlie. "And Mark said, 'Let's give it all away.'"

The decision was partly informed by Charlie and Mark's background. Charlie's parents were members of the Reorganized Church of Jesus Christ of Latter Day Saints, so had a strong belief in giving 10 percent of their income through tithing. Both Mark and Charlie were raised in single-earner, middle-class families with parents who pushed their children through education to help them avoid the same struggles they'd faced. "It was simply foreign to us to be able to retire that early in life," says Charlie. "So the model was very much based on whom we were raised as."

Their identity as an openly gay couple also shaped their giving. The vehicle they chose was a donor-advised fund called Mark and Charlie's Gay & Lesbian Fund for Moral Values, which they established through the Minneapolis Foundation. Through this fund, Charlie and Mark support causes such as women's health and global human rights—things that aren't necessarily LGBT issues, although they'll only consider funding nonprofits that have sexual orientation nondiscrimination policies for board and staff members. Instead of supporting LGBT causes, Mark and Charlie aim to encourage more members of the gay community to give. For this reason they take steps (such as the choice of name for their fund) to ensure their donations are identified as coming from an openly gay couple.

"If you look at gay and lesbian philanthropy in this country, the bottom line is it has to increase," says Charlie. "We all learn from the role models in our lives, so if we don't have open LGBT philanthropists teaching us the power of giving, it's not going to play the role it needs to—that's why Mark and I are out there with our giving."

Assessing the impact of this kind of giving is not easy. "Part of the challenge in the gay and lesbian community is finding us," says Charlie. "We're everywhere in this country, in every county in the U.S.—but some of us are incredibly visible and some of us are invisible, so measuring gay and lesbian philanthropy is pretty much impossible."

If you want to do more to make a difference, measuring the impact of your funding in some way is critical. The trouble is, many of us fail to do any research on our philanthropic investments and few of us seem to care about metrics. In a 2010 Hope Consulting study, 85 percent of the American donors surveyed said that nonprofit performance was "very important"—yet only 35 percent said they did any research on their gifts. Among those who did research, only 5 percent said they used their research to assess the quality of the organization's team.[1]

Part of the reason few of us make efforts to assess the impact of our gifts is that much of our giving is emotionally driven. Too often, we're happy to receive thanks from our beneficiaries, accepting gratitude instead of feedback or performance measurements. And when we view what we're making as a gift rather than as an investment, we can feel awkward requiring any reporting on the impact of our generosity.

It's wonderful to be driven by causes that touch us personally. But at the same time, it's important not to neglect the strategic analysis and assessment we can bring to bear on the process. Otherwise, we're giving in the dark, something that prevents millions (potentially billions) of philanthropic dollars from having the impact they might otherwise achieve.

When thinking about impact, it's important to distinguish between the two sides to evaluating your giving. One part is defining and assessing the impact of your giving portfolio—in its entirety, over time, and including resources of all kinds—as well as of individual gifts made independently. Another is defining and assessing the impact the nonprofits have made through the programs or activities you fund. So first, you need to establish what your own goals are and what giving strategies you'll use to achieve them. This includes identifying nonprofits whose mission and approach match your goals and figuring out how you'll know if your gifts have been successful or not in achieving your goals. Then you need to ask yourself whether the way your grantees define and evaluate their own performance will give you enough information to assess the impact of your donations to them.

Of course, assessing the performance of any nonprofit is difficult, particularly for an individual giver without professional staff. Even in the foundation sector, only a few institutions have sufficient staff and infrastructure to conduct formal evaluations (and for these institutions, such evaluations can cost up to 10 percent of their total grantmaking budget).

However, with so many nonprofits in the world, all tackling different things and going about it in many different ways, you need to be sure the organizations you fund are able to provide feedback—in a form that's acceptable to you—on their activities and successes. This feedback could be anything from anecdotes and stories or metrics and data through to extensive, evidence-based evaluation. Only you can decide what level of analysis is meaningful to you. However, I encourage you to look for more than an emotion-based assessment, such as storytelling, a few photos, or a feel-good anecdote, which can be moving but rarely provide sufficient evidence of impact.

Even if the results you seek are more intangible—as they are for Mark and Charlie as they actively help build a giving movement—defining impact and assessing it are among the most important aspects of your philanthropy. They're tools for learning how to improve your giving and understanding how nonprofits work. They help you define and recognize success and give you insights into why some things work and others don't. It may take many years before you see the evidence of the difference you've made, and your impact may be cumulative rather than the result of a single gift. But if you track your impact carefully, you'll find that collectively, your individual gifts can add up to something big.

SAVING A LIFE OR MOVING A NEEDLE

"If you had one dollar to give, where would you invest it to have the most impact?" This question was recently posed to me by an amazing young tech entrepreneur and new-generation philanthropist—Andrew Mason, the founder and CEO of Groupon, the online coupon company that connects subscribers to discounts on everything from restaurant meals and language classes to spa treatments and karaoke. Andrew was telling me how he wanted to change the world. Of course, in many ways, he already had—millions of people have signed up to Groupon's email service, and he's already using Groupon's corporate reach to create philanthropic opportunities for its customers. In 2010, with a matching grant from the Pershing Square Foundation, Groupon helped subscribers buy credits for nonprofits at half price through DonorsChoose, which helps givers support projects in America's public schools. Groupon also has offered matching gifts—often from community foundations—for local charities such as food banks. Even with these successes, Andrew wanted to do more. He wanted to combine his knowledge of technology to maximize the potential impact of his giving, and was curious to know how I approached the question of impact.

Of course, there is—as I told Andrew—no single answer to his question. With any given problem, you could take any number of approaches and choose from among any number of nonprofits. Do you want to fund immediate needs or support longer-term social change, or a combination of both? The answers may not always be easy. But mapping out your philanthropic path—working out what social change you want to achieve and how you want to go about achieving it—is something you need to do before you can choose your grantees and decide what you'll need from them as evidence of good stewardship of your funding and demonstration and of how it's being used to advance their mission.

You might choose the firefighting approach, in which you give to immediate needs, helping alleviate suffering but not necessarily getting at its root causes. We often call the organizations doing this charities, as they work to ease the pain of a problem such as hunger, rather than finding ways to solve the hunger problem altogether. A charity might be the food pantry that operates out of a church building. Its intention is simple—to provide food to people who can't afford it and who need a basic supply of groceries. Organizations like this often receive small donations and rely on volunteers. They tend not to grow or scale—as that's not their intention. But they provide a vital service that fills a need. And your time or money could help support that service.

Alternatively, you could fund a nonprofit that's working to tackle the root causes of problems. In the case of hunger, that might an organization helping smallholder farmers in developing countries become more productive. Your money might fund irrigation equipment or water filters for the farmers.

On the other hand, if an organization has the potential to expand and make a bigger dent in a particular problem, you might consider a different type of giving—supporting its operations. Nonprofits are like any organization. They cannot run programs or experiment with innovative, exciting ideas unless their infrastructure is stable and strong. However inspiring their mission, they need the basics to support their activities— whether it's training, cutting-edge technology, or simply a reliable supply of printer cartridges.

Unlike businesses, nonprofits have no revenues with which to fund these items (unless they derive a portion of their income from service charges or have a significant endowment), and most have to raise all their operational funds every year. But when philanthropy supplies that funding (ideally on a consistent basis), nonprofits can concentrate on what they do best—executing the programs that deliver the impact you hope to see. Your money (and perhaps your time, too) can help build critical operational capacity, which will help them grow and attract funds from elsewhere. While more intangible, such gifts make a substantial impact.

Of course, this kind of giving doesn't seem all that sexy. A thank-you letter detailing the new computers, office supplies, or executive training purchased with your money (or a utility bill it paid) doesn't necessarily warm or wrench the heart in the way a picture of a smiling or malnourished child does. And certainly, a nonprofit delivering emergency food supplies to starving children in developing countries needs money to purchase and deliver that food. But a grant that could pay for staff training in managing cargo transport logistics or a trip to build a partnership with a corporate distributor could help the organization deliver that food faster and more efficiently, ultimately saving many more lives. Sometimes, the least sexy grants support the most critical services.

I learned this lesson some years ago, when investing some of my family's philanthropic resources in Fresh Lifelines for Youth (FLY), which works to reduce repeat-offender rates among young people coming out of the juvenile justice system. I could have made a gift allowing more children to go through the program. This would've been hugely emotionally rewarding for me, as I could have said that, because of my family, three at-risk teenagers were in the program (for the donation, I'd potentially receive their names and even photographs), and their lives would be improved as a direct result of our money.

However, I took a different approach. Instead, I asked the organization what it needed. It turned out it had no phone system. Staff used personal cell phones, but there was no landline number for young people to call if they needed to speak to someone. What it required was not more money for programs—it was basic technology to help to run the existing program more effectively.

The cost of installing a phone system was $5,000—not a huge amount in proportion to FLY's operating budget. But it was having trouble raising the money, since donors always wanted their funds to be used on getting more young people into the program. I decided to fund the phone system. It wasn't a glamorous gift. I couldn't point to a specific teen I'd helped. But it's one of the gifts of which I'm most proud—by meeting a tangible need in its operations when no one else wanted to, I'd helped an organization with a tremendous track record increase its ability to serve its community.

Of course, you can also combine meeting immediate needs with supporting long-term change. This was the approach Marc and I took when we began making annual gifts to the Stanford Hospital Emergency Department. We had several goals. We wanted to meet a critical need for emergency care that existed in the community in which we live and work. We wanted to help create one of the country's best emergency care departments and support the acquisition of technology enabling everything from IV fluid warming and portable digital imaging and trauma monitors to improved data sharing in the global medical community. We wanted to see advances such as reduced treatment waiting times, improved patient treatment and satisfaction, and excellence in training for medical professionals. We fund an expanded residency and nursing program, and Stanford's medical team now travels globally to share expertise and care for the Haiti relief efforts, a self-sustaining paramedic education program in India, and pre-hospital emergency response in Nepal. We also wanted to fund research and pilot programs in areas such as disaster relief, swine flu treatment processes, and the prevention of injury in seniors—and to help these programs be implemented in other medical centers across the country.

We chose Stanford Hospital because it was the most impressive institution in our area when it came to both research and trauma care, and Stanford had just brought in two of the country's top ER doctors. At the time we were considering our gift, Stanford had also embarked on a major capital campaign to create a state-of-the-art new hospital, so we wanted our gift not only to help build this hospital but also to inspire others to support Stanford's campaign. So our goals combined meeting a critical local need, helping a world-class institution achieve a new level of excellence, and building knowledge and technology that could serve as a model for the entire country and share medical expertise and provide care globally.

Charlie and Mark share our objective of inspiring others to give more through their own example. In their approach to giving, Mark and Charlie were inspired by the Gay & Lesbian Fund for Colorado, part of the Gill Foundation, one of America's largest funders and organizers of LGBT civil rights work. "The Gay & Lesbian Fund for Colorado doesn't give to gay and lesbian causes," explains Charlie. "It's there to get gay philanthropy recognized within the community. That's exactly what Mark and I are doing."

In their giving this way, they've also been empowered by the Gill Foundation's OutGiving program, which—through training, technical assistance, and a national conference—helps LGBT philanthropists become better fundraisers, build stronger boards, develop leaders, and establish relationships with other donors in the LGBT community. A few years ago, Charlie and Mark organized a local Minnesota OutGiving event, and today they continue to use their philanthropy to highlight LGBT giving.

Another form of long-term giving might be funding research work into a certain issue, or supporting the individuals who are working to change the fundamental systems that give rise to problems in the first place. As outlined in Chapter Seven, you could use your philanthropic resources to support activities that bring about long-term social change by influencing public policy and the legislative environment.

When considering which giving strategy will give you the biggest bang for your buck, think broadly. For instance, if your focus is on human rights, you might decide not to give money to your college but to a nonprofit helping free political prisoners from a country run by a repressive regime. Yet the donation to your college might help fund the education of a young person who at school finds a passion for human rights and goes on to become a nonprofit or government leader responsible for bringing about significant progress in reducing global human rights abuses or changing a political landscape.

To maximize your impact, therefore, you need to understand the complex interaction between the way you invest your resources, how they will be used, and how all that supports the ultimate goals you've set for your own giving. I've found that writing up strategies in my giving journal has helped me understand both the impact I want to have and the impact I've achieved through my giving, and I encourage you to do the same. Filling an immediate need, supporting long-term change, working to inspire greater giving by others, or helping change a social landscape are all valid approaches to transforming our world—you have to decide which is right for you.

SHAPING YOUR MEASUREMENT STRATEGY

Once you've chosen your giving approach—and you may want to have several—you can decide what nonprofits to invest in to achieve your goals and what you will require from those organizations in terms of demonstrable impact or formal reporting. Finding out how your money is being used and the difference it's making to a problem or to people you hope to help will increase your confidence in your giving decisions. It will also help you advocate more effectively for the causes you find compelling. Also, when donors hold their grantees accountable for their funds, the resulting level of transparency can help nonprofits attract more funding.

If your favored causes take more of the firefighting approach I mentioned earlier, and your grantee is a charity working to alleviate immediate suffering, it will most likely not make sense to request an evaluation. Nevertheless, you can ask for some simple metrics (or research them from the nonprofit's annual reports or websites) before you give. How many families came to the church to collect food, for example, how many bags were passed out, what types of food were in the bags, and what was their dollar value?

Even for small gifts, you should make efforts to follow their progress. If you've made a financial donation, find out how it's being used and determine whether it's making a difference or not. If you've given time or expertise, find some way to measure the value of those assets to the recipients—and in most cases, the onus of that research is on you.

As discussed in Chapter Two, new and innovative online forms of giving such as the Jolkona Foundation make this kind of information accessible even for those giving small amounts of money. While harder to quantify, the impact of your volunteering is becoming easier to measure through organizations such as Catchafire, whose website tells you the monetary value to a nonprofit of your gift of skills and hours. In fact, the Web has given a new transparency to the nonprofit world, allowing organizations to showcase their results and allowing donors to investigate them.

You may, on the other hand, decide to fund the programs of a nonprofit tackling the root causes of problems. If so, you need to start by finding out whether the organization has a clear plan in place for creating a specific change in its area of focus. This is often called a "theory of change." It sounds complicated but essentially this is a business plan.

Take a clothing store chain that wants to attract more customers. It could do so by beefing up the skills of sales teams, by placing magazine ads, or by creating dazzling new storefront displays. However, it needs to assess potential and actual return on those investments. How many new customers can it attract for every dollar spent on sales force training, advertising, or storefront costs?

For nonprofits, the theory of change is similar. Take a nonprofit that wants to increase literacy among children from low-income households. Ideally, it will first create clear goals—an annual increase in the number of children reading at grade level in a specific community, for example. Then it will form a set of strategies on how to achieve those goals (by, for example, recruiting local university students or professionals to volunteer to tutor children). It will then determine what specific resources it needs (such as classrooms, books, and program data collection) and how it will enroll the children (whether through school outreach efforts or by advertising campaigns). And, perhaps most important, it will define up front what specific indicators or events—such as test scores and increased student engagement and self-esteem—it will use to tell donors how their money is contributing to its mission. Your grantee's programs will be designed to achieve its goals in a way that maximizes the impact of philanthropic dollars and human resources, and it will assess the return on those dollars and efforts both before and after investing them.

To gain this kind of information, you can go to an organization's website to read about its programs in more depth. Look at a nonprofit's mission statement or a description of the results it seeks, statements about the strategies and activities it will use to reach its goals, and information about the resources (funding or volunteers) it needs to implement these. As you investigate nonprofit websites, remember that compelling stories should be backed up by evidence demonstrating that the strategy works. Find out if the nonprofit produces evaluation information and insights that could show you the value of your donation.

If you can't find this information from the organization itself, you can turn to the annual reports of large foundations (the Foundation Center publishes extensive lists of major foundations and the areas they fund). Look for foundations that support the same nonprofits as you—if they have the resources (and not all do), they may have produced detailed public reports or white papers on their grantees' successful programs. If they have not, see what organizations they fund on an ongoing basis (this may serve as an indicator of success).

Once you've started funding a nonprofit, the way you give will influence what evidence you seek from the organization to demonstrate that its programs and approach work. If, for example, you're funding the operations of a nonprofit to help it improve its overall effectiveness—as I did in funding the phone system for Fresh Lifelines for Youth—proof of impact is less easy to obtain. But remember, your funding is helping the organization become better at delivering its programs, so you can ask for some metrics. In the case of FLY, a key metric might be how many teens used the phone to seek help—and, just as important, whether or not the organization can demonstrate reduced repeat offending among the teens it has worked with.

More and more of this kind of information is now online. FLY's website features videos of individuals describing how their lives have changed as a result of the organization's programs. The site has statistics on how the program saves taxpayer dollars (FLY explains, for example, that three months of incarceration costs $21,150, while the equivalent time spent in a FLY program costs only $1,000). You can also read testimonials from judges and school principals on the difference they believe FLY's programs make. Building this kind of online presence has become easier and cheaper and could even be an indication of how accountable a nonprofit is.

Suppose you're funding an organization to support a combination of objectives, ranging from immediate needs to longer-term change (as Marc and I are with Stanford Hospital). This means working closely with the institution to secure the right information and sufficient evidence to demonstrate the gift is being put to good use.

Now, before Marc and I make our annual gift to the Stanford Hospital Emergency Department, I consult with the fundraising staff, head doctors, and nurses. I work with the Emergency Department team to determine what our gift should fund and with the hospital staff on how to evaluate its performance. The hospital gets what it needs financially, and we get what we need in terms of benchmarks against which to measure the success of our gifts. We believe in what the hospital does, so we listen to what it tells us about its requirements, and we agree on the data it will give us to track its progress with our money.

We found, for example, that the hospital was doing some evaluation of the impact our funding was making in improving patient services, and I contributed ideas about other items for it to include in its patient surveys. When funding a nonprofit that seeks to grow, you can play a role in supporting its evaluation capacity *and* holding it accountable for how it deploys your funds, using evaluations to assess the impact of your donation or grant. In the case of Stanford Hospital, that meant requiring written reporting on how our programs were being implemented. Once I saw the impact of our dollars, I also learned more about what the hospital needed, and became more excited to continue our giving. Most important, when you help an organization strengthen its evidence base, you give it a compelling body of evidence with which to attract more supporters.

Even longer-term gifts with little immediate tangible evidence of change can be measured. With advocacy, that could be the passing of a piece of legislation or indications of increased public awareness of an issue. If it's public awareness, an organization could count the numbers in terms of media stories, polling results, or rising voter registration. And for Charlie and Mark, while they can't count numbers, seeing LGBT philanthropy strengthen will be evidence of the value of their efforts. "In the gay and lesbian community, what do we want to be known for right now? We want to be known for being the generation that got equal rights in our country," says Charlie. "But we also want to be known as a community that has helped solve real-world problems."

CLOSING SOME DOORS, OPENING OTHERS

Philanthropy is not a single action or a moment in time—it's a journey, one on which you should ask yourself constantly if there's a better way to spend your money and time. And if giving is a journey, it involves departures as well as arrivals. There will be occasions where you need to consider withdrawing support from an organization. But as long as you're constantly learning, enhancing your knowledge and experience, your money and time are not being wasted. Backed by more knowledge and experience, every new gift has a better chance of making a real impact.

For my friend and fellow philanthropist Alexa Cortés Culwell, a new career prompted a rethink of her giving. As part of her philanthropy, Alexa has taken on many volunteer board roles with nonprofits at local, regional, and national levels, as well as CEO roles with such institutions as the Stupski Foundation and the Charles and Helen Schwab Foundation. Since setting up and running her own consultancy, however, she has decided not to seek new terms on some of the nonprofit boards she was serving and moved from her position as board chair at New Door Ventures—a San Francisco nonprofit that provides at-risk young people with jobs, job-readiness, and a supportive community—to a non-board role as adviser and champion.

In scaling back some of her more hands-on philanthropic activities, she redefined her impact during the transition period. "I wondered what would it mean to be able to say yes to things I can never say yes to because I'm always so busy," she says. "It was a time to step back, but to be able to respond to people who needed me. I created space for opportunities and learning."

Rather than packing her life with organizational commitments, Alexa engaged in other kinds of activities. "I spent a lot of time having lunches and coffees with people who wanted advice and then hooking them up in my network to help them solve problems." While she might not have been as active in some ways, Alexa found she was having an impact in a new way—by passing on her knowledge, advice, experience, and networks to other philanthropists.

In addition to life changes, external factors may prompt you to consider stepping back from philanthropic commitments. The most obvious of these is the emergence of a scandal or a fraud—say, an executive at a nonprofit you support turns out to be siphoning off organizational funds for personal use, for example. However, one person's action doesn't necessarily reflect the values of an organization or the quality of its services, so before making a decision, have a conversation with a board member or another executive to find out how the organization is handling the situation.

You may find that, despite the best of social intentions, a nonprofit you're funding has adopted a flawed strategy that's not advancing the organization's mission or might even be doing more harm than good. This is not necessarily a reason to withdraw support. But before making a new commitment, find out whether the organization is tracking and analyzing its results and using that information to adapt its strategy.

A change of leadership may also prompt a funding reassessment. New management or a merger with another organization may alter the culture, focus, and sometimes the mission of a nonprofit. As a result, it may no longer match your passions or goals. (The good news is that, with an ever-growing number of nonprofits out there, you'll still have an endless choice of options for giving.)

Yet from any giving initiative from which you choose to withdraw, or any gift you regret making, you can learn. And when you stop supporting an organization because it did not deliver the results you wanted, you can still learn from its practices. (Its progressive board diversity policy might be replicable elsewhere, or detailed reporting on its lack of success in one program area could help another nonprofit avoid similar pitfalls.)

While leaders may make mistakes, that doesn't mean an organization isn't doing tremendous work in other areas. It's how a leader handles mistakes that proves critical. When someone takes a wrong turn or a project fails, the leader or board should immediately take full responsibility for it. Other important steps include presenting a report to the board and staff, publicizing the plan the organization has formulated to prevent the same thing from happening again, and changing course on the strategy or decision that caused the problem in the first place. Philanthropy is all about renewal—and this is another opportunity to rethink strategies and move on to a better path.

Even if no mistakes have been made and the organization's mission has not been altered, few funders support any particular nonprofit in perpetuity. If you find yourself wanting to exit a funding relationship, you need to find the best way to exit gracefully.

First, notify the organization at least a year in advance (if not two or three, depending on how long you have been funding it), and consider setting up a matching grant to help cultivate donors to replace you. Explain to the grantee why you're discontinuing your funding and say you're doing so indefinitely to move on to other interest areas. If you don't, the organization may request funding again in a year or two (nonprofits often turn first to past donors for funding). Then evaluate whether or not what you funded was a success, whether that success met your expectations, and how this will influence your future giving decisions.

Your exits—and even failures—while painful, can be valuable. As you experiment with giving strategies and reject those that aren't achieving results, you can share this knowledge, taking your impact even further. Every experience in your philanthropic voyage should inform your giving strategy and future gifts.

FROM THE TANGIBLE TO THE INTANGIBLE

When assessing the impact of her philanthropic dollars, Alexa creates a simple review of how an organization is performing based on three questions: How many? How deeply? How much? "I like to look at how many people, children, or youth are being served; how deeply they are being served, so I can understand the quality and caliber of the program; and finally, at what cost it achieves its results," she says. "Sometimes the cost is as easy as crude math—how much does the organization spend and how many does it serve for that amount," she adds.

Alexa and her husband Travis strive to lead a giving life in everything they do—from giving away 10 percent of their income every year to the hours they spend volunteering. While Alexa has had her volunteer board and CEO roles, Travis has used his MBA and branding expertise to give to nonprofits through pro bono projects, defining the value in the same way he would for his paying clients. Three of Travis's volunteer engagements helped organizations the Culwells support financially with brand consultation equivalent to an additional six-figure donation. (While it is gratifying to estimate the monetary value of such donations of loving labor, you cannot legally take a tax deduction for the market value of your services.)

For the past couple of decades, Alexa and Travis have devoted much of their philanthropic energies and funding to New Door Ventures. "That's been a twenty-year journey of being very committed to that organization time-wise, talent-wise, and financially—really supporting it in every way," she says. Alexa defines her impact broadly as a result. "We try to use our money, time, and talents holistically, lining them up around a series of commitments that we feel passionate about—it's been a great way to live."

While she likes the simplicity of her "How many? How deeply? How much?" formula, Alexa would be the first to point out that not all giving can be assessed in this way. "If an organization does policy and advocacy work or other things that are not easily counted, this is not as simple a formula," she says.

In addition, it's important to think about a nonprofit's general accountability. This includes things such as whether salaries are in line with industry standards, office rent and executive expenses are reasonable, and overhead costs align with mission and activities. Nonprofits should be able to show how they're managing these and other items.

Think broadly about measurement, too. If you make a gift for a specific purpose, such as putting more children through a reading program, you may ask how many children were indeed put through that program. However, those results represent just part of your potential impact. How will that reading program affect those students in the years to come, for example? Did attending that program after school mean they were able to resist the pressure to join a gang? Did it enable a few individuals to graduate from high school, when they otherwise would not have done so?

On the other hand, if your gift is not tied to any specific results, you can measure the same thing that the organization measures, such as the number of children reading at grade level by third grade, and as a result potentially graduating from high school and college, as well.

How you count your impact will be shaped by how you give. So in the same way that you apply different giving strategies to different goals and social issues, you need to apply different forms of measurement to your gifts. For example, if you're giving unrestricted grants to a nonprofit to build its organizational capacity, you will assess everything from its fiscal responsibility to its marketing effectiveness, in addition to the results of the programs and services it provides. Funding to improve operational infrastructure is part of how we help nonprofits make an impact, so we need to measure that, too.

Of course, the impact of certain types of philanthropic investments goes well beyond the success of a single program or the life of a single community. Not everything lends itself to a hard-edged assessment that can be expressed in numbers. Take the philanthropic activities of Charlie and Mark, who are encouraging more of the LGBT community to be philanthropic, to extend the impact of their giving. They also believe that helping people overseas improve their lives is an important part of their impact—because the effect of this kind of giving often extends far beyond the initial recipients. (Giving's ripple effect is true for domestic giving, as well. However, the same dollar invested in developing countries may have greater effect.)

In 2005, the youngest of the four Ecuadorian brothers the couple employed in their bar and restaurant approached Charlie. He told him he needed to go home to raise his two daughters but that there was no work in his home country. He suggested Charlie and Mark potentially invest in a microfinance project that could generate income and jobs in Ecuador because, as he told Charlie, "we can't keep working in your country." Charlie was amazed. "Here's this kid with a third-grade education, and he had it all mapped out. He'd done his homework," he says.

Charlie listened to what the young man had to say, but instead he decided to establish something with Mark that could generate income for Ecuadorians, rather than simply offer them small loans. "Microfinance works well but it's based on agriculture, which is raising chickens or guinea pigs—and that's still going to limit you economically," says Charlie. "You really need something to export, so we're very much focused on creating a micro-enterprise that will grow." The enterprise Charlie and Mark have since created in Ecuador is based on exporting the organic cotton sweaters for babies knitted by village women.

For Charlie, it's all part of a bigger picture. "The solution to illegal immigration is to create clean, safe environments for people to live in and help them to have jobs in their own countries," he says. "Then illegal immigration will be gone in five years. Because people don't want to live in Minnesota in January, they really don't—it's twenty-five degrees below!"

To encourage more Americans to think this way, Charlie is planning to launch another travel company. "What I did for the gay community when I took two thousand gays on a cruise ship, we can do with two thousand Gen-Y people by taking them to developing countries," he explains. "Until you see the face of poverty face to face, it always will remain distant, so we've got to get Americans out to see these issues."

As countless philanthropists have realized, the reason for giving globally goes beyond compassion for our fellow humans. Global challenges such as poverty, poor education, disease, and climate change can no longer be seen as isolated problems. The ripple effect of these things affects us all. In an interconnected world, we need to think broadly about the impact of our giving—for if these issues remain unsolved, global problems end up being our own problems.

Whether you're giving to global causes or creating bigger waves in a philanthropic movement where impact is less tangible, formal evaluations may not help you. Here, it's helpful to think about the ripple effect. When you throw a stone across water's surface, you see changes taking place immediately. These are your tangible impacts, and in giving, that could be metrics, such as the number of hungry people fed or children taught to read.

However, beneath the water's surface the stone creates other ripple effects, deeper changes that you may not necessarily see or be aware of—in giving, that could mean that if fewer children have their lives threatened by hunger, parents can afford to have smaller families, putting less pressure on the earth's natural resources. If more children are educated, teen pregnancy, drug use, and gang violence may be reduced.

This ripple effect is something Cameron, Alexa's son, is also thinking about. On his tenth birthday, he decided to raise money for a cause he believed in. So, in lieu of gifts, he asked friends and family to give to a project to plant trees in a deforested part of Africa through the Jolkona Foundation website.

"I chose an environmental cause because I'm always thinking about our problems in this area," he wrote on his Jolkona page. "I believe all informed people should be concerned about the amount of trees we might have left in even twenty years. Trees fight pollution in many ways. They give oxygen. Provide food. The majority of all things that sustain life." The Jolkona website will keep him updated on the progress of the tree planting, encouraging him to check back for updates, including videos. Even though he was only ten at the time, Cameron already understood the nature of the ripple effect—and with that knowledge, just imagine the impact he can create over the course of his life.

THE GIFT OF KNOWLEDGE

Whether seeking out simple metrics on your own or conducting a formal evaluation after a significant multiyear gift, treat the process not as a test to root out inefficiencies but as a method of empowering a nonprofit to perform even better and to refresh its strategies. And if a nonprofit has no measurement systems in place, you could help fund the development of formal techniques, increasing its transparency to other prospective funders. Remember, the organizations you fund use your dollars to generate positive social change, so this is part of helping them succeed.

Assessing the performance of the organizations you support and partnering with them helps you learn how the programs you're funding function and gives you a sense of whether they can be refined or scaled up. Once you've obtained the right metrics or feedback, you need to decide what actions you'll take. If results don't match your expectations, you may not necessarily withdraw your dollars. But you need to communicate with your nonprofit partners on how to improve those results. You could even set aside some resources for grantees to use in improving areas of operations that emerge as requiring attention. For gifts that didn't meet your expectations, work closely with nonprofits to help them increase their impact—and if this isn't possible, withdraw your funding gracefully.

A key lesson I have learned is that if the results aren't what you or your nonprofit partner expected, other outcomes may emerge that make your gift worthwhile. Say you provide three years' seed funding to a program in which counselors and social workers volunteer at a nonprofit to help educate teen mothers. After doing an evaluation in year three—based on information gathered by the organization—you discover that second unplanned pregnancies among teens in the program are only a few percentage points lower than the national average. You may, at that point, decide not to continue funding the program.

However, if you collaborate with the nonprofit on the outcomes being evaluated, you may find teens in the program achieve higher high school graduation rates and test scores—or they may simply have more self-worth and confidence. Perhaps the evaluation will reveal a disparity in the quality of training delivered by different facilitators or consistency of data collection, helping the nonprofit see how to improve its programs. Then your continued funding will help it to implement these improvements. You could also provide a matching grant for ongoing funding to the program.

Every evaluation—if done in partnership with the organizations you support—is an opportunity to translate knowledge into improved services and increased impact. By learning what does and doesn't work and sharing this with others, you can decrease the risk of failure and increase the effectiveness of your own and other people's philanthropic resources. Knowing a particular social change model is not helping solve a problem (or even has negative unintended consequences) might have far-reaching impact.

In this way, a gift of a few thousand dollars could generate knowledge that helps greatly increase the impact of a few hundred thousand dollars and other resources—or prevent the waste of the same dollars—in the future. The best reason to invest in assessing your impact and that of the organizations you fund is for this learning process. And while it might take several years to determine how effective your gifts are, they each provide an opportunity to learn and build a platform for increased social transformation for all givers in the future.

MAKING IT HAPPEN

What to Ask Yourself:

- How do you define impact for your different gifts and what are your key indicators for success?
- What specific change do you want to create or help create from your gift?
- Do you want to make an impact immediately (by giving to direct needs such as a homeless shelter or by sponsoring a child) or do you want to tackle underlying problems through advocacy, global giving, or support for other philanthropists?
- Do you want your gift to be used to achieve a specific outcome, or would you rather help provide the underlying support that made a nonprofit's activities possible?
- Are you prepared to tolerate the failure of some of the programs you're funding if it means that lessons have been learned along the way?
- What do you and the nonprofit need to invest to make that change happen (money, time, expertise)?
- If you give collaboratively (through a giving circle or venture philanthropy partnership), how will you assess your own impact? And if you single out your own individual role in change, does that matter?
- What form do you want your feedback to take—tangible, measurable, and observable or intangible, emotional, and anecdotal?
- What timelines will you use? In a three-year grant, are you going to conduct annual evaluations to ensure progress matches your expectations—and potentially learn about and improve the program with each year? Or will you evaluate only at the end of the three-year period, so you can decide whether to give another grant to that organization?

(Decisions may depend on whether you're funding a new nonprofit or helping an established program or nonprofit expand, as well as how your gift relates to the overall program or organizational budget.)

- How will you distinguish short-term results from long-term change—for example, between educating a girl in Africa and seeing that feed back into improved health care, education, and income for her family, as well as the avoidance of negative impacts such as the fact that the girl you educated can get a job rather than being forced to become a prostitute or being sold by her family as a sex-slave. (To begin this type of measurement, you can invest through a funding intermediary that has evaluation capabilities. High-impact organizations usually have the resources and infrastructure to measure these kinds of impacts and to assess the accountability and leadership strength of the nonprofits to which they channel your funds.)

Resources for Evaluation and Measurement:

- *The end-of-year grant report submitted by your grantee.* The nonprofit you're funding may already have a robust reporting and evaluation system, in which case you simply need to request specific information or evaluations from it. Many nonprofits post their annual progress on their websites or in the electronic annual reports. However, if the organization is starting a new program, it may need your help in paying for an accompanying evaluation (something to consider, as this is key to your success and theirs).
- *Information submitted by grantees to other funders.* Find out what kind of data the organization submits to the other individual donors and institutions from which it receives funding. If it has foundation funding, it has probably had to submit evaluations to those institutions, and those reports should be good enough for you. Remember, you don't have to reinvent the wheel—your grantee may already have an extensive self-assessment process in place, so be efficient and piggyback on existing data, or have the organization take it to the next level. The last thing you want to do is create unnecessary bureaucratic burdens for your grantees, wasting resources that could be directed toward the mission itself.
- *Third-party evaluation.* If you want to see more than the data a nonprofit has produced internally (data that may or may not be objective or controlled) and you don't have the expertise or capacity to conduct evaluations yourself, you might commission a third party to conduct a professional evaluation (these typically make sense for multiyear grants

of $100,000 or more). When looking for these kinds of evaluators, you can turn to nonprofit consultants. Be sure to select one that works with other foundations and has a strong reputation, as some consultants may lack the relevant expertise to create the feedback you seek. Alternatively, larger staffed foundations funding your issue area might be able to suggest field experts, or if you are co-funding a program with other institutional funders, you can share evaluation design, costs, and results with them.

What to Ask Nonprofits When Conducting Your Own Evaluation:

- How does the organization define success?
- What specific indicators does the organization use to measure the effectiveness (or lack thereof) of its programs—short-term, intermediate-term, and long-term? (If an organization's goal is "making sure all kids in a particular school district are reading at grade level," you will want to ask them specifically, "How will you know if they are?")
- Does the organization currently conduct assessments?
- What form do these take?
- How often are they conducted?
- Are these assessments for internal purposes or are they formal evaluations for submission to foundation funders?
- What changes to your organization and activities have you made in the past in response to evaluations?

Innovation Lab—Ideas to Test:

- Instigate a regular pause in your giving to take stock of its impact on society, as well as its impact on your own life. You could do it, for example, between Christmas and New Year's, during the summer break, or on the first Friday of every month. Put this assessment on your calendar in advance and make it part of your giving journal.
- Take a friend or colleague you admire out to lunch, tell them what you are doing philanthropically, and ask them for their thoughts.
- Pick three nonprofits working in the field you care about (these could include the one you are funding) and go to their websites to compare their transparency levels—that is, how much information they put online about their successes and failures.
- Research what funding intermediaries are investing in, and invest some of your resources through the screened and validated programs that they

measure. At the end of the year, when you take stock in your giving journal, ask yourself if having measurable impact with certain gifts makes them more satisfying than those without specific results.

For the Family:
- As a family, choose one convenience—such as electric lights, water from your faucets, or computers—and go without it for a day. Over a family meal, have each member of the family describe how that experience affected their daily life. Then let your children make a gift to an organization that is providing that "necessity" to families in developing countries.
- Have each of your children choose two nonprofits—one local and one overseas—that provide similar services. Visit the local one with them and volunteer there together, if possible. Choose a dollar amount, and have them assess what impact that gift would have if invested in each organization. Then, let them choose together which one of the nonprofits will receive the funding.
- Ask your children to come up with ten reasons why they value going to school. As parents, come up with ten reasons having an education has benefited you (being able to provide for your family, for example, or enjoying reading the newspaper or making a monthly trip to the movie theater). Get together one evening to discuss your shared gratitude for the educational opportunities that billions of people cannot access.
- Spend a family dinner talking about how your life would change if you lost your home (this exercise is appropriate for kids over the age of sixteen only).

And Remember:
- Assessment is a learning opportunity. Rather than simply counting how many people a nonprofit's programs touched, evaluation and measurement helps it improve its practices and outcomes.
- It's not always appropriate to look for hard numbers. Grants without specific purpose or goals—such as general operating support—might not have measurable impacts beyond increased organizational capacity or funding for specific operating costs. So set your expectations accordingly and assess the role of funds spent on operating expenses, staff salaries, or new equipment in helping the nonprofit execute its mission more effectively.

- If a nonprofit doesn't have the systems or resources to conduct performance measurement, you may decide not to fund it—but you could also use your gifts to help it build the capacity to measure and report on its performance.

- When you help a nonprofit to conduct formal evaluations and produce outcome assessments (or require it to do so), you're also helping it increase its accountability to all present and future donors.

- What you personally count as success can range widely—from the progress of a student whose scholarship you funded to the specific benchmarks for infrastructure development an organization meets to comply with a written grant contract. So figure out how to measure the impact of your funding on personal goals, too.

- For a particular program you're personally and financially invested in, don't underestimate the power of going to see the work and programs in action—you may find indicators, both expected and unexpected, that provide important data for future funding decisions. Personal due diligence can only heighten your passion, and if you want to inspire others to get involved, be sure your accounts are based on credible evidence of impact.

- The more specifically you define both what you want to achieve with your giving and what specific results (in the short, medium, and long term) will indicate that you have been successful, the greater the chance that you will be a high-impact philanthropist.

- Assessing your giving aspirations and impact every year will most likely prove invaluable to increasing your impact over time. Without assessment, how will you know what parts of your giving have the greatest impact?

- By starting with self-assessment, you will be "walking the talk" when you ask nonprofits to assess their results.

- The greater understanding you have of both your own impact and the impact of the nonprofits you fund, the more likely you are to encourage your friends, family, and social networks to give to them, as well—thus increasing the overall ripple effect that your gifts make.

5

GAME CHANGERS
Transform the World with Shared Ideas

Empower others—your impact will be greater in the long run.

Above the door of a small, whitewashed house in the northwest Indian state of Rajasthan are the words "Wel Come," and the walls feature images of a metal pot fringed with mango leaves and topped with a coconut. This is the Purna-Kalasha, the Hindu symbol of abundance. Most of us, however, would not use the word *abundance* to describe this humble place.

This modest dwelling of three rooms and a few simple pieces of wooden furniture is home to a woman called Geeta. Her village, Pachpadra, sits at the heart of the Thar Desert—one of the driest places on earth. It's also one of the most economically deprived. In Rajasthan, the second-poorest state in India, low rates of literacy and high rates of poverty, combined with the strictures of a caste-based society where men hold the authority, make life for women particularly harsh. Water-related diseases, malnutrition, anemia, infant mortality, and maternal deaths are common, as are instances of child marriages, domestic violence, and sexual abuse.

Geeta and her family have no running water and their electricity supply is unreliable. In summer, the heat reaches a burning intensity; in winter, the nights turn bitterly cold. Doing the laundry means filling tin buckets and plastic tubs with water and scrubbing clothes by hand. Long before getting to the laundry, however, Geeta has a long day. Rising at

5 a.m., she puts on her blue floral sari and veil of bright turquoise and stands before the family's Hindu shrine to say a short prayer. With just a glass of tea for breakfast, she packs her two youngest daughters off to school and heads outside to sweep the concrete terrace before embarking on the rest of the morning's chores.

Like many in her village, Geeta, a widow, lives on just a few dollars a day. Her midday meal consists of a small piece of flatbread with a bit of spicy chutney, while dinner—the main meal of the day—is porridge or bread with a few vegetables or dried beans and *karhi*, a thin yogurt curry mixed with chickpea flour.

Thousands of miles away, Peter Cain lives in a nine-story condominium building in Battery Park City, a relatively new neighborhood in lower Manhattan. From his unit, Peter has a view of the Hudson River, the New Jersey skyline, and the Statue of Liberty. On weekends, he heads up to his country home in Rockland, where he likes to go hiking.

Life for Geeta and Peter could hardly be more different. Yet these two individuals are connected through giving. For the money that Peter and others like him donate has helped bring Geeta and her fellow villagers a resource that's critical to their health and livelihood—a resource that in America we take for granted, whether we're in the shower, doing laundry, or simply feel thirsty: fresh, clean water.

CHARITY MEETS A BUSINESS MODEL

The fact that Geeta's home is decorated with the Purna-Kalasha comes as no surprise to anyone who knows her—for this image represents a vessel filled with water. It's a force in short supply there. Geeta's village lies at the heart of the Thar Desert, the world's most densely populated, and is a place where water scarcity is part of daily life. In a lunar landscape, scrubby trees are the only signs of green amid sand dunes and craggy rocks, and at midday the sun blends horizon and sky together in a dazzling yellow haze. In this parched region, summer temperatures soar to more than 110 degrees Fahrenheit, and the average annual rainfall is less than twenty inches.

In most developed countries, it's hard to imagine the physical and mental stress of living without a secure supply of water. Worries over whether there'll be enough for washing, drinking, and cooking can create a permanent cloud over the lives of women like Geeta. Here, water is a precious gift, never to be taken for granted. And extreme scarcity of water is only part of the problem. Groundwater has a high salt content, leaving it with a nasty taste and giving those forced to consume it severe stomach and joint problems.

Happily for Geeta and the other residents of Pachpadra, they now have an alternative. They can collect desalinated water from a small building at the edge of their village where a reverse osmosis plant uses a liquid filtration process to remove the water's impurities. Moreover, with the help of the Jal Bhagirathi Foundation, the Rajasthan-based organization that built the desalination plant, the community has established a series of water outlets in and around the village, making water accessible to far more people.

The project to bring clean water to Pachpadra's residents is not a traditional water aid program—it has a business model. Villagers pay for what they use (although the fee is just a few paise—less than one rupee or a few U.S. cents). And local women run the water outlets, operating them as small enterprises. They buy the water at 8 paise per liter, and then charge their customers 15 paise per liter for collection and 25 paise for a home delivery service.

The idea of using charitable dollars to help foster businesses may be unfamiliar to some philanthropists, but the concept is rapidly gaining momentum. First, donors are recognizing that in economically disadvantaged parts of the world, supporting for-profit entrepreneurs can speed up the creation and delivery of essential services for the poor such as better schools, health care systems, and microfinance loans.

Second, as precious philanthropic dollars become increasingly stretched, some argue that giving away money to address problems that could be solved with a market-based model wastes a valuable resource. It's all part of an important approach to giving—one in which philanthropists are looking to make their charitable dollars go further by harnessing the power of business.

As well as delivering essential services, this development model also provides new income sources, helping people—including women such as Geeta—improve their lives, not through aid or charity, but by helping them generate a sustainable livelihood.

Take sanitation. As unplanned cities sprawl over increasingly large areas, without the necessary infrastructure to support them, slums crop up without sanitation facilities of any kind. Residents risk exposure to infectious diseases such as cholera and typhoid, as well as diarrhea-related diseases and potentially life-threatening parasite-borne illnesses such as schistosomiasis or bilharziasis.

In 2006, Kenyan entrepreneur and architect David Kuria developed an idea to address this—the Ikotoilet, a public toilet that uses waterless biodigesters. However, while using environmentally sustainable technology to run the toilets was one challenge, another was developing a financially sustainable way of maintaining them.

Kuria solved the problem by turning the toilets into businesses—minimalls, with small enterprises clustered around them such as shops selling snacks and newspapers, as well as shoeshine stands and kiosks selling airtime for cell phones. The young entrepreneurs running these minimalls can now become economically independent—and, of course, they have a powerful business incentive to keep the toilets clean so that people keep coming to use them and spending money in the shops afterward. So far, dozens of Ikotoilets have been established in Kenya, and the company has plans to set them up in Tanzania and Uganda.

Some of the business models being tried out work on the principle of cross-subsidization—funding services for the poor by charging those who can afford it. Take the case of Dial 1298 Ambulance—1298 for short—in Mumbai. Until a group of Indian MBA graduates decided to launch an emergency transportation service in Mumbai, getting to the hospital for most people meant calling a taxi or getting in a motor rickshaw. About a thousand ambulances operated in the city—one of the world's most populous, with more than forty thousand emergencies recorded a month—but most were simply empty vans equipped with little more than a stretcher.

Then a team of young, U.S.-educated Indian professionals came up with the idea for an ambulance service accessible to everybody. After securing philanthropic seed funding as well as technical advice and training from the London Ambulance Service and New York Presbyterian Hospital, in 2007 the team launched 1298.

While 1298 still relies on raising money to purchase more vehicles and train paramedics, the service is financially self-sustaining. Those that can afford to pay generate enough revenue to allow the very poor to travel for free. To ascertain who should pay and who should not, the service uses a smart but simple method. People who ask to go to a private hospital pay the full rate, while those heading for the government hospital (where services are free but low-quality) pay a subsidized fare or nothing, depending on their income.

Many of these socially motivated entrepreneurs work in developing countries—but others operate right here in the United States. In Florida, for example, entrepreneur Conchy Bretos provides affordable assisted living services to the elderly. Conchy has found a way of financing retrofits of public and subsidized housing using Medicaid waiver funding—which covers more diverse services by waiving the need to be living in a nursing facility or care home to obtain those services. After three to five years of initial consulting—which includes conducting feasibility studies, retrofitting buildings, recruiting residents and staff, managing the start-up phase, and executing performance and impact evaluations—the management of the facilities is taken over by local housing providers.

Conchy has replicated this model in more than forty projects, serving about five thousand seniors in more than twenty states. And as the physical and cognitive health of residents improves by being at home, rather than in a traditional nursing facility, dependence on medication, hospitalizations, and trips to the emergency room fall, saving Medicaid significant amounts of money.

She does all this, not through a charity, but through MIA Consulting, the for-profit group she founded in 1995. The company receives fees from public housing agencies and nonprofits that want to set up affordable assisted living facilities in their area. After paying senior staff salaries, the company puts its profits toward helping subsidize low-cost and pro bono consulting services.

The individuals and organizations developing these kinds of services are entrepreneurs, but their motives differ from most for-profit entrepreneurs. The prospect of making gains drives these individuals—but not financial gains, social ones. They are *social* entrepreneurs.

You find the term "social entrepreneurship" tossed about a lot these days. It's overused—sometimes misused. But when used accurately, social entrepreneurship describes a relatively new (the field formally gained momentum under this name in the nineties) form of human development driven by entrepreneurs. Equipped with the right tools and networks, these self-propelled businesspeople can build sustainable enterprises that provide longer-lasting solutions to big global problems than aid could alone. Aid, after all, is dependent on political will and donor funding, which can change or dry up at any time.

Of course, the methods vary—and not all social entrepreneurs generate profits. Enterprises could be projects run by NGOs or citizen groups that might, for example, use revenue generation to cover operational costs while seeking philanthropic dollars to fund capital investments for expansion or building critical infrastructure. And social entrepreneurs may not even provide goods or services. They might also be social innovators, coming up with better ways to organize systems—whether a farming cooperative or a health care network—that help alleviate poverty and inequality.

Bill Drayton, founder of Ashoka, which pioneered the idea of identifying and investing in social entrepreneurs, argues that what unites social entrepreneurs is their purpose—one that does not primarily serve their own interests, shareholder interests, or religious or political agendas but that serves the good of all.

Another characteristic of social entrepreneurs is that they treat the communities they serve as customers—not victims. "It's about understanding that people really don't want hand-outs—that they want to make their own decisions; they want to solve their own problems, and that by engaging with them, not only do we create much more dignity for them, but for us all as well," says Jacqueline Novogratz, founder of

Acumen Fund, a U.S. nonprofit foundation that promotes what it calls "ideas worth spreading."[1]

Whatever their model, social entrepreneurs recognize the power of treating the poor and underprivileged as consumers, employees, and businesspeople, giving them a central role in improving their own lives. One organization has tracked the impact of enterprise versus dependence on aid or charity. KickStart, a U.S.-based nonprofit that develops affordable water pumps for poor farmers in Africa, sells its pumps rather than giving them away. While the revenues generated cover some of KickStart's operational costs, it has a far more important reason for selling the pumps rather than distributing them as a charitable donation.

For poor farmers, buying a pump requires an investment and therefore a commitment, which means they are likely to use the equipment to generate income. For this reason, says KickStart, more than 80 percent of its customers use the pumps they buy from the organization to start a small business, compared with research that shows less than 30 percent of people use donated pumps for this purpose. As a result, KickStart has helped almost ninety thousand families start new micro-agriculture businesses.

Designing products that are affordable by the poor is another area of focus for social entrepreneurship. The Stanford d.school (School of Design) has launched several such initiatives through its "Entrepreneurial Design for Extreme Affordability" program. Students and professors work with indigenous populations to create low-cost, life-changing, and life-saving devices such as water pumps, electric lighting, and incubators—often costing less than $30. Products include the high-quality, solar-rechargeable LED d.light lamp and the Tripod Pump, a human-powered irrigation pump.

As a philanthropist, by supporting these entrepreneurs, you can participate in an innovative new way of giving that's spreading across the globe. By giving to them indirectly (through an incubator like the d.school, or via a foundation or funding intermediary), or directly (by engaging firsthand with projects and individuals by becoming a mentor, design coach, or investor), you can become a part of social innovation in action.

FUNDING THE FUNDERS

So what connects Peter Cain to Geeta and her family? He does not make donations directly to her. In fact, he has no personal contact with her or with the Jal Bhagirathi Foundation. He has traveled widely in the developing world but has not visited Rajasthan, nor does he send his money directly to India. Peter donates to Acumen Fund, a New York-based nonprofit. Acumen, which describes itself as a nonprofit venture capital fund for the poor, is an intermediary between donors and the entrepreneurs they would like to fund. The organization pools Peter's money with other individuals' donations and makes investments in the projects of innovative social entrepreneurs.

Intermediary organizations such as Acumen Fund argue that while some of the world's most inventive entrepreneurs possess the wherewithal to get their businesses up and running on their own, others need a helping hand—whether in the form of seed capital, a small loan, or management and technical advice. This is often where philanthropists come in, and in the new millennium a community of nonprofits and foundations has emerged to support the growth of social entrepreneurs.

These organizations use philanthropic funds to invest in business innovations that might be too risky to attract private sector capital and that, because their markets are low-income populations, will never deliver high returns. This allows them to fund projects that support people like Geeta and her village—not through charity but by providing a means of creating small businesses and establishing sustainable livelihoods.

Acumen Fund invests in a variety of entrepreneurs who use diverse business models to reach the "base of the pyramid" (BoP)—or the billions of poor without access to clean water, reliable health services, formal housing options, and other basic needs. However, you can also support a range of other institutions. These include nonprofits or NGOs seeking to scale up their operations and achieve financial sustainability, small and medium for-profit companies in need of capital, and larger companies that are starting specific business units to serve the BoP.

Of course, some donors do invest directly in social entrepreneurs, giving them start-up funding to get an idea going or to scale up their existing operations. However, doing this alone is challenging, even for someone with a business background. First, if you're giving to a social enterprise overseas, unless the organization has a U.S. branch or you are able to complete the complex paperwork for what's known as an equivalency process, you won't get a tax write-off for your donation.

And to give directly, you need to be able to assess what's needed in far-off places and ascertain whether your money has made an impact. Investment dollars must be spent at the right time and projects carefully nurtured before ideas can take root and start to effect change. When you give directly to social entrepreneurs, it's extremely difficult to monitor progress and find out exactly how they used your funds.

If you want to use your money to support this entrepreneurial development model, there's another option—funding organizations that do all the legwork for you. By giving to intermediaries, you can make your money work harder. For a start, your funds are added to a general pool of financing. Moreover, intermediaries will do all the due diligence for you, selecting high-potential projects in which to invest. Let's face it, for individual givers living in America, it's hard to understand the extreme challenges faced by the people we fund. We need organizations working on the ground, employing locals and equipped with local insights, to direct our money where it's most urgently needed.

Many intermediaries and foundations supporting social entrepreneurs do more than invest—they also help project leaders gain access to loans, management consulting services, human resources, mentoring, and fundraising networks. Thus, they give your dollars additional value that you could not necessarily provide when investing directly in social entrepreneurs yourself.

It's a very different strategy from the kind of giving that goes directly to individuals in need. Giving to the foundations and nonprofits supporting social entrepreneurs, your philanthropy is one step removed from the beneficiaries. However, it can enable you to have a bigger impact. If the ultimate grantees of these organizations (the social entrepreneurs) establish successful new enterprises, they'll do more than improve their own lives. They'll also provide vital services to the people around them, generating employment as their business expands.

And if you give one person the ability to earn an income, you'll help improve the lives of their spouse, children, and extended family, spreading the ripple effect of your gift out to the broader community. Unlike traditional aid projects, these businesses provide essential services to the poor that are sustainable and can continue to grow when philanthropic funding is thin on the ground or when government grants have run out.

Bill Drayton was the pioneer in this field. A former McKinsey consultant who studied law at Harvard and Yale, he founded Ashoka in 1980, at a time when few people understood the concept of supporting innovative entrepreneurs.

Ashoka identifies and invests in social entrepreneurs around the world—individuals such as Conchy Bretos—who have come up with innovative and practical ideas for solving big global problems. These "Ashoka Fellows" sometimes require a living stipend so they can quit their jobs, continue to support their families, and focus on developing their innovations. Over its first thirty years, Ashoka has supported almost three thousand entrepreneurs in more than seventy countries and has created a formal network through which its fellows can collaborate, share knowledge, and be part of a bigger community of social innovators.

Ashoka funds individuals creating social ventures in start-up phases. All of them are taking brand new approaches to tackling social issues, from economic development, human rights, and education to health and environmental sustainability. The model also promotes the emerging concept of citizen philanthropy, as any individual can nominate, fund, and mentor Ashoka Fellows.

In 2010, Ashoka launched its Globalizer program. This initiative identifies social entrepreneurs within the global Ashoka network whose innovations have proven a success, are organizationally and financially sustainable, and have the potential to be scaled up and replicated in many communities in different countries, regardless of cultural or geographic differences.

Having identified these entrepreneurs through a rigorous selection process, Ashoka challenges them to refine their models and supports them in this process so that their innovations can be replicated around the globe—providing value that we as individual donors may not necessarily be able to provide alone. At an annual Globalizer Summit, these innovators come together to share their insights.

Among the Globalizer Fellows is Marta Arango, who in Colombia pioneered a new way of preparing children from poor neighborhoods for learning effectively before they enter the school system. Established in 1977 by Marta and her husband, Glen Nimnicht, the International Center for Education and Human Development (CINDE) works by creating networks of support for early childhood education that include families, local communities, and child care professionals.

CINDE has one of the key ingredients Ashoka values in its fellows—a model that can be copied. So far, foundations, Latin American governments, United Nations agencies such as UNICEF, and NGOs such as Save the Children have used its model to design policies and programs aimed at preparing children to perform better in formal and public education systems. In this way, the CINDE model has spread to more than thirty countries making a difference to more than 10 million children worldwide.

Anyone with business expertise wanting to help Ashoka entrepreneurs at an earlier stage in their development can engage directly with them through the Ashoka Support Network. This is a global network of individuals who work with fellows either locally or abroad, visit them, and share their personal and professional networks. Similarly, the Ashoka University program provides college students with the mentoring, resources, peer groups, and community they need to cultivate their own social innovation models, paving the way for a whole new generation of social entrepreneurs to spread their wings and begin to fly. Finally, any individual can give to Ashoka to fund a specific social entrepreneur, to help fund a new Ashoka University at their alma mater, or to give their time and contacts to expand a specific entrepreneurial model.

Since Bill Drayton coined the term "social entrepreneurship," other organizations have joined the movement to support market-based models of development. Among them is TechnoServe, a Washington, D.C.–based organization that seeks business solutions to poverty. As well as running training programs to give entrepreneurs the skills needed to launch or expand an enterprise, TechnoServe connects those enterprises to global markets and works to improve the business environment in which they're operating, working directly with financing institutions to increase access to capital. Focusing on farmers and food producers, TechnoServe aims to help people in poor parts of the world generate income for themselves, their families, and their communities—and ultimately their countries.

At Acumen Fund, the philanthropic money received from donors goes into investments of what is often referred to as "patient capital"—funding that lies somewhere between profit-driven investment and charity. It's funding designed to jump-start innovative ideas with social or economic benefits, generating social rather than financial returns. Yet because these investments are in the form of loans or equity—rather than grants—Acumen can also reap financial returns from the projects, the proceeds of which it plows back into supporting new ideas and helping empower new populations of social entrepreneurs. Each additional cycle of reinvestment begins another cycle of changing lives.

While the seed funding provided by many of the nonprofits and foundations that support entrepreneurs can prove critical in getting an enterprise going, equally important—if not more so—are the other forms of support these organizations provide. This means your donations also contribute to capacity building, giving entrepreneurs assistance on things such as how to manage and run a business more efficiently or gain access to higher-value markets. In fact, in some ways, organizations supporting social entrepreneurs act as management and strategic consultants, guiding them toward greater efficiency—and therefore greater impact.

For some organizations, this consultancy element is central to their mission. Take Endeavor, a New York-based nonprofit. Endeavor works in emerging markets such as Argentina, Mexico, Uruguay, South Africa, India, Egypt, and Jordan, and, like Ashoka, TechnoServe, and Acumen Fund, it seeks out what it calls "high-impact" entrepreneurs.

Rather than raising capital or granting funding, Endeavor devotes all its resources to mentoring the entrepreneurs it selects in areas such as financing, marketing, and leadership development. Mentors include executives on temporary leave from corporations as well as business school students. As a result, small investments have a big impact. In

Brazil, for example, it helped Tecsis, a technology company, to come up with a program for expansion into international markets, resulting in the creation of more than a thousand local jobs.

Aid to Artisans, a nonprofit that supports craftspeople around the world, takes a similar approach. It equips the artisans with business skills, helping them understand disciplines such as sales and accounting, and helps them raise the quality of what they produce before connecting them with markets in the West, where they can sell their products at higher prices.

The organization has even helped open up export markets. In Mexico, it led the Lead Free Alliance to help traditional Mexican potters, whose exports to the United States had fallen dramatically after the country banned their products due to their toxic lead glazes. After the Alliance trained more than a thousand potters in lead-free glaze application, the U.S. Food and Drug Administration lifted the ban. Soon after, export sales of the Mexican potters returned to healthy levels. In 2006, they exceeded $200,000, according to Aid to Artisans, and those were just reported sales (informal sales from family workshops often go unreported).

In supporting these kinds of organizations, your money is contributing to such market-changing initiatives. You're not funding individual entrepreneurs directly. But your funds are pooled with those of others and redistributed by organizations that provide not only funding but also support services to entrepreneurs whose ideas and businesses are having a huge impact. And these entrepreneurs are often doing more than just supporting their own communities—they're also developing models that have the potential to change entire systems.

INVESTMENTS WITH A DIFFERENCE

When engaging in market-based models of philanthropy, another option is to take up a form of giving known as *social impact investing*. As philanthropists, we're not responsible only for philanthropic funds—we can put *all* our money to work for good, not just the funds we set aside for donations. By thinking holistically, we can use personal financial investments to advance issues and causes we care deeply about.

Investing can supplement philanthropy in several ways. By putting it into investments that provide the best return, regardless of social impact, we may generate more money to give away. Alternatively, we can use part or all of our investment portfolios to promote social or environmental goals (which may have lower market value returns), by directing money into sustainable agriculture, accessible health care, financial services, or other social benefit companies, which include B-corporations (companies that use business models to create public benefit), L3Cs (limited liability, low-income corporations), and other market-based models.

The social impact investing strategy is also referred to as the "double bottom line," "aligned capital," "impact investing," or "mission invest-ing." And there is some overlap with other types of investments, includ-ing private equity investing (funds that invest in or buy companies), buying shares in publicly traded companies, or putting money into screened mutual funds or socially responsible investment (SRI) funds.

Some foundations have practiced social impact investing for many decades. A larger movement around this investment model has been spreading rapidly, as individuals and organizations recognize the power of putting their money into vehicles that provide social as well as mon-etary returns (although no tax benefits apply to these investments). Since the millennium, social investing has gained momentum with newer foun-dations taking up this option. It is also spreading to individual giving.

While this kind of investing is related to SRI funds, SRI investment strategies tend to focus on screening out companies that engaged in activities that could damage the environment or do not support human development. By contrast, impact investors look to put their money into enterprises whose business models are promoting environmental conser-vation, education, or social and economic inclusion, while still getting some—albeit not typically market-rate—returns.

Impact investing allows you to address a variety of issues and use for-profit investments to complement your philanthropic efforts. In green or clean tech investments, for example, you can put your money into companies developing clean technologies such as solar and wind power generation. Green investments can be combined with human development if you make for-profit or low-profit investments that promote, for example, a new green revolution in Africa that would banish hunger and help feed the world through greater agricultural productivity.

This approach to investing is rather like an iceberg. As philanthropists, we often invest only the tip of the iceberg every year—annual giving from individuals averaged about 2 percent of disposable income (defined as the amount of income after payment of taxes) in 2010—according to GivingUSA, and foundations are legally required to give away only 5 percent of their assets each year. Instead, we could be putting a larger chunk of the iceberg to work toward our social strategies—a mountain of ice, rather than a few cubes.

You can engage in this kind of investing in a variety of ways. It might be that you use private equity funds to provide growth capital to businesses engaged in your areas of concern, whether that's housing for the poor or improved access to education. Meanwhile, some investment managers are starting to offer impact investments as options to their clients.

If this form of giving is new to you, you can seek the advice of a professional money manager on approaches to it. Another resource to turn to is the Global Impact Investing Network (GIIN). This nonprofit organization was established to promote the effectiveness of impact investing and is developing a rating system—the Global Impact Investing Ratings System (GIIRS)—to give investors an idea of the social return they can expect to get on different investments. In addition, Rockefeller Philanthropy Advisors—under whose auspices GIIN operates—has published a guide called "Solutions for Impact Investors: From Strategy to Implementation," which shows you how to make closer links between your investment decisions and social impact. The F.B. Heron Foundation also has an online library of "Mission Related Investing" resources.

Remember, managing your personal assets may appear straightforward, but if you approach the task innovatively and think about it broadly, you can make it transformational. For if financial returns are the bottom line of traditional investing, social returns are what impact investors hope to achieve. And while this type of investing adds a layer of complexity to giving and may not be for everyone, combining the two makes it possible to use both financial investments and social investments to maximize our total philanthropic bottom line.

MORE THAN MONEY

On his return to New York after several years in London and Paris, Peter Cain started to look for a new way to contribute to solving global problems. He had gained a powerful firsthand experience of social needs in developing countries during a few trips to Nigeria. Like many, Peter had also begun to question whether traditional aid models could really transform the lives of poor people. "I had a sense that a lot of aid is wasted, and ends up with lots of people riding around in Land Rovers not understanding where they are or what they're doing," he says.

Peter's career had given him a good understanding of the need for the public and nonprofit world to work with the private sector. With a background in U.S. public finance, he had spent several years working in the United Kingdom on the Private Finance Initiative, a government program that supported collaborations between business and the public sector infrastructure. "It was the government giving concessions to the private sector to build hospitals and schools," explains Peter. "I've always enjoyed that intersection between government and finance, policy and politics, and how you deliver this stuff."

So when he heard about Acumen Fund's activities, he was very interested. He asked how he could help and was told that the organization needed to raise money. "I committed on the spot," he says. Peter gave generously, at one point, donating about $40,000 a year to Acumen Fund, including funds donated through a matching program run by his company.

Then, on September 15, 2008, Lehman Brothers, one of the biggest Wall Street banks, declared bankruptcy. It signaled the start of the biggest financial crisis the world has seen since the Great Depression. Soon after, America fell into deep recession. As the impact of the crash rippled through the U.S. economy, many donors from the financial sector were forced to scale back their giving, and Peter Cain was no exception. After the crisis, with no new deal-making activity and his company's stock price tumbling, Peter had to stop writing checks.

However, this did not mean Peter cut ties with Acumen—far from it. "I became an informal sounding board for the people who were making the investments," he says. "They'd run things past me and ask questions." On a housing finance scheme in Pakistan, for example, Peter's knowledge of public financing was particularly helpful, since he knew a lot about low-income mortgages and could ask the right questions. "And a lot of times, that's all you need to be—a sounding board," he says.

After Acumen Fund's investment committee had been up and running for a couple of years, the team decided they wanted to prepare more effectively ahead of the formal meetings. Peter would participate by attending run-through meetings ahead of the investment committee itself and helping prep the team by reading memos and asking tough questions.

After doing this for a while, Acumen—which had three board members on its investment committee—needed to find a new independent member, and it invited Peter to join. "I started shadowing it, and I'm now on a committee for a fund called Acumen Capital Markets," Peter explains. "So now Acumen Fund is a significant part of my life. It's one of my communities. It's got a lot of positive energy—and especially with the bleakness of the past couple of years, it's been really fun and rewarding."

Peter goes regularly to the Acumen Fund offices for meetings and quarterly portfolio reviews. He's also joined the Acumen Fund Advisory Council. Along the way, he's been able to get to know the team and see firsthand the way they operate. "It's great to be able to pick up what's going on there," he says.

However, the highlight of Peter's involvement with the organization came when he joined a team of young Acumen executives and fellows for a series of events with some of the organization's grantee entrepreneurs in Nairobi, the Kenyan capital. There, the entrepreneurs—from

India, Pakistan, Kenya, and elsewhere—could meet each other, exchange experiences, and build a community of people with ideas. Outstanding employees from the enterprises received awards, and dinners and coffee breaks gave everyone a chance to get to know each other.

The five-day trip included a site visit to see some of the Ikotoilets installed by David Kuria's company, Ecotact. One of the vast slums in Nairobi left a deep impression on Peter. "It went on as far as the eye could see," he says. "The kids were smiling but the shacks were packed cheek by jowl, across the road was a huge garbage heap, and the sewage ran along the streets in little troughs." Yet in the midst of the chaos stood a neat, clean public toilet surrounded by small shops and a shoeshine stall.

"It was very rewarding to get out there and deepen my understanding of the challenges," says Peter. "And as you learn about these businesses, you see that they're not just creating opportunity but, by treating the poor as customers, they're also giving them dignity."

POWER TO THE COPYCATS

While some social entrepreneurs rely on market-based models of revenue generation, those who do so differ markedly from profit-driven businesses in one important way—their readiness to share their ideas. At Ashoka, the potential for independent duplication by others has even become a key element in the organization's assessment process. Among the questions it asks its fellows in an annual study is: "Has your work been replicated by an individual or group that you did not lead?" An answer of yes would signify success.

This measure of success could hardly differ more from the corporate world, in which any company that has developed a new idea, product, or service will take all kinds of steps to prevent others from stealing the intellectual property, copying it, and using it in their own businesses.

By contrast, for individuals hoping to tackle big global problems, good, replicable ideas are powerful weapons with which to fight everything from poverty and disease to climate change and lack of health care access. When it comes to impact, those who support social entrepreneurs seek out that ripple effect—the small stone that, dropped into water, creates circular ripples that expand outward from where it fell.

Jeff Skoll, who co-founded eBay, has been instrumental in promoting and formalizing the field of social entrepreneurship through the Skoll Foundation. Like winning an Ashoka Fellowship, receiving a Skoll Award brings great credibility to a growing organization. Skoll was one of the first foundations to build a powerful online community—Social Edge— for both social entrepreneurs and their supporters, and the Skoll World Forum attracts individual givers and game changers from around the globe. For anyone giving directly and not through a staffed foundation, mirroring the Skoll Foundation's annual awards portfolio is a great way to make use of its due diligence and get a piece of the action in some of the most exciting models of social change.

Another organization that uses philanthropic funding to develop ideas that can be applied elsewhere is Environmental Defense Fund, a U.S.-based advocacy group. EDF helps big companies such as Walmart and FedEx develop cleaner and more environmentally friendly technologies because it believes that getting large corporations to change their habits will drive environmental change and accelerate the move to a low-carbon, sustainable world.

Funded by grants from foundations as well as from individual donor gifts of all sizes, EDF takes no money from the corporations it works with, even though these companies may benefit from the partnership by, for example, making fuel savings from energy efficiency innovations. This practice assures EDF's independence and the credibility of the joint projects on which it works. But also, instead of asking corporations for money for its consultancy services, EDF insists that any innovations developed jointly must be made public so that other companies can make similar environmentally beneficial changes to their businesses.

Organizations such as EDF and Ashoka take an alternative approach to growth, too. Rather than working to expand their own operations dramatically or to open offices across the world, they keep their organizations small and nimble, and their achievements come through the activities of those they support—individuals and organizations that are formulating new ideas, spreading income generation, and bringing about systemic changes and shifts in policy. They also support a new, open form of philanthropy—one that fosters the growth of ideas others can copy, apply to other parts of the world, and expand.

Take Grameen Bank, the pioneering microfinance institution founded by Nobel Prize–winner Muhammad Yunus to provide small loans to the very poor in Bangladesh. While most of its microloans are made to low-income populations in Asia, the bank has rolled out operations across the world, even in the United States, where it now provides the same small loans to Americans. In another example of the ripple effect, hearing Yunus speak at the Stanford Graduate School of Business was an important inspiration for Jessica Jackley when, with Matt Flannery, she co-founded Kiva.org, the pioneering online lending website.

Meanwhile, the lessons learned through the water project that helped Geeta start her small business could be applied in Africa, too. The project was one of those selected by an initiative called the Ripple Effect. The program—supported by Acumen Fund, design consultancy Ideo, and the Bill & Melinda Gates Foundation—aims to find ideas that can accelerate access to clean water for more than five hundred thousand of the world's poorest people. The Ripple Effect went on to select four Kenyan organizations to test new ideas for delivery and storage of water to other communities that lack access to this critical life resource.

In Mumbai, the 1298 ambulance service has also rapidly expanded. Over the past three years, customers have placed more than a hundred thousand calls to the service, of which many thousands have been by patients that 1298's ambulances transported to medical care for free or at a subsidized rate. The model has proven so successful that regional governments across India are now asking the organization to develop ambulance services in other cities and districts.

When put together, the number of people benefiting from the activities of entrepreneurs is impressive. Take Endeavor's grantees. Since 1997, the more than five hundred entrepreneurs it has supported in eleven emerging market countries have created over 130,000 jobs. In 2010, 83 percent of Endeavor's entrepreneurs are voluntarily giving back as board members and donors to support new-generation entrepreneurs.

Over the past ten years, Aid to Artisans has increased the incomes of more than 125,000 artisans, helping those individuals earn as much as four times their countries' average per capita income. With each job supporting up to four people, the impact made over that decade rises to some 500,000 people.

Herein lies the real power in this kind of giving. Supporting organizations that invest in projects based on smart ideas and that nurture the entrepreneurs behind those ideas means you can make your money work harder, using it to change systems rather than simply to improve individual lives. After all, when it comes to social transformation, an idea that can be copied is something to be celebrated.

Bill Drayton calls the individuals behind these ideas "changemakers." Changemakers work to create game-changing solutions that reinvent methods of delivering essential services and can be replicated, improving millions of lives. "Our job is not to give people fish," he often tells people. "It's not to teach them how to fish—it's to build new and better fishing industries."

In Rajasthan, Geeta's new livelihood demonstrates this principle. Her life has transformed since she's taken charge of running a water outlet. As a widow, her life had been harsh in a society where those who lose their husbands also lose their social status (in some poor rural areas, widows are even expected to shave their heads and remain unseen by men for the rest of their lives). With no other form of income, Geeta had to take on manual labor, often digging wells or breaking up stones on construction sites.

Today, her work is a lot easier. Every couple of days, a truck arrives from the main water filtration plant to fill up her tank. It holds 2,000 liters and costs her 160 rupees (including the transport by truck from the plant). She'll sell that water in two days, and in the summer, she can sell twice the amount. On the side of the bright blue cylindrical tank in front of her house is her mobile phone number, printed in big numbers (while many people come to her house to collect their water, some prefer to call her up and order her slightly more expensive home delivery service).

People see Geeta differently these days—not as a poor widow but as a businesswoman and a respected member of the community. She can now afford to buy more nutritious food for the family and, during the summer, put away a bit of savings for medical and other emergencies.

In a country where many still believe girls are destined only for marriage, Geeta's opportunity marks a tremendous step forward. After they finish school, her girls may embark on careers, become active members of the community, marry later, and, in turn, educate their own daughters, thus breaking the cycle of inequality that so often leaves women in developing countries without voices or options.

This transformation would never have happened with a hand-out. Geeta's change in social and economic status occurred because someone far away gave her the tools and a business model with which to change her own life. And this model is being replicated in dozens of villages in the region.

Geeta has also gained one more unexpected benefit from her role as a commercial water supplier—when women come to her house to collect the water, it's a chance to support one another and participate in a community. While for you and me, this might not seem like much, for a widow once forced to rely on manual labor to survive, a moment's relaxation with friends and neighbors represents something of great significance—a new and better life. And with money to pay for good schooling, Geeta can now give her daughters something she never had—choices.

MAKING IT HAPPEN

What to Ask Yourself When You Want to Give to Entrepreneurs:

- Do more market-based models of philanthropy fit in with your value system?
- How much do you value knowledge sharing and the ability to scale up and replicate successful models?
- Do you want to provide immediate relief to people or to help create the kind of infrastructure that can give communities a sustainable income? (Of course, you can always do both!)
- Do you want to fund social entrepreneurs directly or through an intermediary that provides a greater value proposition (by helping entrepreneurs

with services such as consulting, coaching, and marketing) alongside its grants?

- If giving through an intermediary, are you happy to have your donations be part of a pool, rather than giving directly to a nonprofit?
- What, if any, resources can you give a social entrepreneur in another country besides money?
- If you plan to give directly to a social entrepreneur, how will you know what your money is being used for?

What to Ask Social Entrepreneurs or the Organizations Funding Them:
- What social or system change is the organization trying to achieve?
- What is its model of social change and how is it executing this model?
- What makes its model unique or different?
- How does its model allow grantees to scale up their work?
- How does it measure success in the entrepreneurs it supports? And how does it report on its progress toward that success?
- Does it partner with other organizations, governments, or companies? If so, what are the elements that make those partnerships successful or challenging?
- What is the organization's funding mix (family foundations, individual doors, family members, close friends, corporations, public foundations)?
- How important is financial return to its model?
- Who serves on its board?
- What is the organization doing to share its strategy and successes with other social entrepreneurs?

What to Think About When Considering Direct Investments in Social Entrepreneurs:
- Social entrepreneurs often work in developing countries, where it's harder to obtain the level of transparency and feedback you might with a local or domestic gift.
- Social entrepreneurs tend to be at an earlier stage in their development and often have higher-risk models than nonprofits with long track records. However, their potential to create social change can outweigh the risk that their idea will fail. Figure out what level of risk you're willing to bear— whether you're funding social entrepreneurs creating nonprofits or for-profit businesses that create social benefits.

- While the best ideas of social entrepreneurs are those that can be copied, a model that's successful in one geographic area may not always be translatable into other political, social, religious, or cultural environments.
- When individuals and organizations are attempting to change systems, countless—predictable and unpredictable—external factors can affect their success.

Innovation Lab—Ideas to Test:

- Allocate a certain percentage of your total annual giving to higher-risk grantees. Philanthropy, after all, is considered to be society's risk capital.
- Choose one social entrepreneur to fund each year based on an idea you think has great potential.
- Find a student at your local university who wants to create a new nonprofit and offer to serve as a mentor during the process.
- For an issue you care about, find out what knowledge is created by one of the funding intermediaries working in this area. Give the organization a designated gift (a contribution for a specific purpose or project selected by the giver) and track its progress.
- Go online to find out what local or global early-stage nonprofits professional foundations are funding, and use that information to inform your own giving decisions. Remember, staffed foundations often have field experts who have spent years building expertise in many of the same areas you may be passionate about.
- Use your giving journal to weigh the costs and benefits of giving directly to social entrepreneurs versus supporting them through a funding intermediary.

For the Family:

- Read through a number of online profiles of social entrepreneurs through organizations like Kiva.org or Ashoka with your children.
- Describe some of the world's problems to your children and set them a challenge of coming up with a new idea to tackle one of them.
- Ask your children each month to come up with a "modern convenience" (such as a laptop, medicine, or textbook) and then find a social entrepreneur or organization that is trying to provide access to that or a related convenience to an economically disadvantaged population. Make a

monthly family gift to that organization—perhaps the cost, or a percentage of the cost, of that convenience to your family.

- If your children are in high school or college, fund them (at a typical student-appropriate wage) to spend a vacation week creating a plan for their own social enterprise. Spend the last day of the week sharing your own ideas with them and reviewing the plan together.
- Instead of a beach or ski vacation this year, take a "philanthrocation." Spend a week traveling at home or abroad (perhaps through your place of worship or children's school), and have your family help build a school, hospital, or orphanage for a community in need. The perspective and sense of achievement gained from such an experience could make the holiday one of your family's most memorable.

And Remember:
- When directly funding a social entrepreneur, find out who its existing funders are (such as friends and family versus well-respected philanthropists, established foundations, and corporations), as this can be an important indicator of the model's potential success.
- You don't have to fund social entrepreneurs directly. Organizations such as Ashoka, TechnoServe, Acumen Fund, and Endeavor have done due diligence already, assessing business plans of the individuals and organizations they fund and working with them directly. This provides an accountability that would be hard to achieve on your own and helps make your money go further by having screened and validated opportunities, institutional oversight, and pooled resources.
- If you're considering making a substantial gift to a social entrepreneur, ask to see a strategic plan and make sure the plan includes measurable goals and details of how the entrepreneur is going to achieve those goals, as well as reporting on the use of your funds.
- Social entrepreneurs are trying to change the systems that cause social problems—however, until those systems have been changed, immediate assistance will still be needed. Funding both in tandem is a great opportunity for any philanthropist.
- Your money may fund failure as well as success, even if you give through intermediary organizations that have verified the credibility of the social entrepreneurs to which they're directing your money. Not all investments made by these entrepreneurs—even those with proven track records—will be viable or sustainable. Consider these gifts as "learning grants," and move on to other strategies, ideas, and entrepreneurs.

- Social entrepreneurs may be charismatic individuals, but they don't always have technical know-how or the ability to evaluate their activities. Passion and personal exposure to a social problem are not alone sufficient to make someone a successful social entrepreneur.

- Successful social entrepreneurs are those that have developed proven and innovative methods of advancing social change. By funding them, you can learn from their ideas and even apply some to your other philanthropic investments.

- Social entrepreneurship creates and preserves human dignity, enables people to become self-sufficient, and breaks the cycle of poverty for both present and future generations.

- The best ideas are those that can be copied, and the best social entrepreneurs are those that want to share their ideas with others.

SOMETHING VENTURED

Give and Learn by Getting Together

Join forces for results—shared resources give you a bigger bang for your buck.

For anyone in the business world, the 1990s were a thrilling time. The Internet was opening up all kinds of opportunities for connecting, communicating, and conducting commercial transactions. In 1995, I began studying for my MBA and most of my classmates at Stanford were writing business plans for dot-com start-ups. Like them, I had a burning desire to create my own enterprise. But I wanted to do something different—instead of establishing an organization designed to make money, I wanted to create one to give it away.

After losing my mother to cancer six weeks into my first quarter at business school, I already knew I wanted to build a career in philanthropy and dedicate my time to giving. With her loss painfully fresh in my mind, I wanted to move as quickly as possible to create something worthy of her legacy. I also wanted to make my own mark in the philanthropic world, and earn the credibility to help administer my father's philanthropic resources.

As I looked at the community of potential donors being created as a flurry of technology companies went public, I could see that many of the people around me were in need of support. I watched as a media backlash emerged against the new generation of young high-tech millionaires. Newspapers and TV reports called them the "cyber stingy" and questioned why, with all their wealth, they weren't giving back to society.

Some of this criticism was unfair. For a start, much of this wealth was on paper—it didn't necessarily exist as cash. In addition, most high-tech entrepreneurs were the first in their generation to achieve financial success, and few had families in the background to steer them into giving, as I'd had. Until then, philanthropy had primarily been something you did when you retired, yet these people had gained their economic wind-fall in their twenties, thirties, and forties. This was something new. In addition, most Silicon Valley entrepreneurs came from another state or another country and had no ties to the local community.

I could see that these new professionals needed help in how to give, where to give, and how to do so effectively. They're energetic and highly entrepreneurial, so I thought they'd be attracted to a form of philan-thropy in which social investments would be treated with the same degree of seriousness, accountability, and efficiency as for-profit invest-ments. I had spotted a gap in the market—and I knew how I could help fill it (meeting my own need for a "philanthropy 101" education in the process).

In 1998, SV2 was born. We call it a "venture philanthropy partner-ship" and our donors—our partners—pool their money to give multi-year organizational-capacity-building grants to nonprofits. In grant applications, the nonprofits we fund outline their organizational capacity needs and aspirations, as well as how to achieve them. Together with our grantees, we develop grant contracts that include the strategy, implementation plan, and quarterly benchmarks they need to meet to achieve their goals. While our grantees are accountable to us to achieve and report back on these goals, we are also responsible for helping them achieve their goals by investing our time and expertise in addition to our money.

Our partners are also the decision makers when it comes to allocat-ing funds to nonprofits, and every partner—regardless of the size of gift—gets an equal vote. And new partners can participate immediately in grantmaking. In the grantmaking process, nonprofits—either by invi-tation or by responding to an open request for proposals—present their case to the partners, who assess their needs, their potential to grow, and the impact they might be able to have through additional funding, management support and expertise, and access to the partners' respective networks.

Partners (who come from a wide range of professions, age groups, social passions, and backgrounds) then help choose from among the organizations that apply to SV2 for funding. While this might be a little intimidating at first (particularly when grants involve thousands of dollars), SV2 partners find that the support of their peers soon gives them the confidence to assess nonprofits and their needs and recognize their potential to expand. In essence, the process provides a fast track in learning how to make high-impact grants.

At the same time, SV2 partners can become involved in helping nonprofit grantees not only build the capacity needed to achieve their current goals but also come up with new, more ambitious goals. Partners can also help the organizations come up with strategic plans for growth and present those to the nonprofits' boards. They can meet with the heads of the nonprofits to which their grantmaking panel awarded funds and talk through their objectives, plans, and activities, either over coffee or in more formal meetings. Several of our partners have also joined our grantees' boards (I joined the board of one of our first grantees)—in a few cases even chairing them—and many make individual gifts to them, in addition to the SV2 grant.

Partners therefore have a direct role—both inside and outside SV2—in turning nonprofits with great missions into high-growth organizations that can bring about systemic change in education, environmental sustainability, or international development. We like to frame our investments as "scaling social innovations," in mutually accountable partnership with the nonprofits we fund.

In creating SV2, I was responding to the demands of a dynamic new era in philanthropy—one in which donors are becoming far more involved in their giving. This is certainly something I wanted when I first started giving—and still want now, fifteen years into my philanthropy. My SV2 grants are among the gifts of which I'm most proud, because not only are we transforming innovative, early-stage nonprofits, we're also transforming the way our partners practice philanthropy. Like our partners, I get far greater impact through my SV2 grants than through many of my own gifts (since no staff or professional consultants are helping me with my family's or Marc's and my giving).

In addition, I've also made an incredible new group of friends. Like me, today's donors don't want to give in isolation. Many want to get together to share their ideas and excitement. They want to talk to others about philanthropy, to compare their experiences and problems, and to ask basic questions among communities of people they trust. And often, friendship is what emerges along the way.

ENTER THE VENTURE PHILANTHROPISTS

In 1969, at a congressional hearing about foundation tax reform, John D. Rockefeller coined a term to describe the risk-taking function of private foundations. "Private foundations," said Rockefeller, "often are established to engage in what has been described as 'venture philan-thropy,' or the imaginative pursuit of less conventional charitable pur-poses than those normally undertaken by established public charitable organizations."

In 1997, the phrase gained currency when it appeared in an article in the *Harvard Business Review*. The noteworthy "Virtuous Capital" article (subtitled "What Foundations Can Learn from Venture Capitalists") argued that charitable foundations and venture capitalists faced similar challenges—both chose the most worthy recipients of their funding and left it to those beneficiaries, whether young businesses or new nonprofits, to take their idea and run with it.[1] In addition to putting up capital, the article continued, venture capitalists closely monitor the start-ups in which they invest, giving them management support and strategic advice as they grow.

One of the first people to apply this idea to the nonprofit world was Paul Tudor Jones, a thirty-two-year-old money manager who decided he wanted to fight poverty in New York City. In 1988, with two of his

GIVING
2.0 close friends as co-founders—Peter Borish and Glenn Dubin, both with investment backgrounds—he started the Robin Hood Foundation, putting $3 million of his own money into the project. This was supplemented by $100,000 gifts from his partners and small donors who gave money, sweat (by running the New York City Marathon on the Robin Hood team), or knowledge and experience. Donations of skills not only benefited Robin Hood itself but also the nonprofits the foundation was supporting.

The Robin Hood Foundation pioneered a type of giving that involves much more than money. It's about donors pooling funds, and staff and volunteers going out to work with the foundation's grantees, focusing on everything from youth unemployment to education, health care, hunger, housing, and domestic violence. With the help of Robin Hood's advice, nonprofits can make their programs and organizations more effective and design strategies that will bring about change more rapidly.

The foundation has been both innovative and entrepreneurial, helping define the then emerging field of venture philanthropy, inspiring individuals and institutions across America. It is part of a dynamic approach to giving—one that draws lessons from the business world. "Robin Hood has learned a tremendous amount from successful venture capitalists, angel investors, and later-stage investors," says David Saltzman, executive director of the foundation and a founding board member.

For an individual donor, the work of organizations such as Robin Hood means you don't have to be Bill Gates to make a difference. Because they act like venture capitalists, they choose the most promising nonprofits and community groups to support, so you can be sure your money will go to the most effective recipients. Before Robin Hood invests, it will—as would a venture capitalist—spend time with the organization, scrutinize its strategy and financial statements, and evaluate its management teams. "If you had the time and inclination to spend all your days and nights searching for effective programs, you might choose to do the type of work we do," says David Saltzman. "We make it easy. We do all that work for you—and it's free of charge."

If a nonprofit is selected, Robin Hood helps it with strategic and financial planning, recruiting, legal concerns, and fundraising. If the foundation doesn't have the expertise in-house, it goes out to ask for help in the form of pro bono work from New York firms and individuals.

The effect of both mind and money on the performance of nonprofits can be dramatic. Using a rigorous and innovative measurement methodology, Robin Hood calculates the impact of investing in the nonprofits it supports. Take an education program graduating an additional ten high school students each year (it's thought that high school graduation raises a student's future earnings by about $160,000 over a career). For those ten students combined, the education program would increase earnings by at least $1.6 million. Dividing this by Robin Hood's grant to that nonprofit—say, $200,000—the program raises future earnings by $8 for each dollar Robin Hood spent.[2] This is the venture philanthropy effect—it's all about making a big impact with a small investment.

LIFE AS AN ADVENTURE

In 2005, a group of world-class women athletes turned bitter disappointment into something powerful and positive. Two years earlier, after just three seasons, the Women's United Soccer Association (WUSA) had folded and its team organizations were disbanded. WUSA had ridden on a wave of enthusiasm for women's soccer following America's victory against China in the 1999 FIFA Women's World Cup, in which Brandi Chastain (who is no relation to Alicia Chastain), had scored the winning goal for America. But while WUSA had ceased to exist, the athletes who had been part of this association were not prepared to give up. Brandi and others had seen the impact that women's sports had had on female empowerment and the role models women athletes provided for young girls.

Brandi got together with Julie Foudy, who'd led the team to the World Cup, and Marlene Bjornsrud, former general manager of the San Jose CyberRays U.S. Women's Soccer Team, and started thinking about how bringing more women into sports could fight obesity and low self-esteem. They launched a pilot program, enlisting women's basketball players from San Jose State University to coach teenage girls in an after-

GIVING 2.0 school exercise program. The Bay Area Women's Sports Initiative (BAWSI) was born and started spreading, expanding into eighteen schools in five years. Through BAWSI, young girls have discovered that athletics builds their self-esteem and helps them conquer new challenges. Meanwhile, the organization believes its free weekly after-school athletics programs represent a model that could eventually be rolled out on a global scale.

The individual who first planted the idea of taking the concept global was Joon Yun, a Korean American hedge fund investor. Joon has been deeply involved with BAWSI from its early stages. One day, he and his wife (they met as students at Duke Medical School) came to Brandi's home to meet the founders of BAWSI and listen to a staff meeting. At the end of the meeting, Joon started to talk about how the organization could grow across the nation, anywhere there was a women's sports community. In addition, he said he believed BAWSI had the potential to influence the life of girls internationally, particularly as soccer is so popular across the rest of the world.

"There are so many athletes that are successful and want to give back to women, and the assets they can leave to the young girls are tremendous," says Joon. "And both groups want to be with each other. Women athletes love to be with the girls, and the girls are in awe of the athletes—so bringing them together was the key engagement."

Joon grew up in what he calls the "old world," in a family that had lived on the same land in rural Korea for more than forty generations and in a town populated by hundreds of relatives. "It was a very tribal society and the kind of society you rarely see anymore," he says. "The things you worry about in the modern world, you never worried about there. Today, kids have so much more—but, because marketing messages constantly remind them of what they don't have, there's a sense of poverty. We had a lot less than kids do today but we had a tremendous sense of abundance."

Since Joon's grandfather was a younger son, he was allowed to leave his older brother to take care of the family. So his grandfather left the village, ending up in Seoul as an entrepreneur. Joon's father followed this path too, and took the family to America. "We're the entrepreneurial arm of a very conservative old family," Joon explains. After more than a decade serving on the clinical faculty as a physician at Stanford's Department of Radiology, Joon also entered the world of entrepreneurship and innovation when he joined Palo Alto Investors, a hedge fund investment firm that invests in start-ups and later-stage companies.

As the president and a partner in the firm, his job is to identify innovative ideas that can be turned into successful businesses with global reach. Palo Alto Investors makes long-term investments based on extensive original research, focusing on overlooked or misunderstood parts of markets within health care, energy, and technology. Among the most interesting aspects of his work, he says, is identifying and assessing new ideas that are "hiding in plain sight" by using what he calls "outlier insights"—insights that he can apply to his philanthropy.

It was Ted Janus, a colleague at Palo Alto Investors and a long-term SV2 board member, who introduced Joon to SV2. As Joon recalls, "I knew some of the other folks involved in SV2, but talking to Ted, an incredible philanthropist and investor, I got really interested in the model, and I was blown away by the vision." He could see that venture philanthropy in many ways mirrored his work as a venture capitalist, investing in new ideas so that they can become successful, world-changing enterprises.

He also liked the idea of engaging directly with the nonprofits that SV2 funded. This was also something he could link with his professional life. "In investing, if you're not directly engaged, you might misdirect your capital, so the idea of primary engagement by the partners made sense. In our business, we expect the senior guys to be out there on the road rather than sitting in front of a computer," he says. "The information age is a very challenging environment because in many ways it makes information more liquid but not necessarily more efficient—you have to go see it for yourself."

This is exactly what Joon, as an SV2 partner—and now a board member—has found himself doing. Working with grantees has taken him everywhere, from chaotic offices where start-up education and environmental groups are making up for what they lack in organizational capacity with excitement and enthusiasm, to the homes of athletes such as Brandi Chastain who are pioneering new ways of positively transforming lives and communities.

Whether it's meeting nonprofit pioneers at SV2 or encountering entrepreneurs at his firm, Joon believes he's on something of a roller-coaster adventure. Life, he says, is a "backpacking trip" where nothing is set in stone and new directions and opportunities are there for the taking. While he sees philanthropy as a way of learning, collaborating, and helping change the world, he stresses the need to look to it for something else—fun. "People don't talk about it that much because it feels wrong to have fun in philanthropy," he says. "But we know that fun is what drives people. And people are more engaged and effective when they're having fun."

Joon likes the word *venture*. "It's the root of the word *adventure* and it incorporates the idea of forward looking," he says. "Venture is all about innovation. And because we're working with start-ups, we're often seeing ideas that are at the leading edge of social change."

As well as encountering leading-edge new ideas, Joon—like all SV2 partners—has been on a steep learning curve since joining the partnership, and that feeds back into both his investments and his social investments. But rather than learning from a book or a class, partners learn from each other. This bottom-up approach is something Joon can relate to. "As a kid, I did most of my learning hanging out with roommates and friends, talking about the world. What I learned around the couch—that was my education," he says. "And SV2 is similar. The people are incredible and I've learned so much laterally from my peers. That's really made an impact on my way of thinking about social investment."

He loves learning through collaboration, not only with nonprofit leaders but also with his SV2 partners—collaborations that, on one rainy afternoon, found him in a parking lot with several partners. Together they held an impromptu meeting from the inside of a car, with ideas and insights coming as thick and fast as the rain that was pelting down on the roof. "When we go on these site visits, we build friendships indirectly," he says. "And that intimacy builds into better collaborations."

Joon's next adventure is as one of the founders of the Palo Alto Institute, a nonprofit think tank that is "changing lives by transforming the way people think." The idea behind the institute is to look for truths in unconventional places and promote them through research and education. For Joon, this is a new and exciting form of giving that builds on his experience as a venture philanthropist. "The domino effect for me was how this led to my more direct engagement in philanthropy through the Palo Alto Institute," he says. "And that experience also flows back to SV2."

GETTING TOGETHER TO GIVE

In some ways, venture philanthropy organizations are similar to Ashoka or Acumen Fund: they act as an intermediary between donors and grantees. Organizations such as the Washington, D.C.–based Venture Philanthropy Partners, San Francisco–based Tipping Point, and Boston-based New Profit Inc. pool individual gifts and, after an extensive due diligence and selection process, reinvest those resources alongside pro bono services to help successful nonprofits expand. Individual givers entrust their donations to these organization because they like the high-impact, hands-on approach to supporting nonprofits and community groups. They also like the additional services and support that these intermediaries provide to the nonprofits they fund. In recent years, however, some donors have gone one step further. They also pool their donations with those of others, but they don't want to leave decisions on which nonprofits to fund to intermediaries. They want to do it themselves.

One of the most popular ways of doing this is to join a giving circle—a collaborative group of donors. Emerging across America in recent years, giving circles are typically small groups of donors who put a few hundred to a few thousand dollars (though in some cases much more) into a pool of funds, teach themselves about effective forms of philanthropy and issue areas, and decide collectively how to allocate their money.

In 2007, it was estimated that eight hundred giving circles were operating across the United States. A survey of a subset of these groups—

about 40 percent of the total—found some \$88 million in fundraising since the groups' inception (most since the year 2000) and almost \$65 million in grants to fund community needs.[3] Giving circles are ethnically diverse, and while their membership has tended to be largely female, they are increasingly mixed or all male (some 47 percent, according to the Giving Circles Network).

Giving circles range widely in size, some with a handful of members, others with several hundred. Some larger ones even employ staff to help manage finances and administration. They can be associations formed by former classmates, members of the same place of worship, or simply friends, work colleagues, or neighbors who like spending time together but want to do that more productively. But they all have one thing in common—a passion for humanity and a desire to give more effectively.

The structure of giving circles also varies tremendously. Some are small core groups of fund makers who share decision making. Others have a much larger cohort of members who participate in meetings and donate small amounts of money, but don't necessarily have a say in how the money is to be spent. Others operate membership-type organizations, with joining fees and minimum donation amounts. Some offer volunteering opportunities, too, either to help run the giving circle itself or to go out to work with some of the nonprofits the circle funds.

It's relatively easy to start a giving circle. Once you've identified the initial group, you need to get together to decide on the mission and what the focus of your funding will be. You'll also need to establish where and how often you'll meet, whether in a public place such as a library, recreation center, or restaurant or at members' homes, with each of the group members taking turns hosting.

Beyond that, however, there are plenty of things to consider before getting going. For a start, work out how you're going to give away the funds the group collects. Should your giving circle, for example, decide what to fund based on discussions among the members and members' research? Or will you allow nonprofits to submit applications for funding? How will you do due diligence on the nonprofits you're considering investing in and verify that gifts will be used as intended (this is particularly important for larger gifts)? Will the group require a unanimous decision on the choice of beneficiary? Will members of your group conduct site visits? What kind of feedback will beneficiaries be required to submit as to how the group's money has been spent and what difference it's made?

You also need to settle on the size or range of each member's financial contribution and how much everyone will give over a certain time period. In groups where everyone has an equal say in how the money is distributed, it often makes sense for everyone to give the same amount. However, some groups have tiered donation levels. To look after the money, you can set up a joint bank account, establish a donor-advised fund at a community foundation, or even create a public charity.

You also need to decide whether or not the group can expand and how big it's going to become. Are you going to request that members make a yearlong commitment? Can donors join at any time, or should you allow them to sign up only at certain times of the year? Some giving circles prefer to keep it intimate, restricting membership to the small group of individuals that first came together. On the other hand, once in place, these organizations can grow rapidly to become significant forces for change.

Take Impact Austin, a giving circle founded by Rebecca Powers in 2003 that has spread to cities such as Indianapolis, San Antonio, and Pensacola. Thousands of women each give $1,000 a year through Impact Austin and each of them has an equal voice when it comes to selecting the recipients for grants. In 2010, the organization made grants to five recipients, each of $105,000 and ranging from literacy programs and parks improvement to care for the elderly.

But members do much more than give money. Volunteers participate in everything from organizing mailings and newsletters to chairing meetings, and Impact Austin uses volunteer management software to fit the right member with the right volunteer task. Sometimes members go out to work directly with the nonprofits they fund or participate in advocacy initiatives alongside them.

Some collective giving has gone global. In partnership with the Women's Funding Network—founded by sisters Swanee Hunt and Helen LaKelly Hunt in 2006—Women Moving Millions encourages women to give $1 million or more. Women Moving Millions started a quarter of a century ago with a network of women who realized that, collectively, they could help change the lives of girls and women around the world. In phase one of the campaign, the network garnered the support of more than a hundred donors (both men and women) and dozens of donor circles, raising more than $180 million to support organizations promoting female health, education, antiviolence, and economic development. Women Moving Millions also provides donors with services such as education programs on philanthropy and social issues, training in leadership and fundraising, and donor retreats.

But whether you're part of a large organization such as Women Moving Millions giving away hundreds of thousands of dollars or more a year or a small group of four giving away a few hundred dollars, giving circles and other forms of collective giving are testimony to the power of getting together—a clear case of collaborative philanthropy being more than the sum of its parts.

LEARN, BABY, LEARN!

The further I go into philanthropy and the more I learn, the more I realize how much I don't know. This must be the experience of every philanthropist, regardless of the amount of money they have to give. But if you share your challenges and dilemmas with others, you can get far further, far faster. And when you immerse yourself in philanthropy, moments of learning appear all the time.

Learning is the principle on which the best giving circles are based. Some talk about their experiences and exchange ideas over coffee or dinner. Some groups take turns to research a particular issue area and present their findings to the rest of the team at the next meeting. More established giving circles often organize sessions where they invite expert speakers and nonprofit leaders to talk on particular topics. They also organize site visits to nonprofits or foundations.

Here's a hypothetical example of how collective giving could help you raise your own impact. Let's say you're a retired nurse and you have a small amount of money with which to make charitable donations. As a hospital nurse, you always participated in your United Way workplace campaign. Then, after retiring, you joined a group of women from your church in a giving circle that makes loans to women entrepreneurs in developing countries through a website such as Kiva.org.

But suppose you want to do more, and you've realized that your health care experience could be extremely valuable to people in the countries to which you are making microloans. Then (assuming you have the right qualifications, including a current license to practice) you join a project run by Doctors Without Borders. It turns out to be an amazing trip—one that takes you to the republic of Chechnya, which, after years of conflict between the Russian government and rebel forces, lacks basic health services, particularly in obstetrical and gynecological care. There, you work side-by-side with women at a clinic outside Grozny. Conditions are extremely tough and you're dealing with heartrending cases. It's low-paid work (most participants are not volunteers), yet you find it provides the greatest sense of fulfillment you've ever experienced.

When you return home, you go back to your giving circle and tell stories and show the group your photographs. After hearing tales of the conditions, the group agrees to direct some of its money to the clinic in Chechnya, greatly increasing the resources available for health care for its patients.

This example shows how with limited financial resources but valuable experience, plenty of time, and boundless enthusiasm, you can make a far bigger impact than you could ever have imagined. And what you learn on a volunteering trip—whether overseas or in your neighborhood—you can pass on to other philanthropists in your giving circle, helping them make funding decisions about projects that might otherwise have escaped their attention.

Of course, plenty of professional organizations also provide powerful ways of learning. One of the longest-running programs is the Philanthropy Workshop. Launched under the auspices of the Rockefeller Foundation, today, year-long sessions that are available in London, New York, and Brazil are run by the U.K.-based Institute for Philanthropy. The Philanthropy Workshop West, an independent nonprofit, also runs similar sessions in Silicon Valley.

The workshops give you everything from basic tools such as how to conduct due diligence and evaluate grantee performance to broader skills such as how to foster leadership, pursue policy change, and come up with more effective giving strategies. Meanwhile, site visits—such as trips to the *favelas* (slums) of Brazil or on a boat on the Amazon—expose you to the realities of working on the ground with social and environmental problems. And, of course, one of the most powerful parts of the program is the chance to share your ideas, experiences, and challenges with other philanthropists.

The importance of this networking effect is something emphasized by Jane Wales, the energetic and committed founder of the Global Philanthropy Forum, which runs an annual conference, a summer seminar, workshops, and special events. In the feedback from participants after they've attended one of the GPF events, most cite the importance of contact with speakers and other participants as helping inform their giving strategies.

These kinds of programs do more than give participants exposure to management techniques and best practices and provide an opportunity to hear war stories from seasoned philanthropists. They also create a meeting place for individuals, many of whom may be struggling with the same questions in the context of their own philanthropic activity.

Not all of us can afford an expensive course or workshop. Yet, whether it's the need to acquire knowledge of a new cause or to learn how to assess the performance of your grantees, education is at the heart of new approaches to philanthropy. And collective philanthropy provides a powerful form of peer learning. So if you enjoy meeting up with like-minded, thoughtful, entertaining people over a casual lunch or dinner, giving circles may be for you. If you're looking to learn and expand, why not get together to give together?

PARTNERS IN SUCCESS

The SV2 model is similar to that of Social Venture Partners International. While the two have a strategic partnership (and SV2 has benefited greatly from sharing knowledge with SVPI and tapping into its capacity-building resources), SV2 is not a formal member of SVPI, unlike its other affiliates. SVPI is a network of philanthropists that, like SV2, has recognized what can be achieved when you combine collective grantmaking with nonprofit capacity building, the sharing of time and skills, and the promotion of philanthropic learning and education.

By pooling donations (at SV2, partners each contribute a minimum of $5,000), this collaborative giving model means your money goes further than it would if you made an individual direct donation to a nonprofit. "It's the same reason anyone invests in a mutual fund," says Paul Shoemaker, executive director of Social Venture Partners Seattle, the founding SVP organization. "Everyone puts in a certain amount of money and when we pool that, we end up with the ability to invest in a whole range of nonprofits and with a lot more funding than the partners could give individually."

What's more, the varied skills of partners can be brought to bear on nonprofits at different stages in their development. Those like Joon, who've worked with start-up companies, for example, might become more involved with an organization at the early stage of its development. By contrast, the skills of HR or management professionals could be very valuable for nonprofits at a later stage.

"It's an opportunity for people to really unlock their potential to have the most positive impact they can have," says Paul. "And the way you really amplify people's positive potential is to get them connected to other philanthropists and by engaging them directly with nonprofits. So they're not just making a philanthropic investment—they're buying into a network."

Like Joon, Paul believes that the hands-on nature of this type of giving is part of its power—particularly when it comes to the ability of partners to expand their knowledge and experience. "There's nothing like experiential learning," he says. "When you do a strategic plan or a marketing strategy for a nonprofit you learn a huge amount—you can't put a price tag on that."

In addition, however, what partners are often pleasantly surprised to find is the extraordinary camaraderie generated by a venture philan-thropy partnership. Joining forces on shared goals and meaningful projects is a way of bonding with a group of people who are all happy and enthusiastic about their work. For some, this way of giving can be far better than going it alone. As for donors who join giving circles, half the fun of being part of a philanthropic partnership is simply in being around an energetic, intelligent, and engaged group of people. In the process, people often develop what turn out to be deep friendships.

Moreover, people end up giving more, and more effectively, than they would alone. When we conducted a survey in 2011, nearly 90 percent of SV2 partners reported that their giving had become more strategic as a result of their involvement with the partnership, while 72 percent said this had contributed to greater community involvement. Meanwhile, more than 71 percent said they'd been giving larger amounts of money than they had before joining SV2. For me, there could hardly be a better reward than creating this ripple of philanthropic impact. Many of our SV2 grants, for example, have resulted in nonprofits' experiencing significant organizational transformation because of both the size of our pooled funds and the diversity of our partners' expertise, which is shared with grantees.

For venture philanthropy partners or giving circle members, collaborative giving and hands-on involvement provide the chance to learn a phenomenal amount about high-impact giving in a very short time. It's a model that gives you not only a way to donate your dollars more effectively but also an opportunity to contribute your time and expertise. At every step of the way, you can work in partnership with the organizations that you fund—their success defines yours. And by coming together to give, you can use the power of the collective to deliver measurable results so that, without having to give megabucks, you can have mega-impact.

MAKING IT HAPPEN

What to Ask Yourself When Considering Joining a Venture Philanthropy Partnership:

- How important is learning as part of your philanthropy?
- Would you enjoy working with others on developing your giving?

- Are you prepared to give up a certain amount of control of funding decisions and instead give as part of a group?
- Are you prepared to give up individual recognition for your gifts? In collective philanthropy it is the partnership or giving circle that will receive all the credit for grants, though you will be recognized as a donor to the venture philanthropy organization itself.
- When joining a venture philanthropy partnership, what skills could you bring to a grantee (for example, helping early-stage organizations boost their capacity, advising more mature nonprofits on how to introduce management changes, assisting with event planning, or coming up with a strategic plan for a nonprofit's expansion)?
- Which organizations are the best venture philanthropy grantmakers out there, and what can you learn from them and apply to your own giving?

What to Ask a Giving Circle You'd Like to Join:
- Are its funding decisions made on a collective basis, including all members?
- How are grant decisions made? Do you have to attend certain meetings in order to vote on which grantees the circle funds?
- Is there a minimum donation amount or a tiered structure for donations?
- Does everyone give the same amount and, if so, do all have equal say in funding decisions?
- How often and where does the group meet?
- Do the group's funding decisions require a unanimous vote?
- How does the group resolve a tie or a conflict of interest (for example, if a member is on the board of a potential grantee)?
- Are there volunteering opportunities, either for the management of the giving circle or in the nonprofit grantees' organizations?
- Is the group planning to remain small or will it be expanding to include others?

What to Ask a Venture Philanthropy Partnership You'd Like to Join:
- What learning opportunities does the partnership offer?
- What other experiences can it offer, such as events, site visits, and opportunities to take on leadership roles?
- What sorts of projects do the partners work on with nonprofits?

- Does the organization have any case studies or other evaluation metrics of the grants it has made?
- What does the application process entail?
- Are partners required to commit to working with the organization for a certain period of time?
- What is the minimum annual donation amount?
- What issues is the organization focused on in its grantmaking?
- How are potential grantees identified and selected?
- How does the organization track the impact of its work?

Innovation Lab—Ideas to Test:
- Organize a dinner party and invite your friends to each bring a dish as well as information about a nonprofit and share both with the group.
- Create a giving circle with your best friends (or even with one close friend or relative) and meet quarterly for one year.
- Sit in on a venture philanthropy grantmaking session to meet people and find out how the process works.
- Find out about the ideas and tools used in venture philanthropy and see if those could be applied to one of the nonprofits you support.
- Allocate a percentage of your giving to support organizations that have proven track records but need to expand their infrastructure.
- Make a gift specifically to support an organizational capacity need (such as new software, a printer, a vehicle, or an electricity bill) whose results you cannot measure but that will improve the nonprofit's basic efficiency.

What You Gain Through Shared Giving:
- A means of learning philanthropic skills, such as how to conduct effective grantmaking and evaluation, as well as managing a high-engagement relationship with the organizations you fund.
- Access to a network of like-minded individuals and potential friends.
- The ability to make your money work harder by pooling it with other funds.
- A chance to work directly with nonprofits that you might not have encountered when giving alone.
- The opportunity to give individual time, expertise, and money both to the nonprofits that win funding from the group and to those that do not win immediate funding.

- The possibility of serving on a board or taking up other leadership positions.

What You Give Up Through Shared Giving:
- Individual choice on where to give your money.
- Individual recognition for your philanthropy (although you do get recognition from your venture philanthropy partnership or giving circle).
- Complete choice of issues you personally want to focus on.

For the Family:
- Join a giving circle with your daughter to support women's rights around the world.
- Create a mother-daughter giving circle or a father-son one, and each of you gets to invite one or two other friends to join with their child (or parent).
- Find out if your children might be able to sit in on a grant round at a funding organization in your area.
- Find out if your children's school has a teen philanthropy program—and if it doesn't, consider creating one with your teen.

And Remember:
- Even if high-impact grantmaking and learning opportunities were what drew you to this type of philanthropy, you may also get a lot out of being a part of a community of like-minded people.
- You might make a new friend or meet your future spouse by being part of a collaborative organization.
- Be prepared to be flexible so you can attend meetings in which key voting on grantmaking takes place.
- Pooling philanthropic resources can greatly increase the power of your dollars, but you need to be able to relinquish control and be prepared to share the glory.
- The more collaborative you are with your funding, the more impact you're going to have. This collaboration applies both to the number of individuals you're willing to partner with and to your ability to work with the organizations you fund to find out what they need the most.
- Participating in collaborative funding can expose you to more sophisticated decision-making models and vetting processes, which can inform

funding decisions you make outside the group, dramatically improving your own philanthropic effectiveness.

- The grantmaking process will introduce you to a wide range of nonprofits, so if your partnership or giving circle does not end up funding them, you could do so yourself (even grants made by your giving group long before you joined it can provide you with a potential grantee pool).

- Having a structure through which to build your philanthropic knowledge results in increased impact as you apply your research, experience, and learning to your work with other organizations and investments.

- There is no negative form of learning. All the elements of philanthropy— from refining your focus to improving your decisions—will help your future giving. Without making mistakes, you can't learn from them.

- Giving through a collaborative process can be every bit as compelling as giving to a specific cause, if not more so.

7

CHANGING MINDS

A Tool on the Road to Transformation

Think broadly and embrace a long-term vision—changing minds and policy takes time.

Every time she steps into her office on Spruce Street, Linda Shoemaker (who is no relation to Paul Shoemaker) enters a piece of Colorado history. The mansion housing the offices of the Brett Family Foundation, which she and her husband, Steve Brett, established in 2000, is believed to be the oldest remaining brick home in Boulder. It was built in 1875, and with its classical portico, stucco façade, ornate ironwork, and fine chimneys, it's a magnificent example of the kind of buildings erected by wealthy nineteenth-century Coloradoans. And Anthony Arnett, the man who in 1866 purchased the land on which the house stands—now in the center of downtown Boulder—was not just a rich industrialist. He was also a philanthropist.

Born in France in 1819, Anthony Arnett reached the United States with his family at the age of nine. He left New York for San Francisco in 1849 in search of adventure and gold, rounding Cape Horn on a square-sailed, steel-hulled windjammer, one of the era's grandest merchant ships. Ten years later, following adventures in California, Cuba, Nicaragua, and Panama, he traveled to the craggy mountains, wide plains, and dramatic canyons of Colorado, driven by the rumor of precious metal.

While the Pike's Peak Gold Rush brought him to the Centennial State, his wealth was not amassed through prospecting. In fact, interests

175

in mining, real estate, and freight shipping made Arnett rich. And he was generous with his riches, financing roads and railroads. Perhaps his most important gift, however, was to education. Arnett helped establish the University of Colorado in Boulder by donating not only land for a campus site but also $500 in cash—no small sum in those days—to help the institution get started.

Like Anthony Arnett, Linda Shoemaker is a passionate and ambitious philanthropist. And like Arnett's, her philanthropy extends to the University, where she serves on the CU Foundation Board of Trustees. However, while Linda shares the impetus to give to society with her nineteenth-century predecessor, she does so in ways that are more complex than those of Anthony Arnett. She believes that while directly financing issues such as education, social justice, or poverty alleviation is crucial (and the Brett Family Foundation does make such grants), a critical need exists for a different kind of funding—funding that brings about social change by influencing public policy and the legislative environment.

"I think about giving in a much more comprehensive way," Linda explains. "Because when you have a goal of changing public policy and advocating for change in a public arena, then as a wealthy person you should look for a strategy that includes not just your charitable philanthropy but also what else you can do with your dollars."

What Linda and others like her realize is that philanthropy alone cannot fix the world's problems. To change society, they argue, all players must participate, from civic groups to religious leaders. Business, which generates employment and markets for essential services, is also a leading participant, as those supporting social entrepreneurs and social enterprise have recognized. And there's another party with an extremely important place at the table of social change—government.

Governments are funders, legislators, educators, health care providers, and employers, and as such, they shape the way society evolves. With annual budgets that even in hard times can be larger than the largest foundation endowments, governments have the power to promote education, create economic opportunities, and reduce poverty. Through their legislative powers, they can put a stop to injustices and foster a more equitable society. Yet governments are pulled in countless directions. Their leaders' political views shape their actions. Politicians' desire to gain or hold onto office informs much of what they do. Those funding their election campaigns further influence their policies. The national agenda may hamper their plans at a local level, while bureaucratic inertia may hinder, if not halt, their progress.

Recognizing these roadblocks to positive policy change, advocacy philanthropists such as Linda use funding to nudge the complex juggernaut that is government in new directions—directions that will bring about longer-lasting impact on social problems than a single foundation or nonprofit could alone. "Take homelessness," says Linda. "If you're a direct service grantmaker, you're addressing the current issue, which is the homeless population where you live. But if you're an advocacy giver, your aim is to reduce the need for homeless services in the long term. These problems are long-term problems, and you should fund long-term solutions."

Unlike philanthropists who give their money directly to programs and nonprofit infrastructure, advocacy philanthropists immerse themselves in the world of ideas and information. With their eyes set on more distant horizons, they don't want to limit their funding to direct services— they want to work to ensure those services are no longer needed. They're in the business of changing the world by changing minds.

GOING INTO BATTLE

Advocacy takes many different forms. You can advance your ideas by raising awareness of a cause attracting little attention, or by putting an issue in front of policymakers to encourage government action. To do so, you might file a lawsuit, testify at hearings, organize events, distribute information materials, write letters and op-eds in your local or national newspaper, or publish research reports. Most philanthropists will leave this kind of advocacy to the organizations that they fund.

However, even this type of philanthropy can be highly politicized, pitting left against right, liberal against conservative. Others may not approve of your ideas. And even if the organizations you fund are politically agnostic, people with strong ideas and opposing views may run up against you. For this reason, as an advocacy philanthropist, you need to be certain of your beliefs and prepared to defend your principles. To bring about change, you must be ready to go into battle.

If you're about to embark on advocacy funding by establishing a new organization, you will want to familiarize yourself with the intricacies of U.S. tax law and to think broadly about channels through which to conduct your activities. These include 501(c)(4)s, which are tax-exempt nonprofit organizations that may engage in lobbying as a primary activity, as well as electoral activity. 501(c)(3) organizations are limited in lobbying activities and barred from electoral activity. However, unlike those who give to a 501(c)(3), donors will not receive a tax deduction for gifts to a 501(c)(4).

Less controversial and complex paths do exist in advocacy philanthropy. You might, for example, help enrich a debate in which you believe alternative voices would benefit local decision making. By organizing town hall discussion evenings or sponsoring radio shows, you could help foster greater clarity or better information on a certain issue, not endorsing any one viewpoint but simply promoting a more informed debate, allowing diverse views to be aired. Or you might bring to the table the groups and individuals affected by an impending policy decision.

Your level of involvement will depend on your experience. If you don't feel equipped to engage in advancing ideas yourself, you could turn to established organizations with a deeper knowledge of issues and public policy than you have, using your dollars to support media groups or nonprofits that are advocates for your cause.

However, keep in mind that you may not agree with every activity undertaken by your grantees. Even issues that seem relatively uncontroversial, such as protecting the environment, can present difficult choices for funders—for while some see climate change as the most pressing global environmental challenge, others claim that the threat to water supplies is the world's most urgent problem. In advocacy, there are no easy answers. And your answers can come up against those of another philanthropist—perhaps even someone you know and love.

LIKE WINNING THE LOTTERY

Until 1999, Linda Shoemaker, her husband Steve, and her daughter Emily lived a comfortable but normal life in Boulder. Linda's friends were teachers, lawyers, and small business owners. Steve was working as general counsel at Tele-Communications Incorporated (TCI), and Linda, a former journalist, corporate attorney, and children's advocate, was busy serving as the elected president of a regional school district board covering nine communities including Boulder.

Steve had spent the past year working on a deal to merge his company's operations with those of AT&T. As a corporate lawyer, he'd worked on many such negotiations before and had seen many promising deals fall through, even after months of discussion. It was unclear whether or not this deal would close. Then, in March, the deal went ahead and Steve stood to receive money from the sale of his vested stock options. He had no idea what the final price would be but, confident of some sort of windfall, Linda and Steve decided to share the experience.

Linda and their daughter, Emily, then fourteen, flew to New York to join Steve for the closing, staying at the famous Waldorf Astoria Hotel, where the company executives were staying. While Steve was working, Emily and Linda went sightseeing. After the closing, Steve handed Linda an envelope full of checks and asked her to process them. "We'd still not sat down and figured out how much money we'd be making," says Linda. When she settled into her seat on the plane back to Colorado and opened the envelope, Linda was astonished by the total she found inside. "The checks were only a down payment on what we were going to get," she says. "I felt like we'd won the lottery. I was sitting there thinking: 'Do I go to my bank branch at my local mall and try to deposit these checks?' I didn't even know there was such a thing as private banking."

But if she didn't know much about financial management, she knew what she wanted to do with the family windfall—she wanted to put it to work to help change the world. She'd already been playing a role in shaping civil society by serving on the school board. And she and Steve had always given to causes they cared about. But as she gazed at the checks, Linda felt acutely conscious of the fact that her philanthropic potential had, overnight, been transformed. Millions were now at her fingertips. "With the money came responsibility, and I felt I should use it to change my little corner of the world," she says. Linda also knew what she wanted to fund. Rather than supporting only direct service charitable programs, she wanted to bring about long-lasting change—she wanted to become an advocacy philanthropist.

It was an ambitious choice. "It seemed like a huge leap for me," she confesses. Advocacy, she knew, would take time and yield no immediate results or gratification. Impact would be hard to measure. And Linda had no idea how to go about putting in place the infrastructure necessary to influence policy. She needed to learn how to be a philanthropist.

GIVING TO THE WORLD OF IDEAS

Linda Shoemaker's philanthropic journey was bound to take her into the challenging world of social and political advocacy. However, as an individual donor, you can engage in this form of giving even if you don't have millions to give or wide experience in political leadership. And if you don't want to set up your own organization, you can fund nonprofits whose mission matches your philosophy, pooling your funds with those of others. You may also consider relinquishing your tax deduction to give to a 501(c)(4). By funding these kinds of groups, you get a vicarious seat at the lobbying table.

When considering making this kind of gift, look for organizations that have advocacy as their sole focus or as part of their portfolio of activities. Supporting leadership development is an important part of advocacy funding, so consider funding organizations that use this strategy, as well.

Take the Twenty-First Century Foundation. One of the few endowed foundations focusing on the African American community, it has a range of advocacy programs. These include its "Black Men and Boys" initiative, which promotes health, education, employability, criminal justice, and engaged fatherhood; and "Black Women for Black Girls," a New York City-based giving circle in which investors—black professional women—give money, time, and expertise to support low-income black girls. The giving circle also commissions research studies to inform policymakers about the needs of this population, and members mentor the girls and donate technical assistance to the organizations serving them.

As well as seeking funding from individual donors for its programs, the foundation also allows philanthropists to give to its Twenty-First Century Foundation General Fund. This is an unrestricted fund supporting advocacy, community organizing, and leadership development focused on addressing root causes of social injustice.

Environmental Defense Fund also has a strong focus on advocacy. It has long made its voice heard in Washington as part of its push for stronger environmental laws. While EDF is a 501(c)(3) nonprofit, it has also established a sister 501(c)(4) organization, Environmental Defense Action Fund, which is not limited in what it can spend to lobby for environmental legislation. This has allowed EDF to achieve significant environmental changes in the law. In California, for example, its action helped the first statewide cap on climate change pollution to be passed.

Before making a gift, however, you need to identify organizations conducting advocacy in your issue area. Here, the Internet is again an essential tool. Type the word "advocacy" into the GuideStar or Charity Navigator search engines and you'll find pages and pages of nonprofits with "advocacy" in their title. You can refine your search geographically or by issue. You can perform similar searches on the online version of Publication 78, the IRS's listing of organizations it recognizes as eligible to receive tax-deductible contributions.

On the organizations' websites you can discover whether or not their activities match your giving strategy. Find out if a nonprofit is part of the broader spectrum of groups working in your area of interest. Is it, for example, part of a coalition working in that field? Is it building coalitions?

One of the reasons that, at SV2, we chose to fund the Center for Resource Solutions (whose mission is to change policy around limiting carbon emissions) was that it works hard to bring renewable energy and energy efficiency into debates everywhere, from government and the public to other environmental organizations.

As an individual donor without the time or resources to become an advocacy philanthropist, helping change the law is not out of your reach. With diligent research and a donation, you can participate in democracy in a powerful way.

You don't even have to donate money—you can promote change as an individual by writing to your representative or senator about a bill you'd like them to support. Some advocacy organizations make this easy for you by posting letter texts on their websites—all you have to do is sign and click on the "send" icon.

Today, technology is making advocacy accessible to everyone. With its massive global connectivity, the Internet allows an ordinary citizen to spread a message in a way that was once only possible for organizations with large marketing budgets. Through technology you can raise your hand for a cause, and get other people to raise their hands with you. You can create a spark of social consciousness and watch it catch fire across national, or even global, communities.

Mobile devices are also powerful advocacy tools—something forcefully demonstrated by Erion Veliaj, an Albanian student. In 2003, along with three former high school friends, he founded Mjaft! (which translates as "Enough!") in response to the poor state of public services in his country, as well as rising levels of corruption, poverty, and organized crime. The team used the multimedia tools available on cell phones to send text messages, images, and video to hundreds of thousands of subscribers, creating instant campaigns against corruption and injustice.

A year later, in the 2004 "Orange Revolution," text messages helped Ukrainians protest against the results of their country's presidential election, in which opposition leader Viktor Yushchenko lost, despite his 10 percent lead in the exit polls. As these movements show, wherever you are in the world and however small your financial resources are, you can participate in political and social transformation through virtual campaigns.

More recently, social media was among the forces that sparked the upheavals in the Middle East known as the 2011 Arab Spring. During the Egyptian revolution, for example, Wael Ghonim, a Google executive, helped rally pro-democracy demonstrators as the administrator of a Facebook group called "We are all Khaled Saeed" (named for a young Egyptian who died in 2010 after being arrested by Egyptian police).

The viral effect can be achieved using online tools, too. Social networking technology has opened the door to advocacy. In 2008, the Campaign for Tobacco Free Kids worked with Grassroots Enterprise (part of Edelman, the global public relations firm) to develop a campaign called: "I Am Smoke Free." Using a Facebook app, users could send letters directly to their local officials about the need to protect people from the health hazards of secondhand smoke. Users' activity was posted on the Facebook news feed (where people go to see what friends are doing on the network), and recruits were automatically added to the campaign's mailing list.

Social networking tools are free, effective ways of promoting your cause. They help you attract supporters, create groups of interest, and encourage people already interested in your cause to spread the word to their networks, help raise money for a cause, or write letters to politicians.

Ning, for example, has a discussion forum and advocacy tool for citizens fighting for a wide range of causes. Hundreds of passionate groups and individuals who want to spread their message have established a presence on the Ning network. Environmentalists—one of Ning's many social activist groups—use it to gather everyone from bicyclists wanting to reclaim the streets to citizens promoting recycling or rainwater harvesting. When you're looking for like-minded individuals to connect with, you simply conduct a search on the home page to identify advocates of all kinds.

Microblogging sites such as Twitter also provide forums for fast, compelling exchanges on the issues and causes. Through tweets, you can create buzz and excitement around your cause (or even a relevant ballot initiative or candidate supporting your cause) and also respond to feedback with individual notes or mass communications.

As you do so, the websites of think tanks, nonprofits, government agencies, and academic and research institutes can be critical sources of information about your cause. Many of these organizations conduct research and surveys and produce opinion papers and policy briefs, all of which are often freely available online and provide you with valuable, credible data with which to back up your views and make your arguments. Remember, when investigating issues and developing your own advocacy strategies, you don't need to reinvent the knowledge wheel. You can capitalize on the wealth of existing knowledge other philanthropists have funded—and most of it's free.

Of course, most institutions will have some sort of political agenda (even the nonpartisan ones) or may steer their research in a particular direction, depending on what they're trying to achieve. You'll often find papers on the subject that make opposing arguments. So it's critical to identify studies that match your beliefs and values and are addressing the same issues you want to address. Equally, it pays to learn about the arguments being made against your approach or beliefs—understanding both sides is critical to advancing your own.

If no one has conducted research on the particular issue you're focused on, and you choose to commission your own, the same principles apply—select an institution that shares your values, or an individual at that institution who does. On the other hand, you might want to fund research out of sheer intellectual curiosity and a desire to raise the level of debate on a particular subject.

Whichever form of research you commission or embark on, make sure it's available online once it's completed. After all, advocacy philanthropy is all about people coming together to share thoughts on the things they care about. While you might fund research, it need not require any financial investment—you just need passion, a social networking account, and a few moments of your time to start becoming an activist. This kind of advocacy will grow in strength as online technologies become available to everyone and smartphone apps turn mobile communication devices into tools for social reform. Given the ability to reach such vast numbers of people, anyone with good ideas, strongly held opinions, and a compelling story to tell can start to change minds. Technology is empowering the collective voice for change.

LEARNING TO THINK (AND DRESS) LIKE A PHILANTHROPIST

Back in 2000, before Linda could become an advocacy funder, she had to familiarize herself with a whole new world—a world in which dollars were in abundance. And her first lesson was not in how to write a check for a large sum of money or how to assess a grant application, but in what to wear.

 Realizing she needed support during the sharp learning curve ahead of her, she joined the Women Donors Network, an organization that has evolved from what Linda calls a "random group of wealthy progressive women" to a "dynamic national forum for women's philanthropy." Being part of WDN opened up a whole new world for Linda. "But I remember walking into that first meeting dressed in my lawyer's clothes—a conservative blue suit with a white blouse, pearls, and a scarf from UNICEF, which had pictures of the world's children on it. This in my mind-set was what a wealthy philanthropist would wear," Linda laughs. "Well, everyone looked totally different—they were just in their normal clothes, and I was *definitely* overdressed."

By November that year, when she attended WDN's national conference in Santa Cruz, Linda was no longer worrying about what to wear—she was thinking about how to pursue her goals. The meeting gave her the courage she needed. The message she took away from it was that as a philanthropist, you have capacity, clout, and connections, and those can and should be put to good use. "That's where the whole thing galvanized for me," she says. "I figured out that I was going to start a think tank."

Identifying issues to address was no problem. Education was something Linda cared deeply about. While on the Boulder Valley School

District Board of Trustees, she had been dismayed by a decision to split the neighborhood middle school and put high-performing students into a new charter school. "I was very frustrated," she explains. "There are all kinds of constituencies for the gifted and talented, the disabled, and those who speak English as a second language. But there wasn't anyone to speak for the overall good of public education and what the average student needed."

As well as addressing educational challenges, Linda wanted to help shift policy on the Taxpayer Bill of Rights, TABOR, a constitutional limit advocated by conservative and libertarian groups that severely restrains the growth of the government. Colorado's TABOR is the most restrictive tax and spending limitation in the country, severely limiting state and local spending growth and requiring that all tax increases must be approved by the voters. While some argue that government should play a smaller role in providing public services, Linda believes restrictions like TABOR have a negative effect by limiting the taxpayer revenue available to fund essential services such as public education and health care.

More broadly, Linda also believed policymakers needed better information on which to base their decisions, whether on education, democracy, social justice, equal rights, or the needs of underserved communities. "Most elected officials do a really good job with the information they have—they're honest and work hard," she says. "But they don't always have good information."

To change this, besides endowing the Brett Family Foundation (with $10 million), Linda wanted to establish a progressive think tank and policy institute that would provide Colorado's policymakers, funders, nonprofits, and other decision makers with research and analysis to help them promote effective public policies. It would be an ambitious step in her journey as a philanthropist. And all this sprang from a sudden and surprising financial windfall. An unexpected twist of fate had propelled Linda up to a level of giving on an entirely new scale.

This next step in Linda's philanthropic career was a big one. For a start, by entering the world of wealth and large-scale giving, she had to adopt a new identity. "A lot of women donors are not public," she says.

"But there was no way to do what I wanted to without being public. For fifty years my whole identity was built on being a normal person, and now I'm a wealthy person and a philanthropist," she says. "I still struggle with it."

Moreover, her plan to start a state think tank was ambitious. After all, few have done so alone—think tanks tend to be high-level institutions formed by groups of people, not individuals. Linda knew that for the think tank to be sustainable, she would need the right allies, partners, and investors to commit to the effort for the long term. Linda was about to go from life as a modest giver to engagement in one of the most complex types of philanthropy possible. Her years spent serving as an elected leader, a corporate attorney, a nonprofit board member, and a strategic giver were about to pay off.

Happily, while Linda embarked on her learning curve, she was temporarily able to remain "in the closet," as she puts it, about her new wealth. While Steve had been a senior executive at TCI, he was not sufficiently prominent to warrant mention in news coverage of AT&T's acquisition, so Linda was able to remain on the Boulder Valley School Board until her term ended without anyone knowing about the windfall. The period of anonymity gave her a few precious months in which to equip herself. She started reading all the relevant books and articles she could find. She joined the board of the Women's Foundation of Colorado. She met with the president of her local community foundation to find out what strategies they employed to make change and what kinds of advocacy other philanthropists were engaged in. She talked to anyone who would meet with her and teach her something.

Perhaps most important, she attended a lecture at the WDN conference by Jean Hardisty, author of *Mobilizing Resentment* and founder of Political Research Associates, a national think tank. Professor Hardisty's lecture demonstrated that conservatives had been winning the ideas game for so long in large part through their use of think tanks at the state level. Hardisty challenged the group, telling them that progressive philanthropists needed to catch up. "I listened to her lecture, bought the book right there and then, and grabbed her at lunch the next day after spending all night skimming her book," says Linda. "I told her I was considering taking her advice and starting a progressive think tank in my own state and asked her if she thought I could do it. She said, 'Absolutely!'"

Empowered, Linda got started, consulting with Jean Hardisty and WDN members throughout the country. In the summer of 2000, she hired someone part time to conduct research on existing think tanks and other advocacy organizations so she could determine whether Colorado really needed what she had in mind. Discovering a strong conservative infrastructure but few progressive organizations doing advocacy, she promptly began funding most of the ones whose viewpoints matched hers.

Linda's next step was hiring an off-duty state legislator to draft the think tank's strategic plan, which she used to sell the idea to those who would become her philanthropic partners and members of the nascent board of directors. Linda knew she had only a fraction of the resources to sustain a policy institute over the long term; she had to leverage her contributions by finding others who would share and extend her commitment.

In 2001, Linda and her partners launched the Bell Policy Center, a 501(c)(3) nonpartisan think tank, which she funded through the Brett Family Foundation; as well as a sister organization, the Bell Action Network, a 501(c)(4) funded with her own money. Linda recruited funders who would commit to giving long-term general operating support to both organizations. Named for the Liberty Bell, the think tank uses research and advocacy to promote policies that help Colorado individuals and families access economic opportunities. Meanwhile, to balance her long-term goals with serving immediate local needs, through the Brett Family Foundation; she continued to fund direct service organizations supporting underserved communities, particularly disadvantaged youth and their families.

Her main focus, however, was funding those in the business of changing minds through the four strategies of research, civic engagement, leadership development, and messaging. So it's no surprise that she was among the early funders to The American Independent News Network, which generates and distributes investigative stories to enhance public debate through a series of state-based online news sites. Through training programs, mentoring, and editorial support for online journalists and bloggers, the network promotes high-quality reporting that covers complex and underreported public interest issues.

In 2006, when former journalist David Bennahum founded the network and selected Colorado as one of its two first states, Linda gave it a grant of $5,000 for its first year of operation. That initial seed funding was critical. "Colorado was the first site," explains David, now president and chief executive. "And because it went well in the first few months, it became our calling card." Linda's investment also served as a signal to other potential funders about the organization's value and credibility. Because of its success in Colorado, the network has grown rapidly and now harnesses the energies of twenty-five reporters across the country, with websites in a number of states as well as an award-winning national site.

As newsrooms across America have shrunk and newspapers have gone out of business, the network helps fill the void. More important, in his mission to foster journalism that creates change, David talks about what he calls "impact journalism." To track these kinds of successes, the network has a rigorous process of reporting and feedback on its news stories and features. As well as an annual report, it produces regular email updates and quarterly and annual reports detailing whether or not recent stories have resulted in action being taken to curb an injustice or address a societal need. "The news media is a key driver of debate in any democracy," says David. "And we want to see consequences from our reporting."

Such words come as music to the ears of Linda Shoemaker, who also sees the media as a vital force in any democracy. And the potential for the American Independent News Network to enhance public debate makes it a good example of the kind of organization you can support as an advocacy funder. While you're not the activist, through the organizations you choose to fund and the leadership you help to foster, you're playing a critical role in changing minds—both of fellow givers and the broader public.

MEASUREMENT, COOPERATION, AND COLLABORATION

Although The American Independent News Network can track some of its impact, measuring the consequences of advocacy funding can be tough. Advocacy and policy work requires a lot more energy and investment than, say, writing a check to a relief organization, which might be able to give you immediate feedback on exactly how many hungry, homeless, sick, or injured individuals your dollars have helped. It also requires investment in evaluation so you can track your progress over long periods of time, noting which sorts of policy or advocacy efforts resulted in what kinds of social changes for larger populations—enabling you to help bring about a fundamental shift in the trajectory of an issue that's causing widespread suffering.

What's more, policy change can take years to effect and involves a multitude of constituents, from politicians, donors, businesses, and civil society organizations to the media and voters. Even when policy changes materialize, it's tricky to tease out exactly how much they were due to a philanthropist's actions and funding and how much resulted from political and other pressures. And some advocacy funders have been reluctant to submit their activities to measurement in the belief that evaluating impact by narrow measures, such as legislation passed by a certain date or number of op-eds published, might limit broader advocacy activities, such as building talent or raising public awareness of an issue.

However, a new wave of accountability is sweeping through the philanthropic world. These days, donors and boards want to know their money is being spent wisely and not disappearing into a black hole. It's all part of the new era of giving. Return on investment and performance management are no longer concepts reserved for the corporate sector. As philanthropists today, we all have to track and assess the impact we're making.

And when it comes to advocacy philanthropy, as research reports from Blueprint Research & Design and the Annie E. Casey Foundation highlight, more effective ways do exist to assess whether or not advocacy efforts are making a difference.[1] As an advocacy philanthropist, you can use a number of strategies to do this.

Start by defining what you mean by *policy* or *social change*. (Is it limited to the passing of legislation or can a shifting political landscape and rising awareness of an issue be counted?) It's also useful to define categories of outcome, such as media coverage, increased public awareness, rising voter registration, strengthened alliances, improved organizational capacity, and the passing of legislation. Then establish the role each category plays in achieving your broader long-term goal, whether that's banning smoking in public places or eradicating homelessness.

Other processes include setting timelines or milestones with which to monitor your progress (whether that's actual policy change or improvements in the policy environment), and measuring the effectiveness with which you're reaching those milestones. You also need to be flexible—external changes beyond your control may mean you'll need to set new milestones and let go of others. You may need to adapt your strategy to meet new political realities, shifts in the balance of power, or social developments. And evaluation of your effectiveness helps you understand what's working and what's not.

You may also help win others to your cause; the challenges of measuring impact have often deterred donors from funding advocacy. So by devising a robust form of assessment that demonstrates the difference you're making, you could also help increase the pool of funding available for this form of social change, benefiting causes beyond your own.

As well as bringing in new funders, an advocacy philanthropist needs to be good at working with others. Legal limits on lobbying within a nonprofit context mean you may want to partner with all kinds of entities, including grassroots organizing cooperatives, unions, regulators, political groups, and for-profits. "Encourage cooperation," says Linda. "Think comprehensively, and fund a constellation of different groups that are able to work in partnership with others in order to achieve public policy goals." Some philanthropists even provide extra funding to require their grantees to meet as a cohort and share ideas and strategies—and personal connections can often greatly increase both tangible and intangible impact.

Linda's foundation, for example, funds a nonprofit called The White House Project, a national organization that trains anyone running for public office (with a focus on women). Because The White House Project is a 501(c)(3), and so unable to support its trainees after they assume public office, the organization works closely with the Center for Progressive Leadership, a 501(c)(4) that provides political leadership development programs nationally.

Aside from legal considerations, advocacy is about convincing policymakers that the issue you're concerned about affects everyone, so you need to ensure everyone is at the table, and that all voices are heard.

You also need to be prepared to take a hands-off approach. While in other areas of philanthropy, you might play a direct role—volunteering as a hospice worker or funding the education of an Afghan girl—as an advocacy philanthropist, you are one step removed from the process. "As a funder you are just a facilitator," says Linda. "You have to have respect for the organizations you fund—you have to learn from them. You can't dictate to them; you need to understand the clientele they serve and the strategies they choose to employ."

This is something Linda has had to learn. "I'm very autocratic by nature and like to run the show," she says. "And I've learned that I can't dictate, but that I have to work in partnership with others. I also need to give credit to others."

Above all, your mission as an advocacy philanthropist is not to serve the needy or fight injustice but to help create a world where those services are no longer needed and the injustices no longer take place. And while our egos might tell us that the philanthropic world—at least our corner of it—will collapse without us, in fact, we will have achieved real change when we cease to be the most vital cog in its wheels.

LOOKING THROUGH A LONGER LENS

Perhaps the most challenging part of being a philanthropist is the fact that you'll have to turn down worthy applicants for funding. "What I like the least about my form of philanthropy is saying no," says Linda, "particularly saying no to immediate needs, because with my strategy, I'm sacrificing the immediate needs." For Linda, supporting long-term policy change has meant watching as multimillion-dollar funding short-falls have forced her local schools to cut staff and programs. "I care passionately about education," she says. "But I'm not going to give the schools any money. I'm giving my money to try to change the long-term fiscal landscape in Colorado. That's really hard because people I know are coming to me to ask for funding, and it's very difficult to say no."

However, as Linda points out, you can support nonprofits whose funding requests you have turned down in other ways. You might suggest other resources they might tap. You could even facilitate that effort with introductions to foundation and nonprofit leaders in your network.

To satisfy your need to see immediate results, you can establish some direct giving programs in addition to your advocacy funding. This also allows you to engage in activities that might not be legally permissible through your private foundation. Linda, for example, set up a donor-advised fund at Boulder's Community Foundation, which, because it is a public foundation, can fund certain kinds of advocacy (such as ballot issue campaigns and voter registration drives) that would be impossible for the Brett Family Foundation, which is a private institution. As an individual donor, you can use various legal vehicles to achieve your goals.

And while what defines Linda's giving is advocacy, her portfolio of philanthropic activities is broad. Besides maintaining her donor-advised fund, she continues to volunteer, sitting on the boards of a variety of organizations. She was past president of Boulder Professional Women, which promotes participation, equity, and economic self-sufficiency for working women. A program run by the I Have A Dream Foundation of Boulder County allows Linda and Steve to sponsor forty at-risk students in north Boulder (they're known as the Broadway Dreamers), helping give them tutoring, mentoring, and academic assistance.

Moreover, as with the best philanthropists, Linda never stands still. Her advocacy mission continues to evolve, and she's now building on her roots as a journalist, fueled by a concern for the future of the media and what she sees as its critical role—democracy. "My first ten years was devoted to think tanks," she explains. "In my second ten years, I'm going to be looking at the media sector."

Linda's brand of philanthropy involves immersion and intensity. For the think tank decade, that meant serving as the founding board chair of the Bell Policy Center, helping WDN choose a national think tank for a $1 million grant, and serving on the national advisory board for progressive state-level think tanks, the Economic Analysis and Research Network. For the media decade, she's started by serving on the Advisory Board of the Journalism School at the University of Colorado, which is in the process of reinventing its journalism program for the digital age.

Her ten-year plan is typical of an advocacy funder. Linda stresses the importance of taking a long-term view: "I once expected quick results. I thought social change would happen more quickly," she says. "I'm naturally very impatient and I love to see things happen, but the thing I've learned is that you have to be very patient."

Patience, persistence, and hard work pay off. Through the Bell Policy Center, for example, Linda helped convince voters to ease TABOR's spending limits. After the Bell built a coalition of individuals and organizations keen to modify the legislation, reform moved to the legislature in 2005, with Bell continuing to provide research, analyze options, and support political leaders in their efforts to shape a "Time Out from TABOR" compromise, known as Referendum C. Voters passed this in November that year, preserving vital funding for K–12 education, higher education, and indigent health care for the subsequent five fiscal years. This is the kind of victory for which, as an advocacy philanthropist, you strive. While you cannot shake the hand of a child you've directly helped to educate, your activities may mean more children receive an education.

"The hard truth about Colorado and TABOR," says Linda, "is that it's a continuing battle and a continuing focus for Bell Policy, which has spent ten years doing research, writing reports, building coalitions, and talking to thousands of groups of citizens throughout the state about the continuing need for systemic fiscal reform."

Even if, like many of us, you would be daunted by the prospect of taking on philanthropic commitments with the complexity of Linda

Shoemaker's giving strategy, in other ways, you can still be part of this movement. Whether funding other organizations or starting an online campaign, advocacy philanthropy requires commitment, courage, and depth of knowledge about an issue. You need to pay attention to changes in the world that might demand a re-think of your funding. And you need to be persistent when a new issue distracts attention from your cause. You'll face controversial choices, conflicts, and frustrations.

Advocacy allows you to play a vital role in the evolution of a just and equitable society. Your efforts and investments can help shape decisions that affect millions—and often those people are in communities that would otherwise have no voice. "It's the whole idea of the people's lobby," says Linda. "It's a lobby for opportunity."

MAKING IT HAPPEN

What to Ask Yourself When Considering Advocacy Philanthropy:
- Are you prepared to fight for long-term change, even if in the short term, the tangible results of your funding are hard to identify?
- Are you prepared to face the controversial publicity that may arise when you take a stand on your cause or issue?
- Are you prepared to accept personal enmity on the part of those who oppose your views?
- Do you have sufficient knowledge of an issue to engage directly in advocacy? Or should you fund organizations with an existing infrastructure that espouse policy change as their formal mission?
- Do you want to fund advocacy or give your time and energy by embarking on a community organizing effort?
- Do you need to set up a 501(c)(3) or 501(c)(4) to fulfill your advocacy goals?

What to Ask Advocacy Organizations You'd Like to Fund:
- What is the history of the organization?
- What policy gains or other significant accomplishments has it achieved in recent years?
- How, if at all, has the leadership of the organization changed over its lifetime?

- What is the organization's social change agenda and what are the issues it aims to address?
- What strategies does the organization use (for example, voter engagement, coalition work, policy development and advocacy, public education, social media campaigns, or direct action)?
- Which communities does the organization regard as its constituency, and how does it engage them?
- What is the size of the organization's constituency, and does it plan to expand it?
- What infrastructure needs to be in place to achieve lasting policy change, and how much of this infrastructure does the organization provide?
- What are the areas in which the organization needs most improvement, and how is it working to address those?
- What major programmatic goals does the organization hope to achieve over the next three years?
- What organizational capacities will it need to develop to achieve these goals (for example, a social networking site, a volunteer team, marketing strategy and materials, or media training)?
- How does the organization measure and report on its impact?

Innovation Lab—Ideas to Test:
- Ask a nonprofit you support which policy issues are likely to impact its mission (such as a potential change to tax deductions, a change in political leadership, or a ballot measure)? If the organization does not know, ask it to find out.
- Step up your engagement as a local citizen by working to raise awareness about a policy that may impact you and your community. Perhaps ask friends or colleagues to join you in that effort.
- Identify a group of people who need a stronger voice and find out how you could help give them that voice (by, for example, creating a dedicated social network focusing on the issues they face, helping them write letters to local officials or politicians, or organizing a meeting to bring them together with others who might be able to support them).
- Spend an hour on the website of a think tank researching social issues that interest you.
- Consider supporting a national organization so that you can play a role in bigger policy issues.

- Instead of funding your alma mater's annual fund, direct your support to the research of an individual professor.

Where to Go for Research:

- Research organizations are known as being conservative, progressive, or nonpartisan. Please visit www.giving2.com for a selection of well-respected organizations.

Nuts and Bolts—Channels to Influence and Actions to Take:

- Goal—Policy Change:
  - Channels to influence include state and national think tanks, political groups, academic institutions, and the media.
  - Actions to take include political lobbying in Washington, D.C., helping to shape national media coverage, providing strategic market packaging of ideas in order to influence public opinion, and giving the media information and resources that will inform how they report on issues.
- Goal—Passing a Ballot Initiative:
  - Channels to influence include local and state think tanks, political groups, academic institutions, and the local media.
  - Actions to take include political lobbying at state government level, funding research studies around the public and economic benefits of your initiative, helping to shape local media coverage, and providing humanizing elements to your agenda—such as finding the right faces and stories for the media to profile.
- Goal—Increased Issue Awareness:
  - Channels to influence include grassroots organizations and the local media.
  - Actions to take include local activism, producing reports or white papers (through respected academics or research centers), starting a campaign on sites such as Twitter, Facebook, Jumo, or Ning, and helping to shape local media coverage.
- Goal—Increased Research:
  - Channels to influence include scholars, graduate students, the media, and college newspapers.
  - Actions to take include motivating leadership in scholarship; providing funding for academics to frame historical events or political agendas in new ways; presenting issues from new perspectives; completing

research initiatives; training the next generation of thought leaders; and helping create momentum around policy issues by supporting academic publications. Any of these actions could eventually influence policymakers—especially if promoted through credible channels.

For the Family:

- Bring your children to a town hall meeting or do a tour of the city or state capital.
- Explain the concept of lobbying and how a bill becomes a law, and how elected officials represent certain viewpoints.
- If your children attend public school, discuss with them how they think the school system can be improved and how to bring about these changes.
- Create a campaign on a social networking site for a cause that the whole family cares about and spend an evening a week updating the site, adding news items, and connecting with new members.

And Remember:

- Build a coalition of committed funders who will make multiyear general operating grants to one or more organizations advocating for the social changes you seek—this is especially important when you want to help change government policy.
- Be sure the people and groups you fund are hiring excellent communicators so that they can get their message out as effectively as possible, whether through pamphlets, TV ads, social networking sites, or print media.
- Policy change is impossible to do alone, so encourage cooperation and fund a range of groups that can work in partnership to achieve public policy goals (this also provides an excellent opportunity to give your network to an issue).
- Fund groups using any of the four basic tactics to achieve change—leadership development, civic engagement, media and messaging, and idea generation.
- Engage national groups that have the expertise to help state efforts.
- Since tax law limits charitable 501(c)(3) organizations from doing certain kinds of advocacy, think comprehensively and partner with other kinds of legal entities such as for-profits and 501(c)(4)s.

- Because the political landscape can change at any time, make any benchmarks you expect grantees to meet flexible and achievable.

- Recognize that the best nonprofits doing advocacy are those that have agility built into their structures so they can change strategies when needed. Make sure your own goals are flexible, as well.

- As an advocacy philanthropist, you may sacrifice some privacy and receive more media attention than other philanthropists—the stakes are higher when a voting public is involved and when social good is based on a specific set of beliefs and values.

- Family and friends may disagree with what you're doing as well as with your beliefs and goals.

- Be ready for battle. You never know who will come out in opposition to what you're trying to accomplish and the lengths to which they will go to prevent you from meeting your goals.

- Be patient. Changing hearts and minds, along with public policy, does not happen quickly—but, with time, commitment, and persistence, this kind of giving has the potential to make big and lasting changes to society.

8

FAMILY MATTERS
Gifts That Keep on Giving

Lead by example—the apple falls not far from the giving tree.

Across the Quimby Family Foundation's website floats a series of images of Maine, the place the Quimby family calls home. That diverse landscape, featuring magnificent mountains, undulating sand dunes, and ancient oak trees, is one the family has been intimately connected with since the early 1970s when Roxanne Quimby—the natural products entrepreneur who founded the Burt's Bees natural skin and body products line—bought a small piece of land near the state's center. There, she and her then future husband built a cabin and embraced a life of extreme austerity, living off the land and bringing up two children without electricity or central heating, just lanterns and wood stoves. "It's very undeveloped and incredibly rural," says Hannah, Roxanne's daughter and the woman behind the atmospheric photographs of Maine on the website. "The town I grew up in had just four hundred people. Around it, it's still a really pristine environment."

The family has been devoting its philanthropic resources to preserving that land since 2004 when Roxanne Quimby established a family foundation to protect the landscape she loved so much. The foundation primarily supports nonprofits working to protect wildlife and wilderness areas, but its grantmaking extends beyond the environment to include promoting access to the arts within Maine. It also encourages people to use the landscape for education and recreation—organizations such as the Appalachian Trail Museum Society, which is creating a graphics-based traveling exhibition looking at the subculture of long-distance hiking; or Kennebec Messalonskee Trails, which is helping construct trail surfaces, signage, and a kiosk on an Oakland trail.

Like the Victorians who planted trees that would mature far beyond their own lifetimes, Roxanne established the foundation to help preserve a part of her planet for future generations. But in doing so, she's also creating a legacy of giving. For while the Quimby Family Foundation was Roxanne's creation, it is her children, Hannah Quimby and Lucas St. Clair, who steward her philanthropic legacy now.

For Hannah, the decision to join the family foundation's board of directors came while a board member was on maternity leave. Hannah, then aged twenty-five, was helping out with administration. "One day, I was answering some emails and I realized that this was something I'd love to be part of," she explains. "Because the focus with environmental nonprofits is in Maine, where I was born and raised, and because I have a real love for that landscape and the conservation work that's being done there, it was really appealing."

However, for Hannah, being involved in the family foundation has another appeal. "A piece of it is working with my family," she says. "It's the best thing my mom could be doing for us—having us all work together as a family on a fantastic mission in a place that we all collectively care about. That has so much more meaning than anything else she could have chosen to do." Hannah hopes this process will continue. "I have younger cousins," she says. "And I think they'll become involved. Keeping it going through the generations is really important."

The gifts made by these organizations are extremely rewarding, as Hannah Quimby explains. "I love seeing what the organizations we fund (and some are pretty local) are able to do with a relatively small amount of funding," she says. "It feels great to be a part of that and to see how much can be achieved."

PURPOSE AND PROCESS

When thinking about setting up a family foundation, you first need to assess the amount you have to invest in the foundation. Some philanthropy experts say you shouldn't create a private foundation unless you have at least $10 million in assets. And certainly, given the setup costs, which can be $10,000 to $15,000, starting such an institution is not for those with more modest means. However, many individuals create foundations with an endowment that's relatively small and then build it up over time.

Actually, of the more than seventy thousand philanthropic foundations registered in the United States, more than half are family foundations giving small amounts of money.[1] And one-third of these family foundations were established between 2000 and 2009 (perhaps yours is among them).[2] While prominent institutions tend to make the headlines, about 64 percent of family foundations reported having less than $1 million in assets (and so gave away $50,000 or less per year) in 2009, and of those less, than 10 percent have paid staff.[3] They are essentially formal vehicles for the same type of individual giving that most of us practice each year. Regardless of size or staffing, family foundations like the Quimbys', and perhaps your own, form a powerful—and ever-growing— engine in American philanthropy.

And, as you can see, not having professional staff is the norm— probably because of how deeply personal giving is for us all. Certainly that's the case for my family's foundation, as well as the current plan for the foundation Marc and I are creating. Yet I take that responsibility just as seriously as any paid job I've had (our foundations do not pay family members for board or staff service).

Once you've established what funds you'll use for the foundation, you'll need three more essentials—plenty of tax and legal advice, IRS Form 1023 (through which you apply for tax-exempt status), and a mission. While the first two cover technical matters that involve relatively little choice, developing your mission is a task that requires serious thought on your part.

Your mission will guide your giving philosophy, govern the causes you want to support, and inform your grantmaking strategy. According to the National Center for Charitable Statistics, there are estimated to be more than 1.6 million nonprofits in America alone, so developing a philosophy to shape your funding decisions is critical. Being focused will help you get more satisfaction from your grantmaking. Creating a set of specific guidelines relating to your overall mission—and adhering to your grantmaking policies—also makes it easier to make decisions and to explain why an organization will not receive funding (which saves time, paper, and money for all concerned).

Once you've established your mission and giving principles, think about what kinds of activities your foundation will undertake. With a family foundation, making grants is only part of what you can do to advance your mission. Other activities include hosting meetings and convening leaders in your issue area, commissioning research (or doing it yourself), using your website to share knowledge with other givers, and creating tools to help nonprofits become more effective. You can even launch prizes to encourage and reward excellence and innovation in the nonprofit sector. Think carefully about how you could make the biggest impact on the problems you want to help solve and consider the scale and specificity of those problems against the scale of your financial resources.

Similarly, when it comes to your funding, do some planning before rushing into grantmaking. The advantage of having a private foundation is that while you gain the tax benefits of donating your funds immediately, you don't have to distribute them immediately (although the foundation must make minimum distribution for charitable purposes beginning in the second year after its inception).

Consider what types of organizations you want to fund—their size, location, and organizational structure, and the types of grants you'll make (such as operating costs, capital for infrastructure, staff and leadership training, or research), as well as the tax implications of your foundation's giving.

Say you want to fight cancer. You could help cover the operating costs of a nonprofit working to make the lives of the terminally ill more comfortable and rewarding. You could support a nonprofit providing treatment or post-treatment psychological care for patients and their families. You could fund organizations working in your area or support a larger, national organization researching treatments or cures. You could even fund awareness campaigns or advocate for more government research funding.

A great way to get a sense of what organizations you might fund is to meet leaders from several types of nonprofits working on your issue (tell them in advance the purpose of your visit so you don't set up expectations that you're considering funding them). These leaders will provide valuable perspectives on both your cause and the philanthropic ecosystem addressing it. What they say can be instrumental in helping you construct a great mission and approach—perhaps even one you've never considered before.

For this reason, don't set your mission or focus in stone. You can redraft both as social needs or personal priorities change. As you continue to meet nonprofit leaders and do your own research, your ideas may change as you learn more about needs and how best to meet them. Like so much philanthropy, treat the development of your mission and focus as a journey. These will evolve alongside your strategy, structure, and grantmaking practices as you gain knowledge and experience.

Once you've developed your funding focus, as well as your policies and procedures, consider what information about your foundation you'll make accessible to potential grantees. The easiest way to do this is to set up a website. It could be extensive, carrying details of all your grantmaking and charitable activities, a history of the foundation, and profiles of some of the projects or individuals you've funded. It could include videos, such as clips of you explaining why you're passionate about your mission, educational material about the issue you're funding, or success stories from grantees. However, even if it's a simple noninteractive single page, include all the information necessary for potential grantees to put in a funding request, plus a downloadable application form containing a basic set of questions for applicants. (See "Before You Write the Check" and "What to Ask the Nonprofits You Want to Fund" in Chapter Three for some ideas.)

Hannah Quimby says that establishing the Quimby Family Foundation website has made life much easier. "In the first couple of years we'd get full applications from everyone and they'd come into the post office box," she explains. "We were having to make eight copies of them to send to board members. Having it all paperless has simplified things tremendously." In 2011, the foundation used a system similar to a blog, which allowed the board members to view proposals online, comment on them, ask questions of one another, and vote on them. "Board members can share opinions in the forum before we make final funding decisions," Hannah explains.

With family foundations, as with all forms of philanthropy, you have an opportunity to innovate. While the family foundation is a long-established form of philanthropy, that doesn't mean you can't find new ways to refine and enhance the model, as the Quimbys did by using the Web to connect board members so that they can collaborate more efficiently.

Of course, while online social networks could prove an effective internal working tool, you may not necessarily want to establish a public website for your foundation. You might want to preserve your anonymity, for example. You might also want to keep your funding options open. The Arrillaga Foundation, my family's foundation, chose not to have a website, as we do not solicit grant proposals or accept unsolicited ones, and we work to keep our operational costs to a minimum.

As I write, Marc and I are also in the midst of creating our own family foundation, the Marc and Laura Andreessen Foundation. As part of our plans for our first few years, we'll create a website for our foundation, so that our grantmaking programs, past and current grants, reporting, and knowledge sharing can be done paperlessly. Since I've worked in the sector for so long, Marc and I are developing specific strategies for our grantmaking as opposed to taking a more reactive approach. We want to dive deeply into a few select issues and make the most of the knowledge we'll build in those areas. As a result, we've decided not to accept unsolicited grant proposals, and to base our grantmaking decisions on our own research. However, as our foundation grows and evolves over time, we may change our policies.

Some of the foundations that do call for specific grant applications (or consider all submitted) review proposals only a few times annually, and have submission deadlines for those grant cycles. Others let organizations apply year-round. I recommend reviewing submissions in batches at least three times a year, so you can allocate your dollars using a cohesive strategy, and you do not make nonprofits who might need funding urgently wait as long as a year to hear from you.

Once you've received letters of intent or proposals, the selection process begins. As with individual giving, conducting due diligence on any organization you're considering funding is critical (don't wait until you're funding an organization before assessing its performance). Base your level of scrutiny on the size of your gift (relative to your budget and that of the nonprofit), its focus, and the time period over which the gift will be made (many gifts are one-time only, particularly during economically unstable times. However, a lot of foundations also make multiyear grants).

If you're running an unstaffed family foundation, you might feel equipped to do this yourself or with your spouse, family member, or partner. If they have the skills and interest, your children could participate in the process. You could also establish a grants committee (which may include experts in your focus areas who are not board members) to make decisions based on your foundation's guidelines. Some foundations conduct due diligence even before inviting nonprofits to submit proposals, while others do so as part of the proposal review process.

You might make a decision based solely on the information contained in the grant proposal, or do more thorough research and make visits to potential grantees to meet staff and the people they serve. However, site visits are not a good idea unless you're strongly considering funding an organization. Site visits take up an immense amount of time and effort for nonprofit executives, and these visits can raise hopes for a grant they might not end up receiving.

Most important, as noted in Chapter Three, listen to what nonprofits have to say about their needs. Ask these leaders what type of funding would be most valuable to them. If your foundation has a strong partnership culture, this will extend to relationships with all your grantees. The more trust you build, the more likely it is grantees will be honest with you about challenges they face, helping you play a bigger role in turning those challenges into successes. Remember, we're only successful as givers when our grantees succeed—they are the ones who transform our dollars into social change.

FILLING BIG BOOTS

John Goldman spent a lot of time thinking about how to instill philanthropic values in the next generation, as did his family before him. As a descendant of Levi Strauss, who founded the clothing company of that name and established a philanthropic family that's been in San Francisco since the Gold Rush, he has large boots to fill. John's grandparents established the Walter and Elise Haas Fund. His mother, Rhoda Haas Goldman, was a revered civic leader and philanthropist devoted to cultural, health, and environmental causes who (with her husband, Richard Goldman) established the Goldman Environmental Prize, which honors grassroots environmentalists. Giving, John likes to say, is in his DNA.

When John married Marcia, it gave him a chance to see his family's culture of giving from a new perspective. "She was a bit overwhelmed by all of our philanthropic activities at first and talked to my mom extensively when she was still alive," he says. "My mom told us that you don't have to be ashamed for having wealth. You should enjoy life, but in equal measure, you must give back to the community." John's mother also told her children and Marcia that giving back to the community was like breathing. John adds: "It's a natural response. It's something that we do, or should do, as part of our lives."

However, while John recognizes the benefits of inheriting this culture of giving, he admits that it also brings with it certain pressures. "The expectations are much higher," he says. "And there's that lingering question—can I possibly come close to achieving even half of what was accomplished by my parents and others?"

Among John's many civic and philanthropic activities, he and Marcia set up a family foundation to help disadvantaged and at-risk youth; he served as a third-generation president of the Jewish Community Foundation in San Francisco; and in 2001 he was named president of the San Francisco Symphony. In 2003, he and Marcia established the South Peninsula Jewish Community Teen Foundation as part of the Jewish Community Federation's Imprint Endowment Fund. The program helps Jewish teenagers in the Bay Area develop philanthropic values and learn how to run a charitable foundation or fund. Skill-building seminars help these teens develop leadership capabilities, learn fundraising skills, become effective grantmakers, and understand some of the tough choices that emerge when addressing social justice issues. It also teaches them that philanthropy is about much more than giving away money.

In its initial five years, the initiative—which expanded to four chapters—distributed more than $450,000 (about 75 percent of which the students raised themselves). However, the initiative has also had a profound influence on many of the teens. Rachel Levenson, one of the participants in the South Peninsula chapter, raised $5,000 to start her own education fund and, while applying to colleges, sought to create her own major, combining business, philanthropy, and international affairs. "Philanthropy has really opened my eyes to the issues of the world and the impact we as teens can make," she says. "I just can't sit by and not do something."

However, John believes young people learn from example as much as from formal programs or training initiatives. It's something his family taught him. Discussions around the dinner table usually centered on what was happening to the charitable organizations his parents and grandparents gave their time and resources to. "They talked about people, and the things they were involved in," he says. "So by osmosis we picked up on that."

However, John says that you can only go so far. It's not possible, he argues, to force philanthropy down the throats of your children. However, you can set an example by the choices you make and the actions you take. "There are shades of encouragement, I guess," he says. "We tried to set an example the way we conducted our lives and let our kids know by the things we did what was important to us. They either accepted it or they didn't. There wasn't some master plan."

As it turns out, John and Marcia's children—a son and a daughter, both young adults—are extremely engaged givers, albeit focusing on different kinds of activities from their parents. Both have their own philanthropic funds, but also believe in taking action, too. Around her birthday, for example, their daughter Jessica gathers a group of friends and together they go to bag groceries at Project Open Hand, a nonprofit that helps support people living with serious illnesses and seniors in San

Francisco and Alameda County. Jessica makes this part of her birthday celebration.

"All I can do is smile," says John. "Our kids' value system is fabulous." But, he adds, they learned this value system as he did, by listening and watching rather than by rote. "Marcia and I tried to emulate what my parents did, which was to show our kids by example and by the way we engaged that this is part of their lives too. Because if you want your kids to be good community citizens, it starts with you."

A RICH HERITAGE

You don't have to come from a wealthy background to inherit philanthropic values and instill them in the next generation. Carmen Castellano, born in 1939 in Watsonville, California, says that when she was growing up, "we were poor but we didn't know it." Her father ran a small trucking business and taught his children the habit of giving. "He was one of these people who would bring strangers to the house when they had no food or clothes," she says. "He had such a soft heart, he couldn't resist doing what he could to help them." Another part of her family heritage was music. As children, three of her four sisters played the piano while her brother played the trumpet. "My mother was in love with the arts and music," explains Carmen. "She bought a piano and taught herself to play by ear. So music was an important part of our upbringing."

These two family traditions—love of the arts and a propensity to give—are what Carmen and her husband, Alcario, continue through the Castellano Family Foundation. Even before setting up the foundation, Carmen was an active philanthropist of time and talent. After she married Al and they had children, the couple sat on various boards. They became involved in the American GI Forum, the largest federally chartered Hispanic veterans organization in the United States, which has a chapter in San Jose, where the Castellanos have lived for more than forty years.

Al served for two years in the U.S. Army (primarily in the San Francisco Bay Area) after graduating from high school, then worked in the aerospace industry in the area until 1970. He then became a retail clerk at a supermarket, where he worked until retiring in 1990. Al has a passion for video and photography, and records many GI Forum activities and events, as well as local community parades, music and dance performances, and youth events. He also serves on the board of directors of Latinas Contra Cancer.

In 2001, however, the family's giving underwent a significant transformation following a momentous event: Al won the California state lottery, with a record single-ticket-holder amount of $141 million. Al found out on a Sunday, but he and Carmen didn't turn in the ticket until the Thursday of the following week. Instead, they opened a safety deposit box for the ticket ("We'd never had one before," says Carmen), called all the children, gathered them together, with the grandchildren, sat down with them for several days to work out what to do.

Carmen and Al had already had some idea of what the philanthropic portion of their winnings should fund. "When we first found out we'd won, it was 6:30 a.m., and it was too early to call the children," explains Carmen. "So we sat in the living room pondering what this meant. And one of the first things I did was to make a list of the organizations we'd give to. Because I knew that this would be part of what we'd end up doing."

Later that day, the collective family decision making began. One of their first decisions was how public to be about the winnings. The family decided that the names of Al and Carmen's children and grandchildren would not be made public, and that Al and Carmen would be the ones to step into the spotlight. Then they hired an attorney, an accountant, and a public relations person. "We held our own press conference," says Carmen. "Because we wanted to make sure we crafted the message."

A week later, Carmen and Al called another family meeting. This one was held specifically to discuss their plans to establish the foundation and develop a mission statement. "We told the children that this is what we were going to do, and that our focus would be on the arts and supporting Latino organizations here in Santa Clara Valley," says Carmen.

They also decided to run the foundation without staff (although Carmen now has a part-time assistant). "We decided not to go in that direction because I'm an administrative secretary," explains Carmen, who after working for five years at Cabrillo College, a community college in Aptos, spent thirty-three years as an administrative secretary and office manager at San Jose City College. "I know how to write letters and financial reports and how to manage budgets and talk to people. So we realized I had all the skills it took to do it ourselves." For Al and Carmen, running the foundation themselves also helps them keep their funding focus crystal clear. "We can now read a request for funding, say yes or no, and decide on how much to give in unison," she says. "So it works really well to be clear."

Today, the foundation is dedicated to fostering Latino family values and promoting the arts and Latino culture, leadership, and education. Some of its grants are challenge grants to encourage nonprofits to seek alternative sources of funding. "It's important for organizations to build up an individual donor base," says Carmen. "Sometimes nonprofits rely too much on foundations." The foundation has so far awarded grants to more than a hundred organizations totaling more than $2.5 million dollars.

From the outset, Carmen and Al had in mind creating a legacy to pass on to future generations. So at those early family meetings, they asked the children if they'd be willing, at some stage, to take on that responsibility. The children agreed. For Al and Carmen, this will be the next stage in the journey. For although their children attend events with them, they are not currently playing an active role and do not sit on the foundation's board. "But our plan is that it will become their foundation and that of the generations to come," says Carmen. "So we're now working to develop a transition plan."

Reflecting on those first days after winning, Carmen stresses the importance of having the whole family present. "It worked so well," she says. "The collective thought processes really helped us in making the right decisions."

YOU'RE NOT ALONE

When starting a family foundation, the complexities of establishing a board, organizational structure, mission statement, and grantmaking focus can seem a little daunting, to say the least. But remember, as is so often the case in philanthropy, you are not alone. Other foundations, advisory firms, and philanthropic organizations can counsel you as you develop and execute your family foundation's mission.

For the Quimbys, for example, philanthropy conferences held by Goldman Sachs have proved both helpful and empowering, enabling them not only to learn but also to meet other philanthropists. Rockefeller Philanthropy Advisors was also instrumental in helping the Quimby Family Foundation establish its purpose. "We stumbled along a bit at first," Hannah says. "And then we met with someone from Rockefeller Philanthropy Advisors, which was incredibly helpful. The person we met helped us shape the mission, the vision, and the values for the foundation."

Rockefeller Philanthropy Advisors, a nonprofit that helps individual donors develop, manage, and monitor their philanthropy, and Arabella Philanthropic Investment Advisors, which has a similar mission, are among a growing number of philanthropy consultants (often calling themselves "advisors") emerging in the sector today. Some of these organizations operate from within the wealth management departments of private banks. Some act as independent consultants, such as Tactical Philanthropy Advisors, whose clients include individuals and families who give between $50,000 and $3 million a year to charity.

Others, such as FSG Impact Consultants and Blueprint Research & Design (which was acquired by Arabella Philanthropic Investment Advisors in May 2011), cater to foundations, nonprofits, corporations, and governments, offering consultancy services as well as research resources. Another consultant to the sector is the Bridgespan Group—a nonprofit founded by global management consultancy Bain & Company—which helps philanthropic leaders enhance the effectiveness of their strategies. Bridgespan has a recruitment arm called Bridgestar, which offers nonprofit clients a jobs board and advice on building successful management teams.

These firms can help you bring about social transformation on a significant scale. However, their services are not free (they may charge a fee per project or take as their fee a percentage of the philanthropic assets that they will manage for you), so you need to decide whether or not this is the way you want to spend some of your philanthropic resources. For myself, since philanthropy is my career and my giving is so deeply personal, I prefer to learn while doing and drive my own philanthropy.

At the same time, membership organizations such as the Council on Foundations, the Association of Small Foundations, the National Center for Family Philanthropy, and the Philanthropy Roundtable offer family philanthropists rich seams of information on their websites, as well as workshops, conferences, and research papers. Often these organizations offer paying members a range of private educational opportunities. Joining the Association of Small Foundations certainly helped Carmen and Al, providing them with guidance and a valuable donor network.

While chairman of the Philanthropy Roundtable, Dan Peters, whose family foundation (the Lovett and Ruth Peters Foundation, founded by his parents) is dedicated to reforming and improving K–12 education, saw just how hungry family philanthropists were for support and advice. A meeting in Houston that was part of the Philanthropy Roundtable's first K–12 education program attracted more than a hundred attendees.

As part of the program—which went on to become the Roundtable's most popular, attracting interest among educational reformers around the United States—education experts and philanthropists spoke to the group. One was the late Don Fisher, the Gap co-founder (with his wife Doris) and co-founder of the KIPP network (a national network of free, open enrollment college-preparatory public schools that help students from low-income communities succeed in college), and a visit was organized to a local KIPP school. (Don's son John Fisher continues his parents' remarkable philanthropic legacy with his own wife, Laura, and John is now the board chairman of KIPP.) "That's a wonderful way for someone who's new to the K–12 education business to get a perspective," says Dan. "And there are lots of donor groups or fellow funders that one can learn from."

Of course, sometimes you simply need to call in the professionals to help you to get things going. After Carmen and Al won the lottery, they moved extremely fast to establish their family's philanthropy. "We were really anxious to give this money away—we won the lottery in June, and by December we had the foundation set up," explains Carmen. And just how did they manage to do this so quickly? "We had a *great* attorney," she says.

LEAVING YOUR MARK

Family philanthropy is highly individual. Each family brings its own passions, experiences, research, and priorities to bear on the philanthropic investments it makes and the causes it wants to tackle. Philanthropic goals are the expression of that family's values.

Yet sometimes relatives may disagree on goals and strategies. Some might want to fund immediate needs such as hunger while others prefer to address the root causes of hunger, such as unemployment or homelessness. Issues may also arise if one or more family members have founded a nonprofit or sit on nonprofit boards, or both, since close involvement with specific organizations can influence decisions in one direction or another. Alternatively, if a family member marries someone whose involvement lies outside the foundation's focus geographically, religiously, or in terms of social passions (as when an animal lover marries into a family committed to inner-city public education), tensions may arise around funding priorities.

Other possible points of contention include geographic focus, types of grants (such as programs, physical plant, infrastructure, general operating, annual funds, or endowments), decision-making power, size of grants, and nonprofit affiliations, not to mention how to include spouses, particularly if other family members do not readily accept them.

Setting out the strategy of a family foundation is critical—even if this means a long period of discussion and negotiation. Reaching agreement on how you want the organization to allocate resources and evolve is essential before starting to build up its operational infrastructure or embarking on grantmaking.

One way of doing this, as Carmen Castellano did, is to gather the family together and hold a series of meetings—over a matter of days, if necessary—to agree on a giving strategy. Alternatively, the family member who generated the financial resources may want to set specific requirements about what will and (equally important) what will not be funded in the near and longer term. Some parents may allocate a certain percentage of the annual endowment payout (such as 10 percent of the total 5 percent) to each child and to their own families. Others delegate allocation responsibilities to the child with greatest expertise in giving or knowledge of a particular program area.

Whatever model you end up deciding on, draw up the results of your discussions as a formal statement of intent. This provides a document that can be referred back to should questions or misunderstandings arise in the future—including how you want your foundation assets to be managed and disbursed in subsequent generations after you die. Developing a consensus (even if it means agreeing to disagree) or making these decisions yourself and putting the foundation strategy on paper will minimize conflict and set out practical expectations as well as a guiding philosophy for your family foundation.

Another big question is how to ensure that your values and mission are passed down through the generations. You need to decide whether your foundation—and its capital—will exist in perpetuity or will be a vehicle to channel your assets through and spend down in your lifetime. Even if you choose the latter, creating and running your family foundation over a period of decades, learning as you go, can be a deeply rewarding experience. And you may even decide later that you'd like to change your plans and manage the assets as an endowment so they exist for one or multiple generations to come.

While you're alive, of course, the private foundation structure offers you control over your giving and how you invest your endowment—as founder, you choose the board, investments, and funding decisions. Another advantage of spending down your capital is that certain issues—protection of the environment, for example—may require action and funding now, and not necessarily later. And, of course, giving while living means you maximize the pleasure you get from your philanthropy.

But what happens after your death? How can your philanthropic legacy be continued? The truth is, unless you have a highly specific mission and have set down guidelines, it's hard to predict how the money will be allocated after your death. Your guidelines may become obsolete or be ignored—which often happens after the generation that did not know you personally (your grandchildren or great-grandchildren) takes over board leadership.

So should you set down strict rules—enshrined in a legal document—as to what your foundation can and cannot fund? This would certainly grant you some assurance as to the direction of your legacy. However, remember that needs change over time. Say you set up a family foundation to combat a life-threatening disease. A cure could later be found for that disease, so it's a good idea to set out an alternative mission, or give decision-making power to your children or future board members.

If you want your foundation's funding to reflect specific values (such as a politically conservative or progressive stance on certain issues), be sure to stipulate that those values must be upheld even if the mission evolves. Work with your lawyers to create legal guidelines in your foundation's bylaws and to set up guidelines—often called "donor intent"—in your estate plan specifying exactly what the endowment can or cannot be used for.

Another option is that upon your death (or the death of you and your spouse), the endowment be divided into a certain number of grants to specific grantees (your board has a legal obligation to make those grants). In your estate planning, you can also establish the next generation of board members.

However, sometimes even donors with the best of intentions can set the stage for battles after their death. This is especially likely if the limitations they place around their funding are too restrictive or not restrictive enough. In some cases, families have even filed suits against grantees, claiming they have not used a gift as intended. So build in flexibility that will allow your values to be upheld. While the grants or types of grants may change, and organizational structures could alter, if you've put in place a strong mission, value set, and culture, your original goals and overarching philosophies will most likely remain in place.

As important as any foundation structure or written legacy is the example you set for your children. And putting your money into a philanthropic enterprise, rather than giving it directly to your children, is one way of empowering them. Hannah Quimby certainly believes her mother's money was far better used in creating the family's foundation than in giving her and her brother a large inheritance. Once, while at a philanthropy conference organized by Goldman Sachs, Hannah was asked whether she resented not having a trust fund. Her answer was a resounding no. "If money isn't a concern, you might not find your own passion and work hard at it because you know you can fall back on your money," she says. "And it definitely builds character to work hard and find your passion."

You can also devise activities that will help you encourage your children to become givers. Involve younger members of the family in making grants. Take them on site visits to your favorite grantee organizations. See if they can volunteer at those organizations and consider giving them small discretionary funds (you can increase these as their engagement increases) to support the organizations at which they volunteer. Hands-on involvement is the best education they can get at this stage, exposing them not only to some of the harsh realities of society but also to the fact that there are committed individuals out there working effectively to solve social problems.

You might even devise a new form of philanthropy designed specifically to encourage multigenerational giving, as have a group of mother-daughter givers called ChAngels. The ChAngels was founded in 2007 by Kate, a nine-year-old California girl who invited her friends (including my goddaughter, Lisa, and her sister Sara) to help her change the world—one step at a time. The group collects and earns spare change (hence the name ChAngels) and researches ideas for projects, presenting their ideas at monthly meetings. They have funded help for tsunami victims in Japan, books for libraries in Fiji, and a small farm for sick children to go and play with animals. They volunteer their time when possible, encouraging peers to donate books, helping clean and care for the animals at the farm, and joining breast cancer walkathons in partnership with their mothers.

When it comes to your family foundation, however, one thing to remember is that while you may intend your foundation to be a family activity, family foundations don't necessarily result in familial bonding—and in some cases they can be a source of strife. Spend plenty of time explaining to your children the reasons behind your social commitments and recognize that your passions may not be their passions. Your approach may be very different from the one they want to take. Allow your children to express their individuality and help them discover their own values as they develop their giving—that's what my father did for me. He helped support my choice of a life of service and giving.

Most important, lead by example. Talk to your children about why you feel passionate about giving and the ways in which it's had a positive impact on your life. Expose them to the issues you care about most and encourage their efforts to follow their own passions. Embark on shared family giving projects, and volunteer with them regularly. And show them, as my parents did, that a giving life is a beautiful life. It starts with you.

MAKING IT HAPPEN

What to Ask Yourself:
- Is any of your philanthropy continuing the values of your parents? If so, why is it important to you to promote those values?
- What are the values you want to pass on through your children?
- Do you want to leave financial resources to enable your children to be philanthropic?
- Do you want to give your children control over how those resources are spent or do you want to decide how those resources are spent yourself?
- Would joint philanthropic planning provide an opportunity to share family passions for social change?

What to Ask Your Children:
- What interests them most?
- What individual—either someone they know or a famous person—do they think does the most to help others?
- What do they consider unfair in this world and why?

- What one problem do they hope no longer exists in fifty years' time?
- If they had $100 or $1,000 to give away, what would they do with it?
- If they could rule the world for a week or be mayor of your city, what five things would they do to make it better?

What to Ask Yourself When Considering Setting Up a Family Foundation:
- Setting up a foundation can be burdensome in terms of administration, as you must keep records and file accounts and tax returns. Do you have the time to do this yourself or the resources to employ someone else to do it? (Do some careful budgeting to work out how much of your money will be spent on this.)
- Even if you do hire staff, overseeing a foundation can constitute substantial commitment, so how much time can you give? (Your skills can be as valuable as your money. But remember that in most states, paying family members to do the work is illegal.)
- Will you want to develop strategy, become an advocate for your cause, or manage the board—or all of these?
- Are you prepared to accept that the causes and organizations your children want to support may differ from or even oppose your own values (pro-life versus pro-choice) you support?
- Do your children share your social passions and want to be involved in a family foundation? If so, then proceed together. If not, consider establishing your foundation with a limited life span. Meanwhile, you could create a donor-advised fund for each of your children from which they can allocate funds each year (you can refill these funds annually). You could also establish a next-generation program within your foundation and invite your children and grandchildren to participate in decision making for a set amount of money each year.
- If you plan to leave a foundation to your children, hold long-term planning meetings with them in advance of your bequest to give them time to fully understand your intentions. (Some foundations host annual family "philanthropy retreats" to educate and train children about the foundation's work and mission.) Also, consider making a video about why you chose your foundation's mission and why it's important to you.

What to Ask When Creating Giving Focus:
The more specific you are about how you give money, the greater the ease and effectiveness with which you can pursue your strategy. Start with the following steps:

- What type of grants do you want to make? A family foundation must make grants for charitable purposes, which include funding nonprofits as well as scholarships and grants to non-U.S. organizations (check current laws around reporting and process for funding individual scholarships and NGOs).
- What will your mission statement say? Creating one will help you focus on the purpose of your foundation.
- What are the philosophies, values, and areas of interest you would like your relatives and those who will manage the foundation to preserve after your death? Create a statement of donor intent to establish them. Although this is not legally binding, it will provide them with clear guidelines.

Questions to Ask When Developing Grantmaking Guidelines:
Being specific about your foundation's strategy will make it easier to identify nonprofits to fund and to sift out inappropriate applications for your funding. So in addition to your mission statement, develop a set of guidelines for grant seekers based on questions that include the following areas:

- Your grantmaking focus and procedures:
  - Do you accept unsolicited grant requests or proposals? If so, what are the funding deadlines (for example, the end of each month, the end of each quarter, or by May 31 or November 30, or a rolling deadline)? If not, you can put out RFPs (requests for proposals) or clearly state that you don't accept unsolicited grant proposals.
  - Will your funding be reactive, considering all letters of inquiry that meet your guidelines? If so, you could create a "letter of intent" process in which nonprofits propose ideas, allowing you to invite selected organizations from that process to submit applications.
  - Do you accept grant requests in any form, or only online?
  - What is your foundation's area of focus for grantmaking? If it's education, for example, is it public education, private education, after-school programs, governance reform, or charter schools? (Many foundations have more than one focus area.)
  - Will you have a specific geographic focus (your local community, your home state, a different country, or worldwide)?
  - What size of gifts does your foundation make and to what size of organization? (You could make small gifts to early-stage organizations trying entrepreneurial ideas or a few major gifts to those that

have a five- to ten-year track record and are ready to scale up their operations, either locally or in other locations.)

- What type of projects does your foundation consider (such as general operation, preventative, urgent need, educational, or long-term development programs)?
- How often do you evaluate grantees' activities (quarterly, yearly, or monthly)? And how do those evaluations work (externally or internally, funding mechanism, objectives)?
- How many organizations does your foundation fund every year? (This may vary from year to year.)
- What are your foundation's typical grant sizes? (For example, $5,000 for organizational capacity building, $25,000 in capital building grants, or $10,000 program grants.)
- What is the typical funding lifespan for your foundation's grants (including whether it makes one-off grants only or primarily funds the same cohort of organizations over many years)?
- What organizations did your foundation fund last year? (This is very helpful to prospective grantees.)

- What you require of potential grantees:
  - How many clients should your grantee serve and in which communities?
  - In which geographic area should your grantees be located (nationally, statewide, or only in a particular zip code)?
  - What annual budget range should your grantees have?
  - What range of funding sources should your grantees have?
  - Do you require grantees to have diversity policies for board and staff?
  - How will you and the nonprofits you fund know if they're successfully achieving their social change goals?

- Request the following information on a funding application form:
  - Confirmation of the applicant's 501(c)(3) charitable status.
  - Basic financial information for the applicant organization.
  - Details of the mission of the organization and how it aligns with your foundation's strategy.
  - Details of how the applicant wants to use your money and why it needs it.
  - Details of the community or cause the applicant's organization serves.

- Description of what success will look like for both the organization itself and the grant.
- Accompanying documents to be submitted with a request for funding.
- Details of the format your foundation expects a grant proposal to take (such as number of pages and mode of delivery, whether by mail or email).

For the Family:
- Help your children craft mission statements about changes they'd like to see in the community.
- From the age of five onward, have a "presents for others" component to each birthday celebration for your child or children. Let them choose one of their own gifts each year to give to a needy child their own age. When your child or children start middle school, allow them to decide where to allocate a nonprofit gift each year in their name.
- Read stories and features from the newspaper with your kids once a week and ask what concerns, upsets, or even enrages them about the stories.
- Talk to your children about why you give to the organizations you support and why each one is important to you. (If your gift is significant to the organization, consider inviting a staff member to meet with you and your children when making that gift. Use the time to explain to staff why you chose to give to it and let the staff share what impact your gift will have.) Encourage your children to get together and contribute to a cause as a way of celebrating the birthday of a parent, grandparent, aunt, or uncle.
- Take your kids to visit a community organization once a month—such as a library, a zoo, or a museum—and let them choose which one to donate to.
- Demonstrate to your children that many of the activities your family can do together are a luxury—when you go out to dinner or to the movies, for example, match the money spent with a donation to a nonprofit of their choosing.
- Translate the dollar amount of family gifts into something your child can understand. For example, "This $20 equals five hot meals for homeless people—some of whom may be your age—at the shelter."
- Have your family decide together on a specific cause to support each holiday season.

- Put your child's name, instead of your own, on a donation from your family so mailings, annual reports, and solicitations from the nonprofit will have your child's name on them. Children love to get mail and will be more likely to pay attention to the information if it's addressed to them.
- Bring your children to the toy store and help them select a few toys to give to children in need during the holiday season.
- On each birthday, help your child fill a basket with unwanted toys to give away to a hospital or a homeless shelter.
- Ask grandparents to match your child's allowance for a year, on condition that your child will donate that "matching gift" to a local nonprofit that they visit with you or their grandparents.
- Once a year, invite your children to present two or three verbal grant "proposals" or "pitches" to you and your spouse. Set an amount for each "grant round" in advance, along with required information for each proposal. If your children meet all requirements in their pitch, vote as a family on which proposal from each child to fund.
- Create "giving cards" that people can give to specific organizations instead of holiday or birthday presents (you may send these to friends and work colleagues, as well). These may spark future gifts to these organizations.
- When your children become teenagers, find a "teen giving program" at a nonprofit (community foundations or federated giving organizations might have one) or start a "teen philanthropy circle" at your teen's school or place of worship. Have parents pool resources—for which a group of teens will fundraise matching dollars—and then choose an issue, learn about it, and eventually make a grant together. (Ideally, an outside grant-making professional would facilitate the group.)
- When they're in college, encourage your children to participate in campus service groups, volunteering projects, and nonprofit internships. Offer a "matching gift" of your dollars to their time to support one such effort each year.
- When your children graduate from college, as a graduation gift, sponsor their membership in a giving circle, venture philanthropy partnership, or other service organization. Having a philanthropic peer group has many benefits—most important, support for giving passions from a like-minded community.

And Remember:

- Generally, it does not make sense to start a private foundation with less than $1 million, and $2 million is better, although a lot of private foundations are set up with a small amount of money and the endowment is built up over multiple years. Setup costs are $10,000 to $15,000.

- A private foundation should not make risky investments or hold stock representing more than a certain proportion of a business enterprise. Review the "Recommended Best Practices in Managing Foundation Investments," published by the Council on Foundations in March 2010 and available under the "Legal Information" tab of the "Programs & Services" section of the foundation's website.

- Be as specific as possible about the causes you want to support, the strategies you want to implement, the organizations you want to fund (and in what amounts), and the objectives you hope the foundation will achieve.
- Growing up in a philanthropic family carries unique complexities— including responsibility, guilt, and opportunity. Creating opportunities for your children (from as young an age as possible) to experience both the challenges and privileges of stewarding resources will provide a strong foundation for a giving life.
- Giving your children the opportunity to choose how to give away money, even $5 a month, helps build their confidence in their power to give.
- Make sure your children are volunteering, raising funds, or participating in your philanthropy in addition to giving money—skin in the game is a critical component of instilling long-term giving values.
- Remember that your children might want to support different causes from yours—and that giving values and the intention to be philanthropic is what you're trying to teach above all else.
- While practicing philanthropy with your spouse or children can be one of the most rewarding experiences, it can also be the cause of family arguments, depending on family dynamics, as well as different interests, experiences, and passions.
- If you're not willing to relinquish control over where your money is spent after you die, give it away during your lifetime or create a specific set of guidelines for the allocation of your foundation's resources.
- The legacy and intention of a donor is hard to preserve beyond the first generation of family members (or second, if they knew the donor personally), but the legacy of giving should always be the ultimate intent.
- Include your children in your philanthropic activities. The more you treat them as equal participants and valuable thought-partners, the more they're likely to want to participate in family giving, as well as their own.

- Talking to your children about why you give time and money is just as important as teaching by doing—the example you set in how you live your life is critical to instilling philanthropic values in your family.

- Every giving legacy begins with someone, and for your family, that someone may be you.

9

IN THE TRENCHES
Get Big Results from a Small Nonprofit

Dream lofty dreams—yours may be the next world-changing idea.

When it comes to building self-confidence, few adventures trump mountaineering. After scaling impossibly steep slopes, crossing glaciers, and battling snow and windstorms, nature rewards you with a view from the top of the world.

Elizabeth Martin spent two years of her life pursuing such summits with her friend Elizabeth Davis. While those were years not spent directly helping others, what Elizabeth learned climbing mountains equipped her with skills and knowledge that would prove invaluable when embarking on her next challenge—starting and running an online nonprofit helping victims of domestic violence.

The two Elizabeths climbed mountains from Peru and Ecuador to the Pacific Northwest, ascending Alaska's Mount McKinley unassisted, something few people—and even fewer women—have done. "It was wonderful and challenging and I wouldn't trade it for anything," says Elizabeth. The pair had to do everything from long-term planning to dealing with personal injuries and making smart decisions when bad weather set in. Elizabeth learned to work in a team, solve problems, and navigate the unexpected. She acquired the ability to focus, becoming an effective decision maker and a skilled strategist. "And it gave me confidence in a huge way," she adds.

These were not the only skills Elizabeth acquired that would serve her later. She also discovered how to manage on a tight budget. To fund their mountaineering trips, she and her friend worked in an upholstery shop and rented a cheap one-room apartment. "We took turns sleeping on the bed," she says. "We shopped at the place where you could buy food in dented cans for 25 cents. And when we found small change in the sofas we were re-upholstering, we'd treat ourselves to a soda."

Existing without luxuries meant nothing to the two friends. "We got used to living that way because we were doing it for a reason that we really cared about," says Elizabeth. That reason came into focus whenever they found themselves on top of a mountain looking across a cloudless sky above a striking landscape. Together, they felt the overwhelming sense of achievement that comes from having surmounted seemingly impossible challenges to achieve a goal. It was a feeling Elizabeth would experience again and again in the coming years—it would materialize whenever she learned that another woman had escaped an abusive relationship because of the assistance provided through her online legal advice service.

Elizabeth first witnessed the effects of domestic violence when, after deciding they wanted to do something to give back, she and Elizabeth Davis volunteered at a women's shelter in Washington state. There, they underwent a thirty-hour training course to learn about domestic abuse in the United States and the number of women being subjected to it (for immigrants, the situation would be even tougher, as fear of losing their immigration status made them reluctant to leave even the most violent relationship).

Elizabeth also learned how vulnerable women feel, and how much understanding is needed when trying to help them. "It was eye-opening," she says. "And it's so sensitive—when you talk to someone you need to be prepared and to understand their situation. The littlest thoughtless comment can set them back."

The shelter was run as a collective, with group consensus required for every decision. Volunteers were immediately part of the collective. "You could be as involved as you wanted to be," says Elizabeth. "So we got very involved." The two Elizabeths worked night shifts, helping bring women to the shelter and get them settled in. They also spent time answering the hotline and accompanying women to court hearings.

The house where the women lived, in a secret location, was simple but comfortable. It had plenty of bedrooms for the women, a playroom for the children, a kitchen, and an office, where volunteers would answer the hotline. It was always full and, because the women staying there finally felt secure, it was a happy place.

For Elizabeth, however, knowledge of the horrors of domestic abuse came as a shock. She'd grown up in Charlotte, North Carolina, with loving and supportive parents. She'd never imagined family life could descend to such levels. "I was very sheltered from that," she says. "I didn't know anything about domestic violence and had all the wrong stereotypes about it."

Much of her work at the shelter involved accompanying women to one of the local law courts. There, Elizabeth was troubled by the system's complexity and the difficulties women faced in navigating the intricacies of laws relating to things such as child custody and restraining orders. "It was mind-bogglingly confusing," she says. "Here were these women who'd taken huge, heroic steps to get out of their relationships and to keep their kids safe. They faced so many problems—getting stuck in the procedures of a court system should not have been one of them."

The shelter was unable to meet these needs since its staff had little legal expertise, and their limited time and resources had to be spent dealing with immediate crises. Taking the initiative, Elizabeth wrote out on a single page the procedures for the law court she'd visited with women from the shelter. That was when she had her idea—to make this information accessible to anyone who needed help in escaping abuse. "How can women make a decision on whether to stay or leave when they don't know how it will impact their kids and custody?" she says. "You can't make those decisions without information."

 Elizabeth had spotted a gap that needed to be filled. She would go on to create an online nonprofit called WomensLaw.org, using the power of the Internet to give survivors of domestic violence or sexual assault easily accessible, clear, relevant and state-specific legal information. WomensLaw.org would also provide direct help, linking women via email with other women and advocates across the United States.

Using today's technology to tackle an age-old problem, Elizabeth is a true philanthropic innovator. Before taking her idea any further, however, she realized she had to equip herself with the right kind of information—legal information. Like so many others who want to do something to change the world, she realized she needed to educate herself first. With this in mind, Elizabeth took herself back to school for a law degree.

THE SOUL SEARCHING

Between being inspired to act and taking the momentous step of starting a new organization, you need to ask yourself a lot of questions. The most important: Why do you want to start a new organization? The answer might seem obvious—"Because I care about this issue and want to do something about it." But your questions must go further and deeper.

Should you be starting a new organization at all? After all, others may already be working on your issue or cause. So ask yourself whether you're simply replicating existing efforts. If your social objectives fit closely with those of another organization, perhaps you could provide funding for a new program there as an alternative to creating a new enterprise. Even if you still want to start an organization, could your mission be accomplished more efficiently if you joined forces with another, one that already has a track record of success and is well funded?

Too many nonprofits today are scraping by when others already working on the same cause are fulfilling the mission more effectively. Feeling passionate about something is not a good enough reason for starting a nonprofit. Think carefully about whether what you propose to do is sufficiently innovative and will have a big enough impact on a particular problem to merit diverting the world's limited funds from elsewhere to your organization. In the end, it may be more effective to channel your efforts into supporting an existing organization with the same goals as yours, or helping that organization take a new approach to its work. And in some cases, walking away may be the best thing you can do.

On the other hand, you may feel strongly that you have—like Elizabeth—identified a real and unmet need for the services you want to provide or that you have found a new way of tackling a problem. In this case, ask yourself some tough questions. Are you really filling a gap in the market? Will your idea change the way this problem is tackled? Have you found a potential solution that's genuinely innovative?

To find this out, you need to do some research—pound the pavement, talk to people, read the papers. If your interest is in education, for instance, visit schools. Speak to teachers, parents, staff, school board members, and students. Understand their needs and listen to their ideas about how to solve the problems they face. Look around for lectures or discussions about education policy. Identify local leaders who are committed to education and arrange meetings with them. One thing I've found works well is cold calling people whose work I admire. I ask if I can meet with them and see if I can get involved in what they're doing.

Go online, too, as answers to many of your questions may be readily available. Many foundation websites have summaries of programs they're supporting, grants they're making, and studies they've done. They may even be organizations to which you could apply for funding. Even if not, the information is incredibly useful. You don't need to reinvent the wheel—existing organizations will most likely have acquired rich seams of knowledge and expertise on how to tackle the problem you're addressing.

Think of starting a nonprofit the way you would think of setting up a small business. For a start, who, what, or where is your market? This would be the cause, people, events, or environments that have inspired you to give (in Elizabeth's case it was the women in the shelter and others like them). Then, consider what will really help your market (in Elizabeth's case, this was clear, accessible legal information). The answers to your questions may be complex, requiring in-depth knowledge of your cause, so you may want to hire a researcher or student to help.

If creating a new organization seems daunting, you can prepare for the challenge. For a start, you can build up some local experience. You might start by looking for someplace to offer your time as a volunteer to further your own knowledge of the problem you want your nonprofit to address, as well as find or develop ideas about solutions. This kind of hands-on involvement will also help you understand the complex eco-systems surrounding an issue. These include the organizations and individuals—from existing funders and advocates to political players—that are committed to a particular cause. In addition, there are the political, economic, and market forces that shape how an issue needs to be addressed, as well as geographic and infrastructure constraints and cultural and social influences.

Dipping your toe into the water will help you gain a better under-standing of all these underlying factors and allow you to connect with the problem at a whole new level, bringing you into contact with indi-viduals who are also passionate about finding a solution and giving you valuable experience that will serve you later on. And—as Elizabeth found through mountaineering—any experience will serve you well, whether by preparing you to face challenges, by shaping your ideas as you search for new solutions to a problem, or by helping you discover innovative ways of serving an underserved community.

THE POWER OF YOUR NETWORKS

One summer, while studying for her law degree, Elizabeth Martin took up an internship working with a legal aid organization in North Carolina. As part of this work, she wrote up, in plain English, details of how to obtain a restraining order in the five counties covered by the legal aid organization. She was struck by how much easier this made the applica-tion process. As she had at the shelter, she thought, "Why can't I do this for everyone?"

It was 1999 and the Internet revolution was in full swing. With her father ill, Elizabeth took a job at a North Carolina law firm so that she could be with the family and because she thought the experience would be valuable. It did indeed prove valuable. During her time at the firm, she represented clients pro bono for restraining order and custody cases, giving her a first taste of real legal representation without supervision and a foray into the complicated procedures of family court.

With the difficulties of the women at the shelter still in her mind—Elizabeth's thoughts kept coming back to how she could make legal information accessible to domestic violence survivors. She decided to put it online.

Today it seems obvious—but back then, it was a bold idea. While we now take for granted the fact that we can shop, communicate, and access any kind of information we want online, that was not then the case—especially in the nonprofit and foundation world. Online services were relatively new, email accounts were just becoming the norm, and some questioned whether the people Elizabeth wanted to help would even be able to get online. "My response was that soon everyone would have access to the Internet," she says. "Soon that's where they'd be going to go for information. And you can connect by email without having to get on the phone—that can be an easier first step for many people."

Despite initial skepticism from some, Elizabeth persevered. From her mountaineering days, she knew she could live on very little, so in 1999, after just a year at the law firm, she quit her job and moved to New York to be with her fiancé and because New York—home to many foundations and philanthropists willing to take a chance on an untested idea—would be a great place to start a nonprofit. There, she volunteered with Legal Momentum, a legal defense and education fund that works to advance the rights of women and girls. The work gave her good connections with professionals in her field.

Meanwhile, she rallied friends. Relatives sent small donations with which she bought a fax machine. Others gave their time, helping with the design and technical side of the website. "Luckily I had access to people who understood what I was trying to do—they were not in domestic violence but in the Internet field," she says. "All my friends helped out. They built a template page and showed me how to manipulate it and how to use html. They also gave me three pages in html code, which I spent two weeks replicating for different states."

Elizabeth then set about fundraising. She wrote a letter to a Bank of America executive her father knew—a woman who helped her secure a donation of $25,000. "I had to go through all the hoops because domestic violence was not among the categories they fund, so it was discretionary funding," she says. "But that really got the ball rolling." The Bank of America gift was important for more than the money itself. "That first grant was really critical because it legitimized what I was doing."

Next, Elizabeth started spreading the word about her project and tapping into her networks for help. "I talked about it so much at every cocktail party and wedding I went to," she says. "And people were really interested, whether or not domestic violence was something that [affected] them." She also asked for time and expertise. From among her parents' friends and those of her New York–based in-laws, she identified people with experience in the business world and asked them to become involved. "I had about ten people helping me with the business plan," she says.

As Elizabeth's story demonstrates, when you're ready to start a new venture, one of the most important things to remember is *you are not alone.* Friends, relatives, and colleagues may all be interested in your mission and willing and able to help, so tapping into networks is essential. Think broadly—your networks might include the head of your neighborhood community center, the manager at your local coffee shop, or your bank manager. An acquaintance working at a foundation or an old school friend now employed by a development agency could also offer skills and ideas that you need.

All these people have valuable knowledge, experience, and connections. Even if you've lost contact, social networking sites such as Facebook, LinkedIn, and Ning make it easier than ever to track people down. After all, before social networks came along, you'd have to telephone, write a letter, send email, or meet in person with people you knew in order to tell them about your cause or event. Now, you can reach your entire network with one online post, so people will be aware of the basics about your organization before you get in touch directly.

Access to networks is a gift that's often more valuable than money. The words, "Oh, yes, I know someone who knows someone who can help you," can be among the most important you'll hear in the early stages of starting a nonprofit. And the more personally engaged people are in a cause, the more likely they are to supplement their time with funding.

Don't forget to tell people exactly what you need. If you simply ask for support, people sometimes feel helpless. But if you ask them to do something specific, they feel empowered and are usually happy to help. In Elizabeth's case, this was advice on grant proposals and her business plan. "Don't be shy," she says. "People love to review stuff. They want to feel part of something and that's an easy way for them to do that." And because volunteers are giving a precious resource—their time—they should be treated with the same respect and be shown the same gratitude as financial donors.

The way Elizabeth went about seeking early support for her non-profit showed courage and determination. She thought broadly about networks she could tap into. It takes some nerve to do this, because, while many will be excited about your ideas, you must also be prepared for rejection. But if you have the will and the passion, the resources will come to you. Unbridled enthusiasm is infectious—people will want to get on that train.

GETTING DOWN TO BUSINESS

For Elizabeth, tasks such as filing the certificate of incorporation and nonprofit bylaws and obtaining the 501(c)(3) charitable status for WomensLaw.org were not difficult. "As a lawyer, that part was easy," she says. "And it satisfied my needs for specificity." It's something anyone who starts a nonprofit must do immediately. Obtaining 501(c)(3) status legitimizes your organization in the eyes of the Internal Revenue Service. Once you've chosen its name, you'll need to obtain a federal Employer Identification Number, or EIN, for it, form an incorporating board of directors, hold your board's first meeting, and record minutes. You'll also need to create a set of bylaws (the rules by which your nonprofit will operate), and submit your articles of incorporation and the required fee to the relevant department in your state government.

When it comes to your U.S.-based 501(c)(3), once you've secured its charitable status, you should establish an organizational and financial infrastructure. You might need a chief financial officer, perhaps someone who is already running their own business and has time to spare and experience to share. You might need a corporate secretary and, if you start building a staff, an HR professional to help with things such as developing an employee manual. From the outset, consider paying an accounting firm to produce audited financial statements as well as policy documents, procedures, and controls. In some states, this is not a requirement, but it's a good idea to set a high standard of accountability from day one.

Next, you need to build a board. This does not need to be a large group of people. You could, for example, keep the formal board very small and rely for additional support on a larger group of individuals willing to donate voluntary services such as graphic and website design, marketing and PR services, or technical advice.

And it's important to ensure your board evolves alongside your organization. This means setting term limits for board members, giving you the opportunity to bring in people with fresh resources, fresh ideas, and fresh perspectives through a formal process. If one member is not engaged or fails to meet board requirements, it might even mean asking that individual to step down (make sure you express gratitude for the time and expertise they've given so far). I've also found great value in having all board members conduct an annual self-assessment. This not only helps you manage the team but also helps individuals become accountable and potentially more engaged.

And in the new era of accountability—in both for-profit and non-profit sectors—you need your board to have independent directors and a competent audit committee (whose members must also be independent). Some of these requirements are now enshrined in law, but some are simply good governance practices for all nonprofits (consult the governance section in the charities and nonprofits section of the Internal Revenue Service for more details).

Additionally, set out the key skills your organization needs (such as legal, audit, investment), as well as resources (access to corporate, family, or foundation funding or professional services), and types of members (such as clients and field experts as well as representatives of different genders and ethnic or religious groups). This helps a governance committee identify a pipeline of potential board members who will fit the changing needs of the nonprofit as it evolves.

Most important, of course, you need to establish a set of financial donors. Apart from the people your nonprofit is trying to help, these are your most important constituents. One of the hardest things about running a nonprofit is finding the money to create and execute your mission. It's a task without end. You'll constantly need to find creative ways of supporting what you do—whether through funding or through donations of time (to help with legal, accounting, and other functions) or gifts in kind (such as furniture and equipment). And whatever form of donation you're seeking, never be afraid to ask. You may attract unsolicited donations, but most of the time you'll have to make it clear exactly what you need, how much you need, and when you need it.

When it comes to applying for foundation funding, learn everything you can about the organization before applying for a grant—from what issues and populations it includes in its grantmaking strategy to procedures for making an application. There's no point wasting everyone's time in applying for a grant if your activities and mission don't match a foundation's focus and policies. And think about a portfolio of funders rather than relying primarily on a single gift, foundation grant, or corporate sponsorship. Some organizations may give you one-off grants. With others, you may be able to secure multiyear funding. All will be critical to achieving your mission.

An important part of your funding portfolio will be individual donors (who make up about 75 percent of all giving in the United States), so you need to devise ways of making giving to your nonprofit appealing to them. First, make it easy. Complex forms—whether on paper or online— can easily deter someone who might otherwise have made a gift.

And if you should be specific about the time and skills you require, the same is true for financial gifts. I think of creating "giving products" that individual donors will be excited to purchase. If you have an animal rescue organization, for example, rather than asking donors for general funds, you could suggest that $50 will vaccinate, feed, and house an abandoned dog for a year or that $1,000 will support ten senior citizens in adopting abandoned cats.

Your website will be a critical fundraising tool. There, you can set out your goals, post stories and metrics about your successes, upload photos and videos of the people you're working to help, explain what their needs are, and show how your organization is transforming their lives. When donors get to know more about what you do, they're more likely to want to give. Most donors connect through the heart—so showing pictures of the faces of those in need and telling stories about the injustices or hardships they face can be a powerful way of motivating people to give. Be sure to have a "Donate Now" link on your website, allowing people to make gifts either through a PayPal account or with a credit card.

The Web has transformed what even the smallest organizations can do to connect with potential donors, so use it. For while you may secure foundation grants, individual donors will probably represent a large chunk of your funding, so you must communicate with them in the most powerful way possible.

How you approach different donors is also critical. Donors can get burnt out, so don't ask the same donor for a gift more than twice a year. For the same reason, don't ask again or try to solicit annual funding if a donor has recently given your organization a large gift. Additionally, if a year later you ask someone who made a significant gift to a capital or endowment campaign to increase the gift for the same campaign, that donor might feel unappreciated and might not want to give again. Just one bad experience can turn people away from an organization for years (if not permanently), so make donor appreciation part of your culture from day one. (Consider how you'd feel in the same situation before making requests of others.)

This includes proper thanks to those who've given advice, time, or money. The work of fundraising doesn't stop when you receive the check—that's just the beginning. Donors want updates on what their money is funding and what your organization is doing to advance its mission. You can do this via email or online newsletters and include donors in your activities or hold special events for them. Earlier in this book (see Chapter Three), I laid out details of how individual donors should assess any organization to which they're considering making a gift. As the founder of a nonprofit, you're on the other side of the equation, so if you're thinking about starting a nonprofit, it's worth rereading that section to remind yourself of what donors will expect from you.

I model the way I thank my donors on how I would like the organizations I fund to thank me. Some send donor gifts, such as T-shirts, notepads, or pens with their organization's name on it. But a much more meaningful expression of gratitude (using less of your organization's precious resources) is a hand-written letter from you or from a member of your board. Letters or email responding to donors who are ending their funding of your organization should express just as much gratitude as those for current donors—their funding may well have helped get your organization where it is today. When donors depart feeling appreciated and that they have made a difference, they're far likelier to tell their friends about your work or even give again one day.

At the Stanford Hospital Emergency Department, for example, one of the nurses' daughters created a handmade framed "Giving Tree." In every golden apple on the tree are details of the key needs our annual giving has funded. It proudly hangs in my foundation offices and is a beautiful expression of gratitude that inspires my continued support of the hospital's work.

When it comes to fundraising, finding a connection, however tenuous, with people who can help is critical. After all, it was Elizabeth's willingness to write to a woman she didn't know but who knew her father, that secured that first critical Bank of America funding. As Elizabeth did, you should be willing to put yourself out there—even in potentially uncomfortable situations—on behalf of your cause or community. Frankly, if you aren't willing to do whatever it takes to get your organization going, you shouldn't be asking anyone else for help, let alone money.

However, if you are, let your passion be a source of inspiration to others, whether you're asking them for time or for money. And even if at first you can only secure gifts of time, these gifts can also turn into gifts of money, as Elizabeth found with the individuals who helped her create the initial business plan for WomensLaw.org. "They all eventually became funders," she says. "Because they'd spent time on the project, they felt invested in what we were doing."

HELPING HATCH THE EGG

If getting advice from others is essential when starting a nonprofit, it's also scary, since anyone who knows their stuff will be asking you all kinds of questions—questions you've never considered and may not be able to answer immediately. What infrastructure are you going to need? Where will the organization be based? What kind of offices will it occupy? What are your projected operating costs for the first five years? What equipment is needed? How many people will it take to run it? Such questions are just a starting point. However, answering them will help you to get on the right track and build a better organization as a result.

What's more, starting a nonprofit comes with a set of onerous bureaucratic requirements. As noted, setting up your organization's 501(c)(3) status is just the beginning of work that will include everything from drafting bylaws and setting up an accounting system to developing a budget and forming a board of directors.

All this can weaken the nerve of even the most ardent philanthropist or social entrepreneur. For this reason, it's critical to find a mentor or a set of mentors. In any form of philanthropy, mentors are as important as they are in your professional life, but they are particularly critical when founding a nonprofit. What a mentor provides is a sounding board, wisdom, experience, and the perspective of someone you can trust, but who remains outside your day-to-day work and can give you objective advice.

First, identify someone whose giving strategy you admire. You can choose mentors from among those who've taken a career path you'd like to emulate, as well from among others who've taken different paths. A mentor could be someone who is addressing the same social issue as you or someone whose working practices and ideas you respect, even if they are being applied to a different cause.

Once you've identified a mentor or several mentors, make a point of learning from them. You can do this by consulting them on a quarterly or monthly basis (depending on how much time they have). Ask how they would handle the situations you're encountering. Set goals for your organization, and ask your mentors to hold you accountable to those goals. Seek their counsel during strategy development, as their expertise can provide valuable guidance. Save your questions and requests for advice for important matters; never over-ask for your mentors' time. And, most important, show your appreciation for their time not only when you see them but by following up with letters.

Remember that when starting an organization, you don't necessarily have to go it alone. You might, for example, find a school or other local institution that's prepared to adopt your enterprise at an early stage. Alternatively, you might consider incubating your new nonprofit within a bigger, better-established organization or a nonprofit incubator. Like a business incubator, a nonprofit incubator is an organization set up to foster the development of one or many young nonprofits, helping them share resources—conference rooms, phones, broadband connections, photocopiers, printers, and the like. Sometimes incubators bring a group of small nonprofits together under one roof.

When I first formulated my ideas for SV2, I didn't know much about how to run a nonprofit—my knowledge was based primarily on what I'd learned in Stanford's classrooms and what I'd observed through my limited giving experience. But I knew how to write a business plan. I put one together and showed it to people I knew. I met with venture capitalists, volunteers, nonprofit executives, entrepreneurs, philanthropists, full-time parents, foundation executives, and fellow students, and received invaluable feedback on whether a need existed for my idea and how to make it happen. At every meeting, I found ways to refine and strengthen my plan.

When I took stock of all I'd heard from these people, I felt completely overwhelmed. Questions my advisers and friends had asked me—on infrastructure and equipment, accounting and reporting, staffing and funding—swam around in my head. It was my first solo venture in the field of philanthropy, and I realized I had no idea what I'd gotten myself into.

Then something struck me—if I partnered with an existing institution with a recognized name, an infrastructure, and a community of donors, I'd have access to an amazing start-up support package. I immediately knew the person to approach—Peter Hero, a pioneer in entrepreneurial philanthropy. Peter was a hero in more ways than one. Between 1989 and 2007, as president and chief executive of the Community Foundation of Silicon Valley (CFSV), he turned a small foundation with a handful of staff into a regional center for philanthropy making millions of dollars in grants every year.

I'd met Peter when he first came to CFSV (my mother served on the CFSV board at the time, and I was in college). I admired his work and found his community foundation model compelling. What I didn't know was whether or not he'd consider housing my new organization at CFSV. Armed with more optimism than certainty, I asked to meet with him, and told myself, quite simply, that I wasn't going to take no for an answer. I told him I planned to create a formal giving circle based on a venture philanthropy model and that I was prepared to defend my plan vigorously. Happily, tough talk proved unnecessary. Peter loved my idea, which matched his philosophy and his goals for seeking out and building innovation in philanthropy. So SV2 was born within CFSV's walls.

Peter became one of my most important mentors in those early years. Though he spent much time on the road, helping build the global community foundation movement, when in the office, he always made time to coach me. And while SV2 was technically an in-house start-up organization of the foundation, Peter gave me free rein to operate independently. He also gave me critical feedback, telling me what I was doing right—and what I was doing wrong.

Equally important, Peter and his team gave SV2 a formal infrastructure, financial reporting services, operational expertise, and physical space, as well as other resources such as access to a copy machine and paper. Partnering with CFSV also gave SV2 the public credibility that proved essential to establishing our own funding base.

All this proved vital to our initial success. However, if you do start your nonprofit within the auspices of another one, make sure your mission, values, and approach match those of the institution you're joining. Find an institution that's open to innovation, comfortable giving you independence, and equipped with strong accounting, reporting, and financial systems, an established reputation, a board of directors who believe in your idea, and an executive team you can work with. Finding all this takes a lot of work—and a dose of serendipity. But if, like I did, you find that match, grab the opportunity—it will help you get your nonprofit off to a flying start.

As your organization evolves, so can your parent nonprofit or incubator. If a new executive or board leadership comes in, or the nonprofit goes through a restructuring, creating new objectives, your organization may no longer find it the right fit. Then you need to decide whether to find a new parent or to become a self-sustaining nonprofit. When CFSV merged with another foundation to become the Silicon Valley Community Foundation, we made the decision for SV2 to become a 501(c)(3). Becoming independent was the start of a tremendous phase of growth for SV2, and Silicon Valley Community Foundation supported our evolution all the way.

You may also consider merging with another organization. Some nonprofits resist doing so—sometimes because the founder's ego gets in the way of the bigger mission. But remember why you're doing this—to create maximum impact to address a social problem. So if merging with another organization could help you do that more effectively, you should consider it.

This was what Elizabeth Martin decided to do. Today, WomensLaw.org is part of the National Network to End Domestic Violence (NNEDV). In fact, Elizabeth had always felt merging with another organization would advance the WomensLaw.org mission. "We could have raised more money and scaled up, but it made more sense for it to become housed somewhere else," she says.

However, in the early days, Elizabeth didn't feel she or the organization were ready for a merger. She'd received funding from a nonprofit incubator, Blue Ridge Foundation New York, which housed WomensLaw.org in its offices. "A merger didn't feel necessary," she says. "At Blue Ridge Foundation New York, we were stable. We felt we could move quickly and build as a stand-alone, nimble organization," Elizabeth explains. "We had essentially no bureaucracy, which helped us move fast. However, having no bureaucracy also meant having very small organizational infrastructure, which we knew would ultimately limit our ability to grow. We knew we'd need more infrastructure one day, and we hoped we'd get it by pulling off a merger rather than creating our own from scratch."

In January 2010, Elizabeth knew it was time to join forces with NNEDV. She and her organization had received national recognition, including a 2009 Webby Award Jury Prize for the best website in the law category. As well as helping women in trouble, WomensLaw.org was holding community workshops for women. By January 2010, the website had a new design hosting a vast amount of new information, and a new, more efficient hotline technology allowed women to communicate with the organization in an extremely safe way. "I felt I'd done everything I needed to do," says Elizabeth. So she called up her contacts at NNEDV and set the merger process in motion.

MOVING MOUNTAINS

Like starting any new enterprise, the process of starting a nonprofit is a thrilling ride. You get to build and shape an organization—one that, if you're successful, could make a real contribution to solving an intractable problem or helping a community in need. You get to put your ideas into action, watch your organization evolve, work with dedicated and inspiring colleagues, and look into the eyes of those whose lives have been improved as a result of the services or assistance your organization provides.

When you're thinking about starting a nonprofit, some of the questions you'll need to ask yourself are personal. One of the most important: Am I prepared to put in the time it will take? Think of time in terms of both the number of years you'll need to get the organization established and the daily demands of running a nonprofit.

Be prepared to put in plenty of hard work. While your investment might seem overwhelming as you set out, you can take it one step at a time. Your passion will carry you through the early stages, and as you acquire experience and knowledge, you'll find you can increase your engagement in some areas and delegate in others. And as for any entrepreneur, the creative process provides ample intellectual and physical fuel to get you through even the toughest days and longest nights.

You also need tenacity. If you think that this is something you might do for a couple of years before moving on to something else, think again. Even if you think you've found a new and revolutionary way of addressing a problem, you'll need to test it out carefully—and that can take time. Moreover, turning that idea into a sustainable enterprise is a process that can take a decade or more (how long often depends on founder involvement and other executive team leadership). And you need to be extremely flexible. If you see something is not working, look for new ideas and change your strategy. Be prepared to acknowledge your mistakes, learn from them, and move on.

When you're managing an organization, you'll also be doing everything from budgeting and bookkeeping to managing staff, whether paid professionals or volunteers. You also need to get good at marketing so that potential funders, as well as the people you're trying to help, know that your new organization exists. And, of course, one of your most important tasks will be raising the money to pay for your programs.

You'll expend emotional energy when creating a nonprofit. It will be your baby, in a way, so be prepared to be emotionally involved—not only with its successes but also with the people it serves. In fact, your passion is an important driving force, inspiring others to become involved and donors to give. And the more you can empower others to feel part of your mission, the more sustainable your organization will be, making it less dependent on any one individual.

As it evolves, work for your organization will probably take up much more time than a full-time job. You'll be doing work that can be hard, tiring, and often tedious, so think carefully about your commitment and how far you're prepared to go before embarking on this particular form of philanthropy. As with any relationship, your passion is critical—but so is your staying power.

For the first several years when I was establishing SV2, I found myself working every night and every weekend—creating meeting agendas, photocopying them, addressing envelopes by hand, writing thank-you notes, or drafting content for the website and marketing materials. I had to do what was best for SV2 rather than what I felt like doing. I had to go to social events when I didn't feel social. I encountered many unexpected challenges along the way, and it took me a while to develop my leadership style. I made mistakes, but I worked hard to make each one into an opportunity to become a stronger leader and improve our organization. Sometimes it felt like I was taking two steps forward and one step back.

But eventually you'll get—as I did—that "aha moment" when the pieces fall into place and you see that your efforts *have* made a difference. At SV2, whenever I visited a grantee and met the clients it was serving or heard directly from nonprofit leaders about how our money had helped them achieve more, I suddenly knew what the hard slog was all for. And, looking back on ten years when I ran SV2's operations (I remain an active leader as chairman emeritus), the moments I remember with greatest pleasure are those when I saw or learned that we had given other people—partners, grantees, and their clients—a new skill, a new hope, and even a new life.

MOVING ON

If philanthropy is about looking for opportunities for renewal, this is particularly true of leadership. New leaders bring new ideas and different ways of doing things. If you're leading an organization, it's vital to think about who might support your work in your absence, and who could eventually replace you. In the business world, it's called succession planning, and it's equally important for the nonprofit sector.

Whether in the business or philanthropic world, the idea of stepping down can be hard to contemplate. For a start, if your nonprofit depends heavily on your personality and contacts for fundraising, you may worry about whether it can survive without you. And as a philanthropist, you may have acquired recognition and influence and feel your identity is bound up with your cause or organization, making it hard to let go. Because leading any philanthropic organization requires a deep passion and personal involvement with a social issue, leaving it can be emotionally wrenching.

However, moving on—and doing so in the right way—may be among the most important things you can do to help your organization have lasting impact, and it requires careful planning. Talk to staff well ahead of your departure to prepare them for your absence or transition into a lower-engagement role. Ensure sustainable sources of funding are in place. Establish a talented team and identify a leader who can take over for you. Moreover, do all this with plenty of time in hand.

As an entrepreneur of any kind, you're only as successful as your organization—particularly once you've moved on. As a founder, your support for new leadership is as important as your need to let go of control and decision-making authority. "Founder's syndrome" needs to be carefully managed by anyone who creates and leads an organization over a long period (especially if they continue to serve on the board after moving out of an executive director or chairman role). It's challenging but also liberating to see your organization in the hands of new leaders, who have new ideas about organizational goals, culture, and governance. This is all the more reason to spend at least a few years cultivating and integrating new leadership.

As a founder you'll always feel a powerful connection to your organization and want to invest in its success. But no nonprofit should become too dependent on one individual. Rarely does one person possess all the characteristics needed to lead an organization through its entire life cycle. As a founder, you may be able to create a vision for a new nonprofit or philanthropic organization and build it up into an effective entity. But others may be more skilled at taking it beyond the start-up process into its next high-growth phase.

In the world of social change, it takes a village to run the best organizations. And it takes a village's collective belief in its purpose to guarantee the financial and operational sustainability needed to make a long-term impact.

For Elizabeth, moving on from WomensLaw.org meant putting it under the auspices of NNEDV. NNEDV is a sufficiently large organization to tap into significant federal funding and corporate philanthropy—

funding that was not available to WomensLaw.org on its own. As of 2011, 88,000 unique users were visiting the site per month. WomensLaw.org provides referrals and information to more than 5,000 individuals through the email hotline and community workshops, guiding women through complex legal issues such as divorce, restraining orders, parental kidnapping, and custody.

Elizabeth still works for the organization as an adviser whenever needed. "They want to tap into my original vision and the expertise I developed over the years, so that's good for me," she says. "It feels perfect." By starting a nonprofit, stepping aside, and leaving it in the hands of the right organization, Elizabeth maximized the impact of something that started as one person with an idea.

Looking at what Elizabeth and others like her have achieved, it's easy to feel overwhelmed. The challenges of addressing widespread problems such as domestic violence can seem insurmountable. In fact, the biggest barrier to giving can be our own fear. Yet if we can see that, through our actions, even a few lives have been changed for the better—a few more women have escaped an abusive relationship—we can look at what seem like intractable problems with a new perspective. Then every small triumph becomes part of something infinitely more significant.

MAKING IT HAPPEN

What to Ask Yourself When Considering Starting a Nonprofit:
- Why do you want to set up a nonprofit?
- Do you have the time to commit to starting and running a nonprofit?
- What skills, networks, and personal strengths do you have that will be valuable to this cause?
- What kind of support will you need from others?
- How will you measure your short-, medium-, and long-term success?
- How will you balance what will be a deep emotional involvement in your organization with the other relationships in your life?
- Who are you trying to help?
- Is there a need for what you want to provide, and if you think there is, how do you know?

- Will your organization provide something new, different, and better, and if so how?
- Is a new organization needed in your field, or could you channel your resources into creating a new program at an existing nonprofit, or volunteering with that nonprofit? Could you partner with an existing nonprofit, rather than reinventing the wheel?

What to Ask Others When Considering Starting a Nonprofit:
- How is the population you hope to help being served now?
- What external forces could create barriers to your social goals?
- What organizations exist with which your organization could partner?
- What are the potential nonphilanthropic revenue sources for this idea?
- How could social media help advance your idea?
- Can you talk to your target population about their needs?
- What experts can you talk to about your idea?
- Who are potential board members or informal advisers?
- Could any social entrepreneurs advise or mentor you?
- What professional services firms—such as law firms, accountants, marketers, Web designers, IT companies—could you approach for pro bono work?
- What strategies might increase the impact of your efforts and the efficiency with which you approach this social problem?

What to Look For in a Mentor:
- Someone you know and can trust, and who has experience that you value.
- Someone who has enough time to spend with you on a regular basis.
- Someone whose giving strategy you admire, even if they are working for another cause.

Keys to Success in Working with a Mentor:
- You may choose more than one mentor, but be careful not to overextend yourself by having too many mentors.
- Carve out regular periods of time to spend with each mentor.
- Prepare specific questions and challenges for which you need advice before each meeting with a mentor—and always be respectful of how you use their valuable time.

- Set quarterly, semiannual, or annual goals and use your time with your mentor to hold yourself accountable to those goals.
- Show your appreciation for the mentor's time and thought (the handwritten letter remains one of the greatest expressions of gratitude)—a mentor's generosity is a precious gift.

Innovation Lab—Ideas to Test:
- Meet with an individual who has started a nonprofit and ask about the experience. What pitfalls should you avoid and what key strategies have made the organization a success?
- Explore a virtual way to take action in your issue area (such as creating a website to educate and empower) as opposed to a tangible one (such as providing direct services). By providing information and support, you could help others take action for themselves.
- Before starting your nonprofit, arrange a meeting with three organizations working in your area of interest. Use that meeting to gain a better understanding of the issues that you all strive to address, and explore opportunities for collaboration.
- Conduct interviews with or survey the group of people that you want your nonprofit to help. Ask what they most need and use these insights to determine your own mission. You may be able to reach these individuals through another nonprofit that provides supplementary services to the same population.
- Arrange a meeting with some local foundation program officers and talk to them about the models they have found most effective. Use this information to inform the design of your strategy.
- Do some research to find out if any critical gaps are not being served by other nonprofits working in this area. Consider focusing your organizational mission on those gaps.

Nuts and Bolts:
- Get professional legal and financial advice from day one to ensure that you are doing everything by the book.
- Define the nonprofit's mission and purpose, the need it's filling, the sector of the community it's serving, and the values and philosophies that will guide its activities.

- Decide on a name for the nonprofit, and procure a domain name (website address).

- File a certificate of incorporation for 501(c)(3) charitable status. If you don't think you can handle the necessary tax and legal filings alone, hire an accountant or lawyer or find a volunteer equipped with the right skills.

- Open a bank account through which all the organization's financial transactions will be managed.

- Do an analysis of the existing social change organizations and models currently addressing your target issue area.

- Craft an initial strategic plan for the organization and get external feedback on it from experts in the social or environmental area in which you intend to operate.

- Establish a board of directors made up of individuals with the time to devote to building an organization; the shared belief in the organization's mission and vision; and appropriate expertise—whether legal, financial, organizational, or management skills. Include those people in key decisions.

- Draft a set of bylaws and policies that will govern the operational procedures and decision making of the organization.

- Hold an organizational meeting—at which bylaws will be adopted and directors will be elected—to formally establish the nonprofit. Take minutes of the meeting.

- If you're not using your own money, seek sources of initial financing to cover things such as legal costs as well as infrastructure including office rental, equipment purchases, and staffing.

- Consider potential longer-term funding sources (such as foundations, government grants, and individual donors) and develop a fundraising plan.

For the Family:
- Creating a new organization can consume your personal and professional time. It's impossible to not become emotionally involved, and you may not be able to switch it off at night. Be prepared for your family to become frustrated at times, as balancing your current commitments with your new ones can be challenging. Have a series of family meetings to discuss why starting this new organization is important for society, and

try—particularly for young children—to explain its importance in a way they can easily understand.

- Have a weekly dinner with members of the family and brainstorm ideas during the start-up phase of your nonprofit.
- When your organization gets up and running, invite your children to help you with volunteering projects, such as making a banner for your office, sealing and stamping envelopes, welcoming guests at an event, shopping with you for office supplies, or setting up a Facebook page. The more time they can spend with you on your mission, the more invested they will be in its success.
- If your children are in high school or college, create internship opportunities for them and possibly some of their friends—provided their responsibilities will meet an organizational need.
- Arrange a special monthly outing with your family to express your gratitude for their support. Celebrate them as "donors" to your nonprofit through their understanding, encouragement, and excitement.
- Always make sure that your family knows (through words and actions) that having their blessing and support provides the essential fuel that enables you to work towards social change.

And Remember:
- Ask tough questions of yourself before you make a commitment to assess how it will change your life, your family dynamics, your finances, and your schedule.
- Research everything—from your own motives to what others are doing in your field—before you get going.
- Ask the advice of at least ten respected friends and colleagues about your idea (you may be surprised at how much it will evolve as a result of their insights).
- Ask for insights from at least ten people from the population you want your nonprofit to serve—even if you've been in their situation, your ideas about what they need may differ dramatically from theirs.
- Treat the world as your classroom—engage in activities that will help you learn from other organizations and individuals. And keep doing that, even when your nonprofit is established. Lessons from others will help you become more effective.
- Tap into your networks—and if you ask friends, relatives, or associates for assistance, ask them to help with a specific activity. People love to

help if they know what's expected of them—and the more you ask for, the more you'll get.

- When asking anyone for time, expertise, or other resources, always put yourself in their shoes first—think about how you'd like to be treated both before and after making a gift.

- Listen, learn, and be flexible. Don't make assumptions about what's needed, and be prepared to change tactics when things aren't working.

- Take an evolutionary approach to your organization's growth and your leadership. Push for continuous improvement, refining your model and services and adjusting your leadership practices as your organization evolves.

- The people you're trying to help are your first priority. So be prepared to make a change of leadership (by stepping down) or become absorbed by or merge with a larger organization if this will improve how your programs are run.

- Be aware of founder's syndrome—don't let the organization be driven by your personal concerns at the expense of its mission. It's the mission that counts, not the egos of those driving it.

- Your interests, circumstances, and capacity may change over the years and there may come a time when you want to move on, so succession planning is critically important.

- Few people will give your vision and organization the same level of commitment as you, the founder, so support, value, and celebrate those who do.

- The time and energy you spend empowering your new executive director or board chairman might be the most important investment you make in your organization's long-term success.

- Everyone's contributions—no matter how small—are critical and deeply valuable. Be prepared to acknowledge them all and rarely take credit yourself—even if you deserve it. The stronger an organization's leadership and support systems are, the more assured is its future.

- Express your gratitude for every gift, regardless of its size or form.

- Successful nonprofits are sustainable beyond the leadership and support of one person, so take steps from the outset to avoid dependence on you or anyone else.

- When establishing a nonprofit, little of the work will be stimulating or fun—and a lot of it might be administrative and repetitive. But a few hours of direct contact with the people you're helping can make the seemingly insurmountable challenges, late nights, and endless emailing more than worth it.

- Be ready for the long haul—this is going to take a lot more time than you think.

- What you're about to embark on may not be comfortable or glamorous— but it will be uplifting and compelling. It may become your life's greatest accomplishment or source of pride.

- You are not just changing others' lives for the better. You are also changing your own.

- It's about much more than money—your time, networks, and expertise can be as valuable as your money, if not more valuable. The real gift is you.

EPILOGUE
The Time Is NOW

Giving is a journey, a calling, a way of living. It's not a separate part of life—it *is* life, turning your beliefs and values into action and impact. But making a gift is only the beginning of this journey—every time you give, you have the opportunity to learn; you have a chance to think beyond why and what you give—to think about *how* you give. Doing so can turn your giving from incremental to instrumental, enhancing your potential to bring about positive change. This means you get not only a bigger bang for your philanthropic buck but far greater personal satisfaction, too. For surely there's nothing more rewarding than knowing that because of your gifts a woman has escaped abuse, a child is no longer hungry, a forest has been protected, a family is emerging from poverty—and our world has become just a little bit better.

So where do you start the learning? Well, like many givers, I look to the past for inspiration for the future—in my case, to the extraordinary example of my father and my late mother. They showed me that whatever we give—no matter its form or size—is of value. They showed me that giving is intensely personal, too. For my parents, supporting social change locally, in the communities in which they live and work, was of great importance, as was giving general operating grants. In their deep commitment to volunteerism and willingness to celebrate their blessings by stretching themselves financially, they've served as role models to me and countless others. Most important, they modeled that a life greatly lived is marked not by what we achieve for ourselves but by what we can give to others.

And now I'm looking forward. As I complete this book, Marc and I are embarking on the creation of our own foundation. We're embracing everything we've learned from my parents. We share their commitment to funding local services, general operations, and capacity building. At the same time, fueled by our own passions, we also plan to venture into new areas. We want to expand our commitment to what we call "protecting our protectors"—supporting the individuals who every day risk their lives to provide us all with emergency services (our doctors, police, firefighters, military personnel, and intelligence officers). Through our foundation, we'll also continue to invest in organizations that foster the philanthropic sector and provide educational resources for individual givers at all levels.

Additionally, our shared love of innovation may lead us to launch initiatives that match this exciting new era in philanthropy—a prize for social innovation, perhaps, or a program designed to celebrate new ways of solving old problems. We plan to put details of our giving online so we can share the lessons we've learned with others, and in everything we do, we'll strive to apply the core tenets of this book. Creating the Marc and Laura Andreessen Foundation will be just the beginning of what we want to do to transform our world—for us, life becomes meaningful only if what we give far exceeds what we've been given.

But to give more, and to give more effectively, means going beyond a single action—it takes true evolution—building on what we've achieved already, yet also being prepared to begin afresh, adopting new ideas and rethinking old ones. When I talk about "giving 2.0," I'm referring to a state of mind that embraces constant learning and improvement. For one essential lesson I've learned over the years is that if we want to bring about real change, accepting the status quo is never enough.

It's also important to remember that, as you take your evolutionary steps, life takes its twists and turns. New jobs, new friends, births, deaths, and marriages can all spark new philanthropic directions. While my mother's cancer prompted my family to support patient services at Stanford Hospital, I'd never have started giving to emergency services had Marc and I not worked to identify the critical needs in our community that were most underfunded. Had he never met me, he'd never have started funding initiatives designed to help promote a new giving movement.

You never know what's around the corner. There will be moments when you may have money to give but no time; at others, you may have no money but lots of time. Philanthropy can be as simple as a day's volunteering at the Special Olympics in your home state or as complex as launching a multiyear advocacy campaign to fight injustice in a far-off country. But whatever form it takes, it's a lifelong journey—one with endless opportunities to learn, improve, and create more impact. Once you set out on that path, the people you'll meet, places you'll go, and things you'll learn will change your life in beautiful ways.

You can even use existing activities to make a difference. If you're in a book club, investment club, or hiking group, why not create something similar for your philanthropy—a giving club—or suggest that your group add a giving component to its meetings? When thinking about spending time with family, why not come up with giving projects that involve your spouse, children, or parents? After all, what could be better than sharing a giving activity with the people with whom you love spending time? (See www.giving2.com for what you need to create and lead a "giving club" for twelve months.)

Giving begins deep within our hearts. It's an expression of our love for humankind. But that's a very broad way of looking at it, for it's also about making personal connections—about touching and transforming individual lives. Every gift, however small, matters because it brings with it the potential to change the life of another person—if a gift is significant to you, it will be significant to someone else.

Yet, as discussed, to make the greatest impact, we must put our minds to work as well as our hearts. It is truly important to think beyond why and what you give to *how* you give. Turn your charity into strategic philanthropy. Turn reactive into proactive. By taking stock, equipping yourself with knowledge and experience, and thinking innovatively, you can make your giving an even more powerful force for good. You can apply everything you learn along the way to future gifts, and enhance your potential to bring about change.

Everyone has precious resources to give, and today, new tools, technologies, support systems, information, and models make it easier than ever to contribute to positive change. You can disrupt the present and shape a new future. You can tap into the extraordinary social innovation emerging across the world, and collaborate with others who share your passions.

That's a wonderful thing. It's also critical for our future—whether volunteers, nonprofit pioneers, or social entrepreneurs, our world needs as many philanthropic heroes as it can get. Huge global problems persist—homelessness, poverty, environmental degradation, violence, abuse, war, disease. Natural disasters can throw the lives of millions of people into chaos overnight. Countless people lack what we often take for granted—education, clean water, physical safety.

We all have a responsibility to do what we can to help eradicate these problems, whether they're in our backyard or thousands of miles away. We're in this world together, and we can all make a bigger contribution to its prosperity. So turn your concern into action and your sympathy into passion, and start now—start learning, connecting, collaborating, and engaging. Your only limitation is your vision. So imagine what a better world might look like and start taking steps to make it a beautiful reality. Be ambitious, be bold, be innovative. You can make tomorrow better—and you can start doing so today.

CREATING YOUR GIVING JOURNAL

Taking Stock I—Your Giving Values:

- What motivates your giving? Are your motivations religious, familial, political, social, psychological, intellectual, or based in something else entirely?
- Who are your giving role models or inspirations? Are they your parents, grandparents, children, or friends?
- What personal values and beliefs do you want your giving to express? (I found mapping out my family's giving history, along with my giving motivations and values, was a powerful force shaping my giving mission. My husband and I did the same mapping activities together, as well.)
- What are the five causes or issues you are most passionate about? Are you currently giving to them all?
- What moves you in the world? What excites you? What upsets you? How can you take these emotional reactions and transform them into philanthropic action?

Taking Stock II—Looking Back:

- What are the five gifts you've made over the past two years that make you happiest, and why?
- What gifts did you make in the last few years that inspired you to increase your giving or to start volunteering for an organization?
- Did you encounter any new nonprofits this year that you want to get involved with or start supporting?
- What are the gifts about which you don't feel proud or satisfied, no matter how good or important the cause? (And yes, it's okay to acknowledge this!)

- Have you had a negative experience with a nonprofit? Is that experience affecting your attitude toward giving in any way?
- What gifts did you make last year that you don't feel great about making again this year? (Even if a cause is important to you or someone you love, you may not, in retrospect, be delighted about a gift you make to it.)
- For the gifts you've made over the past year, can you say with any degree of accuracy how your dollars have been used? If the answer is yes, then why is that? If the answer is no, then are you okay with that outcome (or lack thereof)? Or would you like a clearer picture of the impact your money is making?
- Has the focus of your giving evolved over the past five years? If so, how and why?
- What life events have happened this year that might prompt you to change your giving next year?
- What have you learned this year that might change your giving? (Possibly from a lecture, an article, a blog, or a documentary.)

Taking Stock III—Your Giving Decisions:
- Do you make your giving decisions alone or with your spouse or partner? Is your giving a family decision?
- Do you engage in collaborative giving with your friends?
- Which personal or family events have influenced your choice of causes or organizations to give to or the timing of your gifts—such as a health issue, a birth or the adoption of a child, a new wedding, or a new job?
- Do you give to local nonprofits with which you have a direct connection, larger state-based organizations, or national or global causes and organizations?
- What prompts you to give in any given year—solicitations from friends or coworkers, direct solicitations from organizations (via mass mailing, telemarketing, email, or TV commercials), or your own interests, passions, and concerns?

- Do you feel obligation to or pressure from friends or family to give to causes you wouldn't otherwise give to? Do you encourage other friends or family to support causes that are important to you?

Taking Stock IV—How You Make Your Gifts:
- Do you assign a percentage of your assets or income to your giving each year?
- Have you chosen a fixed amount to give every year?
- Do you make one substantial gift every year, several large gifts, or many small ones?
- Do you divide your giving evenly, allocating the same percentage of your giving to each of your chosen causes or organizations?
- Are your gifts one-off donations or recurring gifts?
- Do you give to endowments, annual funds, capital campaigns, or specific programs, or is your giving unrestricted?
- Is your giving largely random, so that you fund a wide array of unrelated organizations or causes each year?
- Are your gifts made from your personal financial resources, or do you use family resources? Or are you in the fortunate position of having both?
- Do you make use of a matching program for donations through your company?
- Do you give nonfinancial resources such as time, expertise, knowledge, networks, connections, or ideas?

Taking Stock V: What You Get Out of Your Giving:
- Has your giving led to any new professional or personal opportunities, for example, a chance to travel or attend educational and social events?
- Have any new friendships arisen through your giving?
- Has giving led you to discover a new community of like-minded people?
- Have you formed any relationships with individuals from the non-profits or foundations you give to?

- Has your giving helped you learn more about an issue and changed your perspective on it?
- Has your faith or spiritual life been enriched by your giving?
- What are the other ways in which your life has improved as a result of your giving?
- Has your giving brought your family closer together through shared experiences, learning, or interest?

Taking Stock VI—Looking Forward:

- What organizations would you like to be involved with that you currently are not?
- What issues would you like to be giving to that you currently are not?
- What issues or organizations do you support to which you no longer want to give?
- Do you want to give money to existing nonprofits or foundations, or start a new organization or philanthropic fund of your own?
- Do you want to give away more or less money than you are currently giving?
- Do you want to become more involved with the organizations you currently give to?
- Do you want to donate more or less time and expertise than you are currently giving?
- If you want to increase your giving, how are you planning to do that?
- Would you like your giving to be more cohesive and measurable?
- Would you like giving to become a family activity and value?
- What are your giving dreams? How will you make those dreams come true?

VEHICLES FOR GIVING

S hould you choose to make your giving financial, the decisions you
will face go far beyond simply what monetary amount to donate.
Appendix II outlines the various issues you will want to consider before
making a financial gift. Only you can decide how important each of these
factors is to your decision-making process (and indeed, you may even
consider additional factors unique to your situation), but ideally due diligence about the costs and benefits of using any vehicle for giving should
be a part of your philanthropic plan. The following table—including a
list of vehicles for giving and potential considerations—should help get
you started.

	Tax Benefit	Due Diligence and Expertise	Resource Pooling
Direct giving to U.S. 501(c)(3) nonprofit	50% / 30% (50% cash / 30% long-term real estate & securities)	Donor	Yes, but self-driven
Direct giving to overseas nonprofit		Donor	Yes, but self-driven
Private foundation	30% cash 20% long-term real estate & securities	Donor or staff	Yes, but self-driven
Federated giving program	50% / 30%	Provided	Provided
Funding Intermediary	50% / 30%	Provided	Provided
Donor-advised fund at community foundation	50% / 30%	Provided	Provided
Donor-advised fund at financial institution	50% / 30%	Depends on fund size	Varies
Supporting organization	50% / 30%	Yes, but self-driven	Yes, but self-driven
Charitable trust	Depends on vehicle	Donor	N/A
501(c)(4)	None	Donor	Donor
Social impact investing	None	Donor or financial adviser	Yes, but self-driven

GIVING VEHICLES: KEY

Note: See Chapter Two, "Making It Happen," for a detailed explanation of these vehicles for giving.

Vehicles for Giving

- Nonprofit 501(c)(3) (there are over 1.28 million nonprofits in the United States—including community-based organizations, local affiliates, national umbrella organizations, and religious institutions):[1]
  - Service organizations (Rotary Club, Lions Club, AARP, Junior League, Kiwanis Club, Elks Lodge, college and high school service clubs, fraternities, and sororities)

Donor Community	Administration and Legal Matters	Investment Control	Payout Requirement
Yes, but nonprofit-driven	Donor	N/A	N/A
N/A	Donor	N/A	N/A
N/A	N/A	Donor	5%
Varies	Provided	N/A	N/A
Varies	Provided	N/A	N/A
Yes	Provided	Depends on fund size	N/A
Varies	Provided	Depends on fund size	N/A
Yes, if at community foundation	Yes, if at community foundation	Depends on fund size	Sponsor organization's legally required payout rate
N/A	N/A	Varies	Varies
N/A	Donor	Donor	N/A
N/A	N/A	Yes	N/A

- Philanthropic Associations (Global Philanthropy Forum, Philanthropy Roundtable, Women Donor Network, Association of Small Foundations, Council on Foundations, Association of Fundraising Professionals, National Center for Family Philanthropy, Independent Sector, and similar organizations)
- NGO overseas (unless an NGO has a U.S.-based affiliate, you will not receive a tax benefit for contributions to an international NGO)
- Private foundation (such as a family foundation)
- Federated giving program (United Way, Jewish Federation, Catholic Charities, and similar organizations)

- Funding intermediary (Global Fund for Women, Global Fund for Children, Ashoka, Acumen Fund, Robin Hood Foundation, and similar organizations)
- Donor-advised fund—community foundation
- Donor-advised fund—financial institution
- Supporting organization—typically based in a community foundation
- Charitable trust (a charitable remainder or annuity trust)
- Nonprofit 501(c)(4)
- Social impact investing (such as investing your assets in a sustainable fishery or a clean-technology mutual fund, where you earn a return for doing something beneficial)

Donor Considerations

- Tax benefit: What is the charitable tax deduction for donors giving to this type of vehicle?
- Due diligence and expertise: Who drives the due diligence process to evaluate giving decisions?
- Resource pooling: Does this vehicle have an opportunity for donors to formally pool their dollars with those of other donors?
- Donor community: Does giving through this vehicle provide you formal opportunities to meet and share ideas with other donors?
- Administration and legal matters: Who drives the legally required setup procedures, ongoing administration, and annual reporting when you give through this giving vehicle?
- Investment control: Who controls the investment of your fund's principal or endowment (that is, the money in your vehicle that is not given to nonprofits each year)?
- Payout requirement: Is there a legal payout requirement for this type of giving vehicle? If so, what is it?

You may also want to consider the level of engagement you can have with the nonprofits your dollars ultimately fund. Does this vehicle provide formal opportunities for you to get personally engaged with the nonprofits that ultimately receive your money?

RESOURCES FOR GIVING

Further Reading

- Paul Brest and Hal Harvey, *Money Well Spent: A Strategic Plan for Smart Philanthropy* (New York: Bloomberg Press, 2008).
- Charles Bronfman and Jeffrey Solomon, *The Art of Giving: Where the Soul Meets a Business Plan* (San Francisco: Jossey-Bass, 2010).
- Bill Clinton, *Giving: How Each of Us Can Change the World* (New York: Knopf, 2007).
- Jim Collins, *Good to Great and the Social Sectors: A Monograph to Accompany Good to Great* (Boulder, CO: Jim Collins, 2005).
- Joel Fleishman, J. Scott Kohler, and Steven Schindler, *The Foundation: A Great American Secret; How Private Wealth Is Changing the World* (New York: Public Affairs, 2007).
- Peter Karoff, *Just Money: A Critique of Contemporary American Philanthropy* (Boston: TPI Editions, 2004).
- Peter Karoff with Jane Maddox, *The World We Want: New Dimensions in Philanthropy and Social Change* (Lanham, MD: AltaMira Press, 2006).
- Tracy Kidder, *Mountains Beyond Mountains: The Quest of Dr. Paul Farmer, a Man Who Would Cure the World* (New York: Random House, 2003).
- Mark Kramer and Leslie Crutchfield, *Do More Than Give: The Six Practices of Donors Who Change the World* (San Francisco: Jossey-Bass, 2011).
- Bill Shore, *The Cathedral Within* (New York: Knopf, 1999).
- Bill Somerville and Fred Setterberg, *Grassroots Philanthropy* (Berkeley, CA: Heyday Books, 2008).
- Tom Tierney and Joel Fleishman, *Give Smart: Philanthropy That Gets Results* (New York: Public Affairs, 2011).

- William Verducci and Susan Damon, *Taking Philanthropy Seriously: Beyond Noble Intentions to Responsible Giving* (Bloomington: Indiana University Press, 2006).
- Dan Zadra and Kobi Yamada, *One: How Many People Does It Take to Make a Difference?* (Compendium, 2010).

Academic Centers

Based at universities and colleges, these institutions all have websites (please visit giving2.com for direct links) that are great places to find the latest research on different issues and forms of philanthropy. They include:

- The Stanford Center on Philanthropy and Civil Society
- Center for the Study of Philanthropy and Voluntarism, Duke University
- The Center on Philanthropy at Indiana University
- Center for Strategic Philanthropy and Civil Society, Duke University
- Hauser Center for Nonprofit Organizations, JFK School of Government, Harvard University
- Center for Civil Society Studies, Johns Hopkins Institute for Policy Studies
- The Center on Philanthropy and Public Policy at the University of Southern California
- The Center for High Impact Philanthropy, University of Pennsylvania
 - Center for Civil Society, UCLA
- Program on NonProfit Organizations at Yale University
- Center on Wealth and Philanthropy, Boston College
- Center for Public and Nonprofit Leadership, Georgetown University
- Center on Philanthropy and Civil Society, City University of New York
- Udall Center for Studies in Public Policy, University of Arizona
- USF Institute for Nonprofit Organization Management, University of San Francisco
- RGK Center for Philanthropy and Community Service, University of Texas

- Dorothy A. Johnson Center for Philanthropy and Nonprofit Leadership, Grand Valley State University

Philanthropy Consultants

These organizations charge for consultancy, but their websites offer useful information (please visit giving2.com for direct links):

- Center for Effective Philanthropy ("publications," "research," and "assessment tools" sections)
- Rockefeller Philanthropy Advisors ("media" section)
- Tactical Philanthropy Advisors
- Monitor
- Arabella Philanthropic Investment Advisors
- Blueprint Research & Design (part of Arabella Philanthropic Investment Advisors)
- FSG Social Impact Consultants ("webinars" and "ideas")
- TCC Group
- Bridgespan ("articles" and "case studies" section)

JARGON BUSTER

501(c)(3) A tax-exempt *nonprofit* or charitable organization established to promote human, societal, or environmental welfare. Donations made to a 501(c)(3) are tax-deductible, unlike those made to a *501(c)(4)*.

501(c)(4) A tax-exempt *nonprofit* organization that, according to the Internal Revenue Service (IRS), must be working for the promotion of social welfare, with all its net income devoted to charitable, educational, or recreational purposes. These organizations may engage in lobbying as a primary activity, as well as electoral activity, although some political activities may be subject to tax. Unlike gifts to a 501(c)(3), gifts to a 501(c)(4) do not entitle individuals to tax deductions.

—A—

Advocacy Attempting to change the behavior of an institution or group of individuals; in the context of philanthropy, includes speaking out on issues of concern, working to raise awareness of those issues, and taking action (by *lobbying* or engaging with lawmakers or businesses) to change regulations and policies in an area of concern.

Articles of incorporation A legal document that creates a specific type of organization under the laws of a particular state. All nonprofits must file articles of incorporation as part of the process of legally establishing themselves as organizations.

—B—

Ballot initiative Allows citizens who have gathered sufficient numbers of signatures to propose legislative measures or a change in the law to be voted on by elected officials (rules vary among different states and municipalities).

Bequest   A gift to be disbursed upon the death of a *donor*.

Blog   A personal or professional online journal and commentary that is frequently updated, intended for public consumption, and to which readers can often contribute comments.

Blogosphere   The online world of blogs.

Business plan   In the context of philanthropy, this is a summary of what a *nonprofit* plans to do and how it will do it—including, but not limited to, a *mission statement*, description of services or products to be offered, description of the problem it will address, results of a *needs analysis*, description of how the *nonprofit* will be organized and managed, marketing and fundraising strategies, list of potential funding sources, and an annual and projected budget. Some distinguish between a strategic plan (what an organization is doing to change the world) and a business plan (how it expects to finance and execute its strategic plan).

—C—

Capacity-building funds   Funding that helps build up an organization's infrastructure—including financial systems, fund development, marketing, IT, HR, legal affairs, strategic planning, staff and board leadership development, *program* development, and evaluation—in order to run more effectively and efficiently.

Capital   An organization's or donor's resources—financial, intellectual, social, or human.

Change agent   An organization or individual who acts as a catalyst for change.

Changemaker   Term used (among others) by the *nonprofit* Ashoka, referring to individuals and *social entrepreneurs* developing new, system-changing ideas along with models for implementation.

Charitable lead annuity trust (CLAT)   An irrevocable trust directed by appointed trustees who each year allocate funds to high-impact nonprofits. At the end of the trust, the remaining funds revert to the donor's heirs.

Charitable lead unitrust (CLUT)   An irrevocable trust through which your chosen nonprofit receives an annual income for a specified time period and at the end of this period the trust's remaining assets go to the donor's heirs, another noncharitable beneficiary, or a charitable beneficiary.

Charitable remainder annuity trust (CRAT)   With this type of trust, the income you receive is either a preset dollar amount or a percentage of the trust's initial fair market value, and must be a minimum of 5 percent of that value. You cannot add new funds to this trust after you've set it up.

Charitable remainder trust (CRT)   An irrevocable trust (one that can't be changed without the consent of the beneficiary) that provides an annual income stream for a set period of time (a certain number of years or a lifetime) to the one whose assets are used to set up the trust. At the end of the trust, the remaining principal goes to a designated nonprofit or other charitable entity.

Charitable remainder unitrust (CRUT)   With a CRUT, the income stream is based on an annual valuation of the trust's remaining principal. You can also contribute additional funds to a CRUT. At the end of the trust, the remaining principal goes to a designated nonprofit or other charitable entity (your private foundation or donor-advised fund).

Charity   Aid for those in need, particularly given to relieve immediate suffering.

Civil society   Collective description of society's voluntary, nonprofit, religious, and *nongovernmental organizations*, as well as *advocacy* groups and groups of citizens with shared concerns.

Collaborative funding   When a *foundation* or *donor* partners with other funders on a specific social initiative or grant, thus increasing the overall funding amount as well as potentially sharing evaluation and administration costs.

Community-based organization (CBO)   A *nonprofit* that operates in a single local community.

Community foundation   A public foundation that manages philanthropic funds established by individual *donors*, families, or corporations (these funds can include *donor-advised funds, charitable remainder trusts*, or *supporting organizations*). A community foundation generally focuses on a specific geographic area, usually no larger than a state (or a region), and has an *endowment* dedicated to that area's community needs that the foundation's *program* staff deploy. Donor-advised funds at community foundations, however, are not limited to a specific geographic area.

Crowdsourcing   Using the general public to come up with new ideas (or provide funding or other resources), which are usually contributed online.

—D—

Deduction   (Specifically, an income tax deduction): In the context of philanthropy, the total amount of charitable donations that are subtracted from a *donor*'s income at the end of the tax year, resulting in a lower amount of taxable income for the donor (the deduction amount depends on the type of giving vehicle used).

Development   The process of raising funds for a *nonprofit* organization.

Development director   The staff member in charge of managing fundraising for a *nonprofit*.

Direct lobbying   Presenting a case for or against a piece of legislation and asking a legislator to vote a certain way.

Direct public support   Financial contributions received directly from the public, including funds received from individual *donors, foundations*, trusts, corporations, estates, public charities, or raised by a professional fundraiser (this type of support does not include earned income or government contracts).

Discretionary grants   A certain amount of money that a member of the foundation's staff or board can grant each year without seeking formal approval from the CEO or board (grant approval structure will vary by foundation); can also refer to grants that lie outside an organization's core strategy (but that might require the same approval process).

Diversity policy   An inclusive hiring policy an organization (of any kind) follows to ensure that its staff and board members include individuals from a range of geographic locations, racial and ethnic backgrounds, religions, sexual orientations, disabilities, and possibly other characteristics.

Donor   In the context of philanthropy, an individual who gives time, money, knowledge, expertise, or gifts in kind, or networks toward social good.

Donor intent   The explicit intentions of a *philanthropist* for how a certain gift or *bequest* should be used or allocated. In less specific cases, the donor intent might simply be the ideas and values the philanthropist hopes will be honored in future allocation of the resources in question.

—**E**—

Endowment   The financial gifts, resources, and *bequests* that a *foundation* or *nonprofit* possesses, also known as corpus or principal (sometimes endowment resources include nonfinancial resources, as well). A foundation is required by law to pay out a minimum of 5 percent of its net investment assets every year toward social good. (This percentage may change in future legislation; refer to the IRS website for the current percentage.) An organization has the potential to increase the value of its endowment by investing it.

Equivalency determination   When an international grant is made from a private foundation or a *donor-advised fund*, the *grantor* must prove that the foreign grantee is equivalent to a U.S. public charity. Alternatively, the *grantor* can conduct a thorough evaluation of where the grant dollars go and how they are used, and then submit that information in an *expenditure responsibility* report to the IRS for approval.

Evaluation   A formal, often external, assessment of the internal practice of a *foundation* or *nonprofit* and its effectiveness; formal assessment of the effectiveness of a *grantee*, either for *program* design or social impact.

Executive committee   A subset of *trustees* on a board with a higher level of authority and decision-making power than the others; the executive committee often consists of the board officers (chair, vice-chair, treasurer, and secretary), and possibly the chairs of board committees.

Executive director   One possibility for the title of the highest-ranking staff position at a *nonprofit*, often abbreviated as "ED." Some nonprofits with national or global scope and satellite or local offices use this title for regional or local directors, and these EDs often report to a CEO or president at the national or global headquarters.

Expenditure responsibility   Generally speaking, an assurance that is legally required of a foundation when it is funding an organization not classified by the IRS as a public charity (including foreign organizations and private corporations). Making this assurance involves filing reports to the IRS demonstrating that the funds will be used for their intended charitable purposes.

—**F**—

Family foundation   A *foundation* whose funds are derived from members of a single family, with at least one family member serving as an officer or board member (and frequently family members hold a majority of the board seats or control). Relatives—often second- or third-generation family members—may govern or manage the organization, often serving as *trustees* or directors.

Fiduciary duty   The legal duty of a board member to act in the best interests of the *nonprofit* or *foundation* (and thus of society), including overseeing investment, allocation of financial resources, and grantmaking in a transparent and fiscally responsible manner.

Foundation   A nongovernmental entity whose primary purpose is to make grants to other organizations for scientific, educational, cultural, religious, or other charitable purposes. Legally, there are two types of foundations: a private foundation, which derives its money from a family, individual, or corporation (in each case, a single source), and a grantmaking public charity, or public foundation, which derives the majority of its money from diverse sources. Some foundations are endowed, and other foundations are funded on an annual or as-needed basis.

Funding intermediary   In the context of global giving and social entrepreneurship, an intermediary is a grantmaker that pools the resources of its *donors* and, according to its organizational mission, distributes them to *nonprofits, nongovernmental organizations (NGOs)*, or *social entrepreneurs*. In the *foundation* sector, the term is often used to refer to a local, regional, or smaller organization that a foundation uses to disburse its grants, in recognition of the fact that the intermediary may have greater expertise on local or regional needs or specific issue areas.

—G—

General operating support   Unrestricted funding that a *nonprofit* can use for any purpose (among the hardest funds for nonprofits to raise).

Giving circle   A group of individuals who meet regularly to pool their donations, teach themselves about causes and issues, make grants collectively, and seek deeper engagement in the process of giving.

Governance   Legal, financial, and managerial oversight of an organization, generally administered by the board of directors.

Grant agreement   A formal agreement made between a *foundation* or *donor* and a *nonprofit grantee* on how the funds will be used and, possibly, evaluated.

Grant proposal   A document written and submitted by a *nonprofit* or an individual to apply for funding from a *foundation* or individual.

Grant round   A competitive process in which a *nonprofit* submits a *grant proposal* to a foundation—in response to a *request for proposal*, or *RFP*, or an invitation—in an effort to obtain funding from a grantmaking organization. In the grant round, members of the grantmaking organization decide which applicant is the most appropriate recipient of the funding. Grant rounds typically take place annually or at set times during the year.

Grantee   An individual or organization that receives a grant.

Grantor   An individual or organization that makes a grant.

Grassroots lobbying   Encouraging the public to urge their elected officials to support a stated position on an issue.

—**H**—

Human capital   A person's ability to perform labor and intellectual capabilities; in philanthropy, human capital is donated through *volunteering* time, skills, or expertise.

—**I**—

Impact   The change or improvements that *nonprofit* organizations and their funders seek to achieve; the change in society that occurs as a result of a philanthropic gift and the effect of a *program* or set of activities.

Income   *Nonprofits* have various ways of generating income to cover their costs (such as charging fees for services, obtaining grants, fundraising, or executing government contracts) to deliver *programs*, *services*, activities, and operations. For a *foundation*, income can include investment interest, capital gains, or other financial returns.

Indirect public support   Indirect donations from the public that are generated by the campaigns of federated fundraising agencies (such as the United Way) or by an affiliated organization.

In-kind contribution   A donation of goods or services rather than money.

Intellectual capital   In the context of philanthropy, this is the knowledge, skills, and experience that can be put to work (often through *volunteering*) to accomplish certain goals.

—J—

Junior board   A grantmaking board established by a family foundation for younger family members. These can be set up for training purposes, and members are not legally part of the main foundation board.

—L—

Lobbying   Interacting with elected officials and their staff to express a position on a particular piece of legislation or influence their policy decisions.

—M—

Matching grant   A grant or gift made with the specification that the amount donated must be matched on a one-for-one or two-for-one basis or according to some other formula.

Microfinance   Offering financial resources such as loans to low-income populations to start and run their businesses, manage their risks, and become economically independent.

Mission creep   When a *nonprofit* takes on work beyond its mission without formally reassessing its mission; often occurs when a *donor* offers a significant gift to start a new *program* that is not aligned with the organization's existing *services* and social objectives.

Mission-related investing   Funds invested by a *foundation* in a way that is strategically aligned with its social mission. This type of investing is also known as mission-driven investing, aligned capital, and impact investing.

Mission statement   A description of the declared goals of a *nonprofit* or *foundation* and how it intends to fulfill them.

—N—

Needs assessment   The process by which a *nonprofit* determines whether or not there is a need for the *services* it proposes to provide. Also the process by which an organization evaluates the requirements of the community it serves.

Nongovernmental organization (NGO)   A *nonprofit* organization pursuing social goals that operates independently from government, often in countries outside the United States.

Nonprofit   A tax-exempt organization that uses its resources (including philanthropic dollars, earned income, volunteer time, and in-kind gifts) to pursue social goals.

—O—

Operating principles   The way a *foundation* implements its strategic goals. Such principles include, but are not limited to, how foundations assess grants, what type of grants are made, what *programs* are created, and what research will be generated.

Operating programs   Activities—such as research, service provision, and awareness building—through which an organization aims to accomplish its mission and goals.

Organizational capacity   An organization's ability to apply its human and physical infrastructure (such as staff, skills, management, IT systems, and other resources) to accomplish its mission and goals.

Organizational strategy   An organization's plan for achieving impact.

—P—

Partner   In the context of venture philanthropy, a partner is a member of a *venture philanthropy partnership* who donates not only money but also time, knowledge, experience, and skills.

Patient capital   Funding that lies between profit-driven investment and charity and is designed to jump-start innovative ideas with social or economic benefits, generating social rather than financial returns; can also refer to the longer time horizon of the philanthropic investment.

Payout requirement or minimum distribution   The minimum amount that a private *foundation* has to spend for charitable purposes each year—such as grants and certain administrative costs that support its social mission, as required by law and the IRS.

Perpetuity foundation   A foundation that plans to exist indefinitely.

Philanthropic strategy   An overarching plan for how to achieve desired social, environmental, or other change.

Philanthropist   Anyone who gives any personal resource, regardless of its amount or form. Philanthropy can include, but is not limited to, gifts of expertise, money, time, talents, knowledge, influence, compassion, or networks.

Philanthropy   Charitable efforts to improve the welfare of others (from the Greek *philanthropus*, which translates as "love of humankind").

Planned giving   A method through which a *donor* can commit to a gift of money or assets to be made at a future date or upon death, such as *bequests* and *charitable remainder trusts*. Depending on the structure, the donor may receive the tax benefits associated with the gift from the time of commitment and may also have eventual estate tax savings.

Pledges and grants receivable   Money that has been promised to a *nonprofit* from *foundations*, individual *donors*, and others, and that has not yet been received by that nonprofit.

Private endowed foundation   A *foundation* that uses income from its *endowment* to make grants or fund *programs*. The law requires a percentage (currently 5 percent) of its net investment assets to be distributed annually.

Private operating foundation   A *foundation* that uses most of its resources on *programs* or *services*, such as conducting research or running a library, museum, or historic property.

Program officer   A staff member of a *foundation* or corporate giving program who may do some or all of the following tasks: recommend policy, review grant requests, manage the budget, and process applications for the board of directors or contributions committee.

Program-related investment (PRI)   Investments (with below-market-rate returns) that a *foundation* makes in a *nonprofit* or individuals to further the foundation's social mission. PRIs can include, but are not limited to, high-risk or low-interest loans to students, loan guarantees to nonprofits, low-interest loans to small businesses run by members of and for the benefit of disadvantaged communities, investments in for-profit companies that have significant social benefit, and deposits in banks that provide loans to low-income populations. PRIs can also be used as an element of *mission-related investing*.

Programs (see also Operating programs)   Clusters of activities through which an organization aims to accomplish its mission and goals.

—R—

Re-grant   A *funding intermediary* takes the money given by a *donor* and distributes it to *social entrepreneurs, nonprofits,* or *nongovernmental organizations (NGOs)*.

Report out   *Nonprofit* executives present organizational updates including finance, operations, programs, and development to the board (sometimes information that is provided in addition to or instead of a written report).

Request for proposal (RFP)　A funder's invitation to a *nonprofit* to submit a *grant proposal*.

Ruling year　The year the IRS grants an organization its *501(c)(3)* status.

—S—

Seed money　A grant or loan used to start a new project, organization, or enterprise.

Self-dealing　Activities of a *foundation* that financially benefit one of the board members or *donors*. Self-dealing is illegal, and it includes practices such as lending money, selling or leasing property, making unreasonable compensation to board members, providing scholarships, and funding family travel expenses to "disqualified persons," which include foundation board members, donors, or employees with authority to disburse foundation assets and act on the foundation's behalf.

Services　The *programs* a *nonprofit* provides to benefit society.

Site visit　A visit made to a *grantee*—a *nonprofit*, a *nongovernmental organization (NGO)*, or *social entrepreneur*—to better understand the organization and its operations and activities.

Social entrepreneur　Someone who seeks to apply market-based approaches to address social and economic problems and create solutions that are self-sustaining and do not rely entirely on philanthropic funding. Social entrepreneurs create organizations that can be revenue-generating businesses, *nonprofits*, for-profit enterprises, local government entities, or hybrid organizations. Note that definitions vary, and some apply the term to individuals or organizations that do not necessarily employ market-based approaches but that have found innovative new ways of changing the systems that create social problems.

Social innovator　An individual or organization devising new ways of tackling social and economic problems. A social innovator may also be a *social entrepreneur*, but is not necessarily one.

Spend down or sunset   A *foundation*'s decision to pay out all of its assets and close its doors by a certain date.

Strategic philanthropy   A type of philanthropic practice that may include, but is not limited to, the following elements: having clear goals, a strategy by which to achieve those goals, and measurement metrics to assess progress toward those goals and the resulting social return on investment. It may also include creating a *business plan*, budgeting for different initiatives and *programs*, soliciting feedback, monitoring the activities of *grantees*, measuring results against a set goal, learning from the experience, applying that knowledge to future grantmaking, and sharing knowledge with others.

Succession planning   Formal process by which an organization plans for a future leadership transition (among the executive team members, board officers, or board members).

—T—

Tax saving   The reduction in taxable income allowed to a *donor* as a result of a charitable deduction.

Technical assistance   Help given to a *nonprofit* to improve its management and operations in areas such as budgeting and financial planning, legal and tax matters, fundraising, IT, or marketing.

Theory of change   A hypothesis or theory about how to create a specific social change. The equivalent to a "strategy" in the corporate sector; refers to the relationship between actions taken and their effects. However, while in the business world, effects are relatively easy to define (for example, the number of new customers resulting from a marketing campaign), the results of actions are harder to measure in the social sector (for example, whether mentoring teenagers reduces their likelihood of committing a crime).

Trustee   A *foundation* board member or officer who exercises fiduciary responsibility, employs the chief executive, sets policy, approves strategy, and helps plan and approve the budget. Sometimes, foundation trustees help make grantmaking decisions and, depending on whether or not the foundation has salaried staff, may play an active role in running its affairs. Trustees or board members are also responsible for the financial oversight of the foundation. Some *nonprofits*, particularly educational institutions, use the term *trustee* for those individuals serving on its board of directors.

—U—

Unrestricted or undesignated gifts   Donations that a *donor* does not require to be used for specific purposes.

—V—

Venture philanthropy   A form of high-engagement and high-impact giving that includes, but is not limited to, the following key elements: investment of financial, intellectual, and human capital; multiyear grants designed to build *organizational capacity*; outcomes-based measurement of mutually determined—by both *grantor* and *grantee*—strategic objectives; annual evaluation; exit strategy; and mutual accountability between the *grantor* and *grantees*. In addition to providing funding, venture philanthropy funders give *grantees* management support and strategic advice. Venture philanthropy is often based around an entrepreneurial business model and is sometimes tied to *social entrepreneurship*.

Venture philanthropy partnership   An organization that pools financial, intellectual, and *human capital* from *donors*—often called *partners*—to execute *venture philanthropy*. In the partnership model, *donors* work closely with the partnership's *grantees* to build up their *organizational capacity*. A venture philanthropy partnership's mission also includes the education of its *donors* to help them be more effective in their own philanthropy.

Virtuous capital   Money invested in order to bring about improvements in society or the environment.

Volunteering   Giving one's time without receiving payment.

A NOTE ON SOURCES

A number of sources proved invaluable in compiling this glossary (please visit giving2.com for direct links). These include

The Internal Revenue Service website

"Glossary of Terms Used in Application Materials," Skoll Foundation website

Paul Brest and Hal Harvey, *Money Well Spent, A Strategic Plan for Smart Philanthropy* (New York: Bloomberg Press, 2008)

"Glossary of Philanthropic Terms," Council on Foundations website

"Glossary of Grant-Making Approaches," Ford Foundation website

"Guide to Funding Research," Foundation Center website

Introduction

1. "A team including Dr. Jorge Moll of the National Institutes of Health found that when a research subject was encouraged to think of giving money to a charity, parts of the brain lit up that are normally associated with selfish pleasures like eating or sex." Nicholas Kristof, "Our Basic Human Pleasures: Food, Sex and Giving," *New York Times*, January 16, 2010.

2. Data on household giving per the Center on Philanthropy at Indiana University, cited in the American Express Charitable Gift Survey, Fall 2007: http://www.philanthropy.iupui.edu/research/giving_fundraising_research.aspx.

3. Fidelity Charitable Gift Fund, 2009, described in "Women Take the Lead in Couples' Charitable-Giving Decisions," *Chronicle of Philanthropy*, May 19, 2009.

Chapter 1

1. "Do Good Live Well Study: Reviewing the Benefits of Volunteering," UnitedHealthcare/VolunteerMatch, March 2010.

2. Stephen G. Post, "It's Good to Be Good: 2010 Annual Scientific Report on Health and Happiness and Helping Others."

3. "The Health Benefits of Volunteering: A Review of Recent Research," Corporation for National and Community Service, May 7, 2007.

4. Grey Matter Research, "Heart of the Donor," Russ Reid Company, March 2011.

5. Deloitte Volunteer IMPACT Survey, 2010.

Chapter 2

1. Stephanie Strom, "Foundation Lets Public Help Award Money," *New York Times*, June 26, 2007.

2. "Convio Online Marketing Nonprofit Benchmark Index Study," March 2011.

3. Peter Panepento, "Guest Post: How Nonprofit Groups Can Benefit from Foursquare," *Chronicle of Philanthropy*, April 5, 2010.

4. Raymund Flandez, "Groupon Garners New Members and Cash for Museums," *Chronicle of Philanthropy*, February 25, 2011.

5. Jennifer Valentino-DeVries, "FarmVille Crops of a Cause," *Wall Street Journal*, March 28, 2011.

6. Cody Switzer, "To Spread Its Message, a Charity Invites Hackers to Use Its Data," *Chronicle of Philanthropy*, April 15, 2011.

7. Monitor Institute and Knight Foundation, "Connected Citizens: The Power, Peril and Potential of Networks," April 2011.

8. Philip Rucker, "Learning to Give at a Young Age," *Washington Post*, January 8, 2008.

9. Stephanie Strom, "Confusion on Where Money Lent via Kiva Goes," *New York Times*, November 9, 2009.

Chapter 3

1. Claude Rosenberg and Tim Stone, "A New Take on Tithing," *Stanford Social Innovation Review*, Fall 2006.

2. Arthur C. Brooks, "Religious Faith and Charitable Giving," *Policy Review*, Hoover Institution, October 1, 2003.

3. Andrew W. Hastings, "2010 Donor-Advised Fund Report," National Philanthropic Trust, n.d.

4. Emma L. Carew and Ben Gose, "A Surge in Donor-Advised Funds," *Chronicle of Philanthropy*, July 11, 2010.

5. Jacob Berkman, Raymund Flandez, Holly Hall, Heather Joslyn, and Maria Di Mento, "How Different Causes Fared in 2010—and What 2011 May Bring," *Chronicle of Philanthropy*, June 19, 2011.

6. Fareed Zakaria, interview with Bill Gates, *Global Public Square*, CNN; aired October 5, 2008.

Chapter 4

1. Hope Consulting, "When Metrics (Don't) Matter," presentation at the ANDE Metrics & Evaluation Conference, June 2010.

Chapter 5

1. "Jacqueline Novogratz Invests in Africa's Own Solutions," TEDGlobal, filmed July 2005, posted October 2006; available online: www.ted.com/talks/jacqueline_novogratz_invests_in_ending_poverty.html.

Chapter 6

1. Christine Letts, William Ryan, and Alan Grossman, "Virtuous Capital: What Foundations Can Learn from Venture Capitalists," *Harvard Business Review*, March 1, 1997.
2. "Measuring Success: How Robin Hood Estimates the Impact of Grants," February 27, 2009, p. 65.
3. Linda Daily, "Just Causes—The Giving Back Gang," *Delta Sky Magazine*, January 2007, cited on www.givingcircles.org.

Chapter 7

1. Blueprint Research & Design, "The Challenge of Assessing Policy and Advocacy Activities: Strategies for a Prospective Evaluation Approach," funded by and prepared for the California Endowment, October 2005. Organizational Research Service, "Guide to Measuring Advocacy and Policy," prepared for the Annie E. Casey Foundation, 2007.

Chapter 8

1. Foundation Center, "Key Facts on Family Foundations, Revised Edition," January 2011, pp. 1 and 3.
2. Foundation Center, "Key Facts on Family Foundations," January 2011, p. 3.
3. Foundation Center, "Key Facts on Family Foundations," January 2009, p. 3; Foundation Center, "Key Facts on Family Foundations," January 2011, p. 3.

Appendix II

1. Giving USA, Giving USA Foundation, Executive Summary, June 20, 2011, p. 19.

NOTE OF GRATITUDE

Our world abounds with astounding generosity. It flows from sources of all kinds, including the nonprofit, corporate, volunteer, and government sectors. The vast majority, however, comes from the gifts of countless individuals—parents, students, employees, young adults, retirees, entrepreneurs, volunteers—who all display extraordinary readiness to give. This book celebrates every one of them.

Giving 2.0 is also the culmination of a journey of both heart and mind on which I embarked many years ago, when I committed to leading a giving life. Along the way, I've received unbounded support from family, friends, fellow philanthropists, and academic colleagues. Countless people have stood by me, encouraging me to go on, offering advice and insights, and pointing me in new directions whenever I hit roadblocks. *Giving 2.0* was possible because of their generosity of time and spirit.

First and foremost, immense gratitude goes to my sensational editor, Sarah Murray—her brilliance of pen compares only to the beauty of her soul. Sarah helped me find my written voice, shape the direction of the book, and make it a reality. *Giving 2.0* could not have happened without her. In Sarah, I have a treasured partnership and wonderful friendship.

My huge thanks also go to the brilliant Amanda "Binky" Urban, literary agent extraordinaire at ICM. Binky believed in me and in my roughly formed first draft and shared my conviction in the potential for a new kind of book on giving. Her tough love helped me undergo an evolution in thinking that influenced the form the book takes today. The ICM team—including John DeLaney and Paige Holtzman—has also given me valuable support at every step of the way.

I could not have asked for a better publishing team than the individuals at Wiley's Jossey-Bass, especially Karen Murphy, a skilled and thoughtful editor whose belief in social change literature is a true gift to our society. She empowered me to be the best I could possibly be on the page. John Maas, (the marvelous) Mary Garrett, Erin Moy, Amy Packard, Meredith Stanton, Alina Poniewaz, Adrian Morgan, and Cedric Crocker are also among those at Jossey-Bass who have taken a lead in publishing by embracing the importance of giving and supporting a wide range of literature on philanthropy and the social sector. The world is changing because of their values.

This book would not be what it is without the philanthropists who shared their passions and stories and allowed me the privilege of celebrating their giving on these pages. In every case, I found their generosity to be matched by their humility. God bless them all for what they do for our world.

Connecting me with this incredible group of givers were helpful friends and philanthropy colleagues, including Roxie Jerde, Henry Berman, Patricia Evert, Donna Hall, the media teams at AARP and IBM, and, indirectly, Lowell Weiss and Mario Marino.

The opportunity to teach at Stanford Graduate School of Business (GSB) provided me with a tremendous channel for learning—and this learning is at the heart of *Giving 2.0*. It all started in Bill Meehan's kitchen, where Professor David Brady first proposed the idea that I should teach philanthropy at the GSB. Dave believed in what I could teach the future generation of philanthropists even before I did. Our conversation that January evening resulted in my first faculty appointment, in 2000, and in giving me this honor, he changed the course of my life.

Bill not only shared Dave's belief in me but also spent many hours mentoring me, helping me become the educator I am today. And Bill's gentle influence, along with the support of Susan Ford Dorsey, a philanthropic leader and president of the Sand Hill Foundation, gave me the confidence to found and lead Stanford PACS (Center on Philanthropy and Civil Society), which I now chair. Founding Stanford PACS would not have been possible without Paul Brest's immense support, and Paul's mentorship has been instrumental throughout my professional evolution. Our founding and current board is a dream team, and the commitment of these individuals to the vision and work is inspiring. Our stellar team at *Stanford Social Innovation Review* does a fantastic job of presenting powerful and provocative ideas, especially Eric Nee and Regina Ridley. My immense gratitude goes to Kim Meredith (our executive director), who is a superb partner, remarkable leader, and stunning friend.

Supporting my research and teaching at the GSB and Stanford University has been a group of exceptional leaders and professionals, including Dean Garth Saloner, Associate Dean Glenn Carol, former Dean Bob Joss, former Associate Deans David Kreps and Mary Barth, as well as Margot Sutherland, Kriss Deigelmeier, Deborah Stipek, and John Shoven (who assigned me my first research assistant—a significant show of support—and under whose leadership I teach my undergraduate seminar at Stanford Institute for Economic Policy Research).

Particular thanks go to Stanford University President John Hennessey, Provost John Etchemendy, and Jeff Wachtel for promoting an academic agenda that includes philanthropy and service.

If teaching is an opportunity to learn, much of that learning comes from one's students. The commitment to social change of two of my former students and past and present research assistants—Lauren Wechsler and Allison Fink—continues to inspire my teaching. I thank them both for their support and contributions to my work. Also, Stacy Walder, one of my top former GSB students, now brings her poise, grace, and dedication to all of my philanthropic work as my first program director.

SV2, the venture philanthropy partnership I founded, has given me many of the insights into high-engagement philanthropy that helped in creating *Giving 2.0*. Over SV2's thirteen-year existence, I have partnered with a series of awesome individuals. Peter Hero and Barb Larson helped me take SV2 from an idea to a reality. All past and present partners and board members have contributed knowledge and time to its development, not least Lance Fors, an individual with incredible energy and vision whose leadership of the board since my transition to chairman emeritus has kept SV2 moving forward spectacularly. Our sensational SV2 executive director, Lindsay Austin Louie, provides outstanding leadership for our partnership, and she amazes me every day. Among the philanthropists (and dear friends) who, from the outset, have supported our work at SV2 are Jeff Skoll, Karla and Steve Jurvetson, Mark and Diane Parnes, Akiko Yamazaki and Jerry Yang, and Laura and Gary Lauder. My special thanks I give to Sally Osberg, whose support, mentorship, love, and friendship have been a gift throughout my leadership of SV2 and far beyond. We have accomplished so much, and we have so much more important work to do in the years to come.

Many people took precious time from their busy schedules to read this book. Their feedback improved it immeasurably. At this project's beginning, Simone Otus Coxe (my close friend) shared her social change expertise and guided me in focusing on an audience of individual philanthropists. Margit Wennmachers gave enthusiastic support and counsel throughout the publishing process. John Goldman (close friend and fellow philanthropist) provided support and wisdom at every step of *Giving 2.0* and throughout my career in philanthropy. Lindsay Austin Louie (former star student, research assistant, and now SV2 executive director) read drafts of the manuscript so many times that we've both lost count, and she has provided essential input throughout the writing process. Ben Horowitz (my husband Marc's best friend, business partner, and an unofficial member of our immediate family) and Regina Kulik Scully (an incredible philanthropist and spiritual sister) gave me first-rate feedback on draft one.

At every step of the way, Alexa Cortés Cullwell (a dear friend and colleague) brought her intelligence, ideas, and expertise to bear on my efforts, while Susan Liautaud (my treasured friend, soeur, and mother to my godchildren) offered keen insights and a global perspective that helped me put my thoughts into a broader context. And, as the book evolved, Jacob Harold (my former student and now philanthropic colleague) provided expert insights when polishing the "Jargon Busters" section.

Dr. Judith Rodin (my magnificent mentor and loving friend) spent days of her invaluable time helping me enhance the book and supporting my professional evolution. And without the superb insights of Herb Allen Jr. (aka Herbilicious), I would never have found the giving principles that were right before my eyes (nor, indeed, would I have met Binky Urban).

In giving their time and expertise, the generosity of these individuals was inspiring, and it kept me going during my most exhausted moments.

From friends and family I have received love and guidance through those moments in life—personal and professional, joyful and tragic—that inspired me to write this book. Thanks beyond measure to my godmothers—especially Patti Davis, Kathie Alden, and Maddy Stein—and godsisters—Diana Beltramo Hewitt and Vanessa Roach—who took care of me and whose pure love sustained me after I lost my angel mother. Much beauty, support, and care surrounded me in recent years—Dr. Lisa Pasquirello Turvey, Mark and Pattie Davis, Barbara and Arnie Silverman, Sarah Rakonitz Stein, Michael Ovitz (TBL), George and Stephanie Tenet, Marc Glimcher, Phillipe Vergne, Mark Zuckerberg and Dr. Priscilla Chan, Sheryl Sandberg, Edwardian Norton and Shauna Robertson, John and Marcia Goldman, Johnny and Regina Scully, Simone Coxe, Susan Ford Dorsey, Charlie Rose (BFC), Delphine Damon, David and Colleen Anderson, Dan Rosensweig, Jeff Berg and Denny Luria, Steve and Laurene Powell Jobs, Susan and Bernard Liautaud, Laura Foster Whitaker, Scott Norton, Jenny Ward, and Dr. Neda Pakdaman each contributed to that light.

In addition to those I adore and value mentioned above . . .

My dearest friends Peter Thiel, Charlie Knowles, Ted Janus, and Greg Waldorf have each given me much along my path that has enabled me to be the person I am today. Laurene Powell Jobs and Nanci Bakar Fredkin (both of whom stood beside me at my wedding and are the most unconditionally loving of friends to me on a daily basis) believed in this book from the start and, as friends, mothers, wives, and philanthropists, continue to be my role models for leading a giving life.

To my family, who are by God's grace too numerous to count, I give my deep gratitude for their love and support—especially to my immediate Arrillaga family, including my father's wife, Gioia (who makes simply scrumptious meatballs). My brilliant brother, John Jr., has been quietly giving society his time since an early age and has been an exceptional friend to me, and his wife, Justine, founder and chairman of the Teak Fellowship and mother to three gorgeous boys (Jack, Finn, and Ben Arrillaga), is a dedicated social entrepreneur. My love to them all.

I would never have been a philanthropist or a philanthropic entrepreneur without the extraordinary example of my parents. My mother, Frances Arrillaga—my light, my angel, my soul mate—showed me what it was to lead a life of service. And with his generosity and philanthropic acumen, my father, John Arrillaga Sr., has taught me what it means to be a transformational giver. His encouragement, support, and love have enabled me to take my life's path. My love and gratitude to them are boundless.

Most important, I give my infinite gratitude to my beloved husband, Marc Andreessen. His gifts of unerring patience, sage counsel, incessant encouragement, and incomparable support enabled me to create *Giving 2.0*. Marc is my partner, my best friend, and my truest love, and I am immeasurably grateful for our life together. Not a day passes when he does not amplify my knowledge, split my sides with laughter, fill me with joy, and love me completely. His extraordinary mind is surpassed only by his beautiful soul, both of which I cherish. I am beyond blessed to share my giving life with him.

Laura Arrillaga-Andreessen is founder, chairman emeritus, and former chairman (1998–2008) of SV2 (Silicon Valley Social Venture Fund), a venture philanthropy partnership. Under her leadership, SV2 built a portfolio of twenty-five grantees and nearly four hundred investors and won the Silicon Valley Association of Fundraising Professionals Philanthropic Organization of the Year in 2008.

Laura is founder and chairman of Stanford PACS (Center on Philanthropy and Civil Society), a global research center committed to exploring ideas to create social change and publisher of the *Stanford Social Innovation Review (SSIR)*. Her faculty appointments include lecturer in business strategy and philanthropy as well as associate of the Center for Social Innovation at Stanford Graduate School of Business; lecturer in public policy; and lecturer at the Stanford School of Education.

Laura is president of the Marc and Laura Andreessen Foundation and director of the Arrillaga Foundation. She is a board member of the Sand Hill Foundation, Stanford University School of Education, SIEPR (Stanford Institute for Economic Policy Research), and Women's Health at Stanford Medical Center. In 2008, Laura was selected as the only individual philanthropist in the Aspen Institute Philanthropy Group—an agenda-setting body of twenty national philanthropy leaders, who come together annually to identify issues that would benefit from sector-wide deliberation among grantees and grantors and among social enterprises and their investors. She is a member of the Donor Effectiveness Network, an invitation-only network of twenty leaders committed to strengthening the field of donor education, and an Advisory Council member of the Global Philanthropy Forum.

Laura holds an MBA from the Stanford Graduate School of Business, an MA in education from Stanford School of Education, and a BA and

MA in art history from Stanford University. She received the 2001 Jacqueline Kennedy Award for Women in Leadership, and in April 2005, she became a Henry Crown Fellow of the Aspen Institute. She was awarded the President's Volunteer Service Award from the Points of Light Foundation in June 2005 and the Children and Family Services' Outstanding Silicon Valley Philanthropist Award in 2009. In 2010, Laura was honored with Castilleja School's Distinguished Alumna Award and, in 2011, the World Affairs Council honored her and her husband with the Global Citizen Award. A native of Palo Alto, California, Laura lives with her husband, technology entrepreneur and venture capitalist Marc Andreessen, near Stanford University.

To learn more about Laura, please visit www.giving2.com.

INDEX